de Romanis

BOOK 3:
scriptores

ALSO AVAILABLE FROM BLOOMSBURY

de Romanis Book 1: *dei et deae* by Katharine Radice, Angela Cheetham, Sonya Kirk and George Lord

de Romanis Book 2: *homines* by Katharine Radice, Angela Cheetham, Sonya Kirk and George Lord

Essential GCSE Latin by John Taylor

Latin Stories by Henry Cullen, Michael Dormandy and John Taylor

Latin to GCSE Part 1 by Henry Cullen and John Taylor

Latin to GCSE Part 2 by Henry Cullen and John Taylor

Aeneas: Virgil's Epic Retold for Younger Readers by Emily Frenkel and illustrated by Simon Weller

Selections from Virgil's Aeneid *Books 1–6: A Student Reader* by Ashley Carter

Selections from Virgil's Aeneid *Books 7–12: A Student Reader* by Ashley Carter

Companion to the Aeneid (3 vols), Christopher Tanfield

Supplementary resources for *de Romanis* Books 1, 2 and 3 can be found at
https://bloomsbury.pub/de-romanis

Please type the URL into your web browser and follow the instructions to access the Companion Website. If you experience any problems, please contact Bloomsbury at onlineresources@bloomsbury.com

---

The teaching content of this resource is endorsed by OCR for use with specification GCSE (9–1) Latin (J282).

All references to assessment, including assessment preparation and practice questions of any format/style, are the publisher's interpretation of the specification and are not endorsed by OCR.

This resource was designed for use with the version of the specification available at the time of publication. However, as specifications are updated over time, there may be contradictions between the resource and the specification, therefore please use the information on the latest specification and Sample Assessment Materials at all times when ensuring students are fully prepared for their assessments.

Endorsement indicates that a resource is suitable to support delivery of an OCR specification, but it does not mean that the endorsed resource is the only suitable resource to support delivery, or that it is required or necessary to achieve the qualification.

OCR recommends that teachers consider using a range of teaching and learning resources based on their own professional judgement for their students' needs. OCR has not paid for the production of this resource, nor does OCR receive any royalties from its sale. For more information about the endorsement process, please visit the OCR website.

de Romanis

BOOK 3:
scriptores

KATHARINE RADICE,
ANGELA CHEETHAM,
SONYA KIRK AND
GEORGE LORD

BLOOMSBURY ACADEMIC
LONDON · NEW YORK · OXFORD · NEW DELHI · SYDNEY

BLOOMSBURY ACADEMIC
Bloomsbury Publishing Plc
50 Bedford Square, London, WC1B 3DP, UK
1385 Broadway, New York, NY 10018, USA
29 Earlsfort Terrace, Dublin 2, Ireland

BLOOMSBURY, BLOOMSBURY ACADEMIC and the Diana logo
are trademarks of Bloomsbury Publishing Plc

First published in Great Britain 2025

Copyright © Katharine Radice, Angela Cheetham, Sonya Kirk and George Lord, 2025

Katharine Radice, Angela Cheetham, Sonya Kirk and George Lord have expressed their right under the Copyright, Designs and Patents Act, 1988, to be identified as Authors of this work.

Cover design: Terry Woodley
Cover image: Mosaic of a poet 'inspired by the theatre' currently in The National Bardo Museum, Tunis, Tunisia
Photograph: Keren Su/China Span/Alamy Stock Photo

All rights reserved. No part of this publication may be reproduced or transmitted in any form or by any means, electronic or mechanical, including photocopying, recording, or any information storage or retrieval system, without prior permission in writing from the publishers.

Bloomsbury Publishing Plc does not have any control over, or responsibility for, any third-party websites referred to or in this book. All internet addresses given in this book were correct at the time of going to press. The author and publisher regret any inconvenience caused if addresses have changed or sites have ceased to exist, but can accept no responsibility for any such changes.

A catalogue record for this book is available from the British Library.

A catalog record for this book is available from the Library of Congress.

ISBN: PB: 978-1-3504-6267-0
ePDF: 978-1-3504-6269-4
eBook: 978-1-3504-6268-7

Typeset by RefineCatch Limited, Bungay, Suffolk
Printed and bound in India

To find out more about our authors and books visit www.bloomsbury.com and sign up for our newsletters.

SOURCES OF ILLUSTRATIONS

13.1 Prisma/Universal Images Group via Getty Images; **13.2** REDA & CO srl / Alamy Stock Photo; **13.3** Culture Club/Bridgeman via Getty Images; **13.4** wildwinds.com; **13.5** Sedmak via Getty Images; **14.1** Dennis Jarvis; **14.2** Carole Raddato; **14.3** Art Media/Print Collector/Getty Images; **14.4** Mondadori Portfolio/Contributor via Getty Images; **14.5** only_fabrizio via Getty Images; **15.1** FrankCJones; **15.2** WikimediaCommons/Didier Descouens; **15.3** Heritage Art/Heritage Images via Getty Images; **15.4** wildwinds.com; **15.5** WikimediaCommons; **16.1** Following Hadrian; **16.2** Commonists; **16.3** VCG Wilson/Corbis via Getty Images; **16.4** Lawrence Alma-Tadema; **16.5** Victor Manuel.

CONTENTS

scripta are printed in **red** in the chapter lists below

Preface to Book 3 viii
  Structure of Book 3 viii
  Reading the *scripta* in Latin ix
  Building vocabulary skills ix
  Understanding idiom x
  Notes for teachers preparing students for GCSE and A Level qualifications x
  Bibliography xii

13 Cicero and Caesar – Eye-Witness Accounts of Civil War 1
  Introduction 2
  Read the *scripta* in English 7
  Core Language Vocabulary List 9
    4th and 5th declension nouns 10
    Consolidation: case endings 11
    Deponent verbs 12
    Consolidation: *fero* 14
    Compounds of *fero* 14
    tollo 15
    New irregular verbs: *malo, coepi* 16
    Pronouns: *idem, ipse, quidam* 17
    Unusual adjectives: *alter, nonnulli, solus, totus* 18
  scripta 19
    Meet the *scriptores*: Cicero and Caesar 19
    Reading original Latin note 1: Getting started 20
    scripta 13.1: Caelius Rufus fears the outbreak of civil war 21
    scripta 13.2: Cicero's loyalty to Pompey 23
    scripta 13.3: Caesar requests a meeting with Pompey 25
    scripta 13.4: Cicero urges his wife and daughter to think of their safety 27
    Reading original Latin note 2: Cognate nouns 29
    scripta 13.5: Cicero is angry at Pompey's decision to leave Italy 29
    scripta 13.6: Caesar's victory in Spain 31
    scripta 13.7: Caesar wins the civil war 34
  Questions for Discussion 36
  Additional Language 37

14 Virgil and Ovid – Epic Poetry 47
  Introduction 48
  Read the *scripta* in English 53
  Core Language Vocabulary List 55
    Semi-deponent verbs 56
    Further notes on tenses: time relative to the main verb 57
    Participle tenses: future participles and deponent perfect participles 58
    Translating participles into idiomatic English 59
    Consolidation: ablative absolute 60
    Consolidation: infinitives 61
    Present passive infinitives 61
    Indirect statements: present passive infinitives 62
    Perfect active and perfect passive infinitives 63
    Indirect statements: perfect active and perfect passive infinitives 64
    Future infinitives 65
    Indirect statements: future active infinitives 65
    Consolidation: indirect statement 66
  scripta 67
    Meet the *scriptores*: Virgil and Ovid 67

Reading original Latin note 3: Latin verse 68
Navigating adjectives and participles 68
scripta 14.1: Dido's love for Aeneas 69
scripta 14.2: Aeneas kills Turnus 74
scripta 14.3: Pentheus is torn apart by his mother 77
Reading original Latin note 4: Poetic expression and emphasis 80
scripta 14.4: Pyramus and Thisbe 80
Reading original Latin note 5: Rhythm 85
scripta 14.5: Arachne confronts Pallas Athene 86
scripta 14.6: Hercules dies 88
Questions for Discussion 90
Additional Language 91

15 Tacitus, Suetonius, Pliny – Writers and the Emperors 101

Introduction 102
Read the *scripta* in English 107
Core Language Vocabulary List 110
    Sentence structure: subordinate clauses and phrases 111
    Why it is important to distinguish between clauses and phrases 112
    Consolidation: subordinate clauses 112
    New subordinating conjunctions 113
    Labeling subordinate clauses 114
    Tenses in subordinate clauses 115
    Consolidation: subordinate phrases (indirect statement, ablative absolute) 116
    Gerundives 118
    ad + gerundive 119
    Consolidation: expressions of time 120
scripta 122
    Meet the *scriptores*: Tacitus, Suetonius, Pliny 122
    Reading original Latin note 6: Latin's concision and sentence length 123
    scripta 15.1: Tacitus discusses the challenges of writing history 124
    Reading original Latin note 7: The importance of indirect speech 125
    scripta 15.2: Tacitus describes the political uncertainty at the prospect of Augustus' death 126
    scripta 15.3: Tacitus comments on the emperor as a god 128
    scripta 15.4: Suetonius describes how Claudius became emperor 130
    Reading original Latin note 8: Vividness 132
    scripta 15.5: Suetonius describes Agrippina's murder 133
    scripta 15.6: Tacitus describes the great fire in Rome 136
    scripta 15.7: Tacitus describes Nero's treatment of the Christians 138
    scripta 15.8: Pliny writes to the emperor Trajan 140
Questions for Discussion 143
Additional Language 144

16 Catullus, Horace, Tibullus, Martial – Shorter Poems 153

Introduction 154
Read the *scripta* in English 158
Core Language Vocabulary List 160
    Further notes on tense: aspect 161
    The aspects of the Latin verb 162
    The subjunctive 164
    Fear clauses 165
    Further notes on verbs of fearing 166
    Purpose clauses and indirect commands 167
    Demonstrative adjectives and adverbs 168
    Result clauses 170
    Subordinate clauses introduced by *cum* 171
    Question words 172
    Indirect questions 174
scripta 176
    Meet the *scriptores*: Catullus, Horace, Tibullus, Martial 176
    Reading original Latin note 9: Displays of literary skill 177
    scripta 16.1: Reflections on the role of poetry 178

Reading original Latin note 10: Patterns in word order and sound 181
scripta 16.2: Religious poetry 182
Reading original Latin note 11: Implication, inference and wit 184
scripta 16.3: Roman customs and daily life 184
Reading original Latin note 12: Extended imagery 187
scripta 16.4: Death, grief and fear 188
Reading original Latin note 13: Cultural values and symbols 190
scripta 16.5: Love poetry 191
Reading original Latin note 14: Power play 194
scripta 16.6: Insults 194
Questions for Discussion 197
Additional Language 198

Appendix 1: Advanced Syntax 209

Gerunds 209
Future perfect indicatives 209
Future passive infinitives 210
The impersonal passive 210
Present and perfect tense subjunctives 211
Present and perfect subjunctives in subordinate clauses: sequence of tense 212
Main clause subjunctives 213
Extended indirect speech 213
Sequence of tense in English 214
The subjunctive in conditional sentences 214

Appendix 2: Latin Metre 215

Reference Grammar 217

Vocabulary List 259

English to Latin 259
Latin to English 272

Preface to Book 3

Book 3 of *de Romanis* aims to help you develop the ability to read and appreciate original Latin texts.

The thematic focus of each chapter is centred on a distinct genre or time period for Latin literature. These focuses are:

- Chapter 13: Cicero & Caesar – Eye-Witness Accounts of Civil War
- Chapter 14: Virgil & Ovid – Epic Poetry
- Chapter 15: Tacitus, Suetonius, Pliny – Writers and the Emperors
- Chapter 16: Catullus, Horace, Tibullus, Martial – Shorter Poems

STRUCTURE OF BOOK 3

Book 3 is similar in structure to Books 1 and 2 but with some differences in approach. The structure of each chapter is as follows:

- **Introduction:** this discusses the thematic focus. At the end of each Introduction there are **Read the *scripta* in English** questions, designed to help you explore the content of the *scripta* in a way that is similar to the Sources to Study material in Books 1 and 2.
- **Core Language:** as in Books 1 and 2, each chapter contains vocabulary to learn and notes on new grammar and syntax. Practice sentences are included throughout. Unlike Books 1 and 2, however, there are no Latin stories in the Core Language sections; original Latin reading material is provided instead, called *scripta* (see further below). The Latin reading material is calibrated to the vocabulary and grammar content of the course and there are signposts within the Core Language section to indicate when you could look at each set of *scripta* in Latin.
- *scripta*: this section provides reading material. The section opens with a **Meet the *scriptores*** introduction: this contains biographical information about the most famous writers for the relevant genre / time-period. The reading passages within the *scripta* sections come directly from original Latin texts with minimal or no adaptation. Idiomatic English translations accompany each text and this means that **you can choose whether you read these texts in English or in Latin**.

Within the *scripta* section are notes on **Reading original Latin**: these will help you learn how to translate complex, idiomatic Latin. The notes will also help you understand key aspects of literary style.
- **Questions for Discussion:** each chapter ends with five broad questions for discussion. These are designed to explore your interpretation of the *scripta* or to focus on aspects of literary style.
- **Additional Language:** as in Books 1 and 2, the Additional Language materials are sub-divided into three sections:
  - Section A focuses on new vocabulary for the chapter;
  - Section B practises individual details of new grammar, making use of vocabulary from recent chapters;
  - Section C contains English into Latin sentences and offers more wide-reaching practice for new material, using vocabulary and grammar from throughout the course.

Unlike Books 1 and 2, macrons are not used to denote the length of Latin vowels other than in the Reference Grammar and Vocabulary Lists on pp217 and 259. This is in keeping with the convention that original Latin is printed without macrons.

Further notes about the overarching design of this course are included in the **Teacher's Guide**, provided on the Companion Website.

READING THE *SCRIPTA* IN LATIN

If you choose to read the *scripta* in Latin, it is possible to engage with them in different ways: you might choose to cherry pick interesting Latin words or phrases, you might choose to translate a text in a very literal way or you might explore the differences between English and Latin idiom which these texts reveal.

The texts have been chosen to fit with the Core Language grammar syllabus. Their vocabulary, however, is broader than the *de Romanis* vocabulary lists; some of this vocabulary is glossed underneath, but some of it is left unglossed to develop deduction skills. Full vocabulary lists and translation notes for each text are available as an additional resource on the Companion Website.

Further guidance on different ways to approach the *scripta* is given in the **Teacher's Guide** on the Companion Website.

BUILDING VOCABULARY SKILLS

Underneath each *scripta* help has been given for unfamiliar vocabulary. Only some of the words are glossed, however, based on the following principles:

- words whose meaning can be deduced from English derivations or related Latin words are not glossed; this is because developing the ability to deduce the meaning of an unfamiliar word is an important skill.

- two principal parts only are given for verbs unless a form appears in the Latin text which uses the perfect stem or supine stem.

The derivations task at the end of each *scripta* will help you get quicker at using one language to understand the other; in addition, the word deduction tasks in Additional Language Section A will help you practise working out the meaning of a new Latin word from one you already know.

UNDERSTANDING IDIOM

The idiomatic English translations are there to help you explore the difference in idiom between the two languages. At times, these English translations will be very different from the most literal translation of the Latin, and – in particular – you will often find that the grammatical shapes of the sentence have been changed (e.g. a noun like 'flight' may have been turned into a verb in English such as 'they fled', or a participle may have been turned into a finite verb). Noticing this will help you think about the differences between the languages and the impact of constructing a sentence with one set of grammatical shapes rather than another.

There may be times when you disagree with aspects of the idiomatic translation: this is an important part of developing your own translation skills. It will be really constructive to think about how and why a different translation might be better.

NOTES FOR TEACHERS PREPARING STUDENTS FOR GCSE AND A LEVEL QUALIFICATIONS

Book 3 supports preparation for GCSE and the progression to A Level. It can be used in different ways depending on the teaching time available and the needs of the students. The online **Teacher's Guide** offers detailed guidance about the individual chapters, but it may be helpful to remember the following principles.

Preparation for GCSE

- **Vocabulary and grammar syllabus:** by the end of Chapter 16 students will have met all Eduqas and OCR GCSE vocabulary and grammar but there is some material contained in these chapters which goes beyond the syllabus requirements (for example, the gerundive of obligation is introduced in Chapter 15 but in OCR GCSE Latin language papers, students will only meet *ad* + gerundive to express purpose). See Appendix 1: Advanced Syntax for notes on material that is not included in the GCSE syllabus.
- **Passages for translation:** the original Latin texts are designed as preparatory reading practice to support the transition to GCSE set texts; they are, however, much more demanding than the level of Latin set for GCSE unseens. **Students preparing for GCSE will benefit from practising continuous translation calibrated to**

- **GCSE language requirements**, either via exam board past papers or the practice materials in books such as *Latin to GCSE* or *Essential GCSE Latin*.
- **Translating set texts:** the idiomatic translations printed next to the Latin texts can be used in a variety of ways: students may enjoy reading some of these texts in English only (similar to the Sources to Study sections in Books 1 and 2) or the translations could be used to provide context for a teacher keen to focus on just a few phrases or details in Latin for further study. It should be noted, however, that when students move to GCSE set text work, translation questions and questions requiring comment on content and literary style require a **literal – rather than literary – translation**; the idiomatic translations printed here should **not** be taken as a guide for how to translate a set text in the context of a GCSE (or A Level) exam.
- **English into Latin:** the Additional Language English into Latin sentences are much more challenging than the English to Latin requirements at GCSE. In line with the approach in Books 1 and 2, these sets of sentences are designed to offer practice material which helps pupils understand grammatical principles in both Latin and English. Teachers are encouraged to be flexible in how they approach this material. Full translation into Latin is likely to be suitable only as extension material for the most ambitious students; alternatively, the sentences could be used as a quick way to cement understanding of grammatical rules. Students could be asked – for example – to identify which nouns would be accusative and why, or to label the tenses in English without any need to translate into Latin.

Further details about the fit with different GCSE syllabuses is available on the Companion Website.

Transition to A Level

Teachers may like to use some of the material in Book 3 for broad extension sessions, designed to inspire students to choose the subject at A Level. In addition, at the start of Y12 the original Latin text materials could be used to facilitate the transition from GCSE to A Level. In particular, Book 3 supports the following skills:

- **Building confidence in reading original Latin:** the short extracts and the careful selection of passages which are not too demanding means that this reading material will help students develop confidence in their ability to translate original Latin.
- **Using commentaries:** The online notes for each *scripta* will help students develop the skills needed to use commentaries as an effective guide to translation.
- **Understanding of historical context and genre:** students are likely to get more from their A Level set texts if they have an awareness of the literary genre and historical context for these texts. The Introductions in Book 3 are designed to offer an overview of this material; the range of authors contained in each chapter will offer a useful contrast or context for whichever author is studied in depth at A Level.

Bibliography

Caesar (1914), *Civil Wars*, trans. A. G. Peskett. Loeb Classical Library 39. Cambridge, MA: Harvard University Press.
Catullus (2007), *The Shorter Poems*, trans. John Godwin. Aris and Phillips Classical Texts. Liverpool: Liverpool University Press.
Catullus, Tibullus, and *Pervigilium Veneris* (1962), trans. F. W. Cornish (Catullus), trans. J. P. Postgate (Tibullus) and trans. J. W. Mackail (*Pervigilium Veneris*), revised by G. P. Goold. Loeb Classical Library 6. Cambridge, MA: Harvard University Press.
Cicero (1986), *Selected Letters*, trans. D. R. Shackleton Bailey. London: Penguin.
Dio Cassius (1914), *Roman History, Volume III: Books 36–40*, trans. Earnest Cary and Herbert B. Foster. Loeb Classical Library 53. Cambridge, MA: Harvard University Press.
Dio Cassius (1916), *Roman History, Volume IV: Books 41–45*, trans. Earnest Cary and Herbert B. Foster. Loeb Classical Library 66. Cambridge, MA: Harvard University Press.
Hornblower, Antony, and Antony Spawforth (eds) (2003), *The Oxford Classical Dictionary 3rd edition*. Oxford: Oxford University Press.
Holland, Tom (2004), *Rubicon, The Triumph and Tragedy of the Roman Republic*. Ilford, Essex: Abacus.
Johnston, Patricia A. (2013), *Epigrams and Satire in Latin Poetry*. New York: Oxford University Press.
Lewis, Charlton, and Charles Short (1897), *A Latin Dictionary*. Oxford: Clarendon Press.
Martial (1943), *Select Epigrams of Martial*, trans. Walter C. A. Ker. Cambridge, MA: Harvard University Press.
Morwood, James (1999), *Latin Grammar*. Oxford: Oxford University Press.
Ovid (1985), *Metamorphoses Books I–IV*, trans. D. E. Hill. Aris and Phillips Classical Texts. Liverpool: Liverpool University Press.
Pliny (1972), *Letters II*, trans. B. Radice. Loeb Classical Library 59. Cambridge, MA: Harvard University Press.
Propertius (1986), *The Poems*, trans. W. G. Shepherd. London: Penguin.
Plutarch (1917), *Lives, Volume V: Agesilaus and Pompey. Pelopidas and Marcellus*, trans. Bernadotte Perrin. Loeb Classical Library 87. Cambridge, MA: Harvard University Press.
Plutarch (1919), *Lives, Volume VII: Demosthenes and Cicero. Alexander and Caesar*, trans. Bernadotte Perrin. Loeb Classical Library 99. Cambridge, MA: Harvard University Press.
Seager, Robin (2002), *Pompey the Great: A Political Biography, 2nd Edition*. Oxford: Blackwell Publishing.
Simpson, D. P. (ed.) (1982), *Cassell's Latin Dictionary*. London: Cassell & Company.
Suetonius (2001), *Suetonius: Divus Claudius*, ed. Donna Hurley. Cambridge: Cambridge University Press.
Suetonius (1957), *The Twelve Caesars*, trans. Robert Graves. London: Penguin.
Tacitus (2012), *Annals*, trans. Cynthia Damon. London: Penguin.
Tibullus (1972), *The Poems of Tibullus*, trans. Philip Dunlop. London: Penguin.

CHAPTER 13
CICERO AND CAESAR – EYE-WITNESS ACCOUNTS OF CIVIL WAR

Chapter 13: Introduction

Chapter 13 focuses on the **civil war** between **Gaius Julius Caesar** and **Gnaeus Pompeius Magnus**. As you read in Chapter 9, the civil war between Caesar and Pompey was a pivotal moment in Rome's evolution away from the Republican principles of shared and limited power. Rome's political structures cracked in the face of Caesar and Pompey's rivalry; after his victory, Caesar secured a position of king-like dominance, lasting until his assassination in 44 BC.

Julius Caesar remains one of the most widely known Romans today, but in many ways **Pompey's career was more exceptional**. If you would like to find out more about Pompey's extraordinary early success, there is an additional resource on the Companion Website: **Pompey's rise to power**.

> The Latin noun *ordo* means *rank, class*. Explain the meaning of *extraordinary*.

This period is one of the best documented in Roman history. The texts (*scripta*) for this chapter are taken from contemporary, **eye-witness accounts** of the conflict. The *scripta* are printed on pp19–35. You can read them in English alongside this Introduction and you may find the questions on p7 a useful way to think about each text.

The Latin versions for each *scripta* include grammatical forms which are introduced in the Core Language section. As you work through the chapter, there will be signposts to indicate when you could look at the *scripta* in Latin; alternatively you could wait until the end of the Core Language section and read the *scripta* then. On p36 there are questions which will help you think more broadly about the texts and aspects of their genre or literary style.

Caesar and Pompey: an alliance disintegrates

During his early career, **Pompey had amassed huge personal power** as a talented military leader, winning a series of significant victories which included exceptional campaigns in the Mediterranean and the east. Caesar and Pompey's remarkable achievements made them rivals, but they had not always been enemies. In 60 BC, **Caesar** and **Pompey** had formed an **unofficial alliance** with **Crassus**, the richest man in Rome at that time, combining their wealth, political power and influence to steer the Republic's decisions in their own interests.

During the 50s, however, **relationships between these three men deteriorated**. Caesar was away in Gaul and Crassus died after a crushing military defeat at the Battle of Carrhae in 53 BC. In addition, Pompey's

FIGURE 13.1 Bust of Pompey

Gnaeus Pompeius Magnus, better known as Pompey the Great, is shown in this early 1st-century-BC bust at around the age of fifty. His hairstyle, with defined locks of hair, was said to have imitated the hairstyle of Alexander the Great, whom Pompey admired. This bust is currently in the Ny Carlsberg Glyptotek in Copenhagen.

wife – Caesar's daughter, Julia – had died in childbirth in 54 BC; this ended an important personal connection between Pompey and Caesar. Pompey remained in Rome, able to influence Rome's political decisions in person, but the mechanics of government were becoming increasingly strained by corruption, coercion and intimidation.

Rome descends into violence

By 52 BC **the Republic was in freefall**. Mob violence on the streets of Rome had disrupted the elections and Pompey had been established as sole consul in an attempt to regain political order. **Julius Caesar knew that returning from Gaul to Rome could be dangerous** for him: without the legal protection of a military command or a political role, his opponents could move against him via criminal trials in the law courts. He needed to secure a seamless transition from the *imperium* of provincial command to the *imperium* of political office. In 52 BC he secured a law granting him permission to **stand for the consulship** *in absentia* at the end of his time in Gaul, thus protecting him from a potentially dangerous return to Rome.

> The Latin adjective *solus* means *alone, only*. Explain the meaning of *sole*.

Unfortunately for Caesar, by 50 BC hardline members of the senate, such as Cato the Younger, who feared Caesar's growing personal power, were demanding that **Caesar disband his legions** now that his conquest of Gaul was complete. Moreover, the decision to allow him to stand for the consulship *in absentia* was also revoked. Caesar argued that he would only disband his armies if Pompey – who held military power over the legions in Africa and Spain at the time – did the same. Pompey and the senate refused. In *scripta* **13.1** and *scripta* **13.2** you will read about the **tension** prominent Romans felt at this time and their fear of a seemingly inevitable war between Pompey and Caesar. In *scripta* **13.3** you can read Caesar's version of his attempts to negotiate a peaceful resolution.

In early January 49 BC the senate passed the **senatus consultum ultimum**, a decree which declared the state to be in danger and gave power to the consuls to do whatever it took to protect it from further harm. In response, Caesar marched Legion XIII across the Rubicon. **Civil war** had begun.

49–48 BC: Civil war begins; Pompey leaves Italy

As news of Caesar's declaration of war reached Rome, there was chaos and panic. In *scripta* **13.4** you will read of Cicero's indecision about whether it would be safest for his family to remain in Rome or to flee. The senate immediately looked to Pompey, as their greatest general, to save them, despite previous disputes and years of mistrust. Pompey had two legions at his disposal, but he was well aware that Caesar could be marching on Rome with ten of his own experienced legions. **Pompey made the bold decision to abandon Rome** and withdraw east. Pompey's decision to leave Rome had huge military as well as symbolic implications.

FIGURE 13.2 Column inscription commemorating Julius Caesar's crossing of the Rubicon

Here we see a *cippus*, a raised stone with a flat top and an inscription. This *cippus* is intended to memorialise the moment when Julius Caesar took his army across the Rubicon river, sparking a civil war. This *cippus* is believed to have been made centuries later. It can be seen in the town of Rimini in northern Italy.

Chapter 13 Cicero and Caesar – Eye-Witness Accounts of Civil War

> The Latin adjective *vetus* means *old* or *experienced*. Explain the meaning of *veterans*.

The man who, despite his extraordinary political career, had always claimed to put the Republic first was now seen to be abandoning it in the face of Caesar's approaching army. In *scripta* **13.5** you will read about **Cicero's anger** at Pompey's decision.

From a military perspective, however, abandoning the city made sense. Pompey's newly raised soldiers would have been no match for the battle-hardened veterans of Caesar's Gallic legions. He needed time to gather support, drawing on favours from allies and clients gained during his successful campaigns in the east, and he needed time to train his soldiers. Many of the senators chose to join Pompey in Greece rather than wait for Caesar's arrival in Rome.

FIGURE 13.3 Julius Caesar crossing the Adriatic Sea

Pictured here is an artist's rendition of Julius Caesar crossing the Adriatic Sea in pursuit of Pompey. In this image, created in 1938, Caesar wears distinctive red boots and a billowing red cloak. Caesar appears to be alone except for one man steering the boat. There is no sign of the fleet which carried his army in stages to Brundisium.

Fighting in Spain and Greece

Caesar made straight for **Brundisium** in southern Italy, the port Pompey and the senators were using to withdraw to **Greece**, but he was too late. Pompey, and many of the most influential senators of the day, including Cicero, successfully arrived in Greece. Instead of following Pompey east, Caesar went in the opposite direction. He marched to **Spain** with his army, with the aim of defeating the five Republican legions there so that Pompey would not be able to call on them at a later point in the war. In *scripta* **13.6** you can read about **Caesar's victory in Spain**.

While Caesar was campaigning in Spain, Pompey gathered a large army and fleet from all over the Mediterranean, including Greece, Egypt, Syria and Turkey. By the time Caesar arrived back in Brundisium in the winter of 49–48 BC, he was faced with a **difficult choice**: should he wait in Italy for Pompey's inevitable spring invasion, or should he take the fight to Greece, preventing Pompey from growing any stronger, but braving a dangerous winter crossing of the Adriatic Sea? Caesar, ever the risk-taker, opted for the latter. Caesar's fleet was not big enough to transport his whole army; he had two crossings and – despite the success of his first crossing – the Pompeians were able to delay the second, leaving Caesar stranded in Greece with only half his army. The other half of his troops were still at Brundisium under the command of Mark Antony, one of Caesar's most loyal allies.

Caesar's position in Greece was precarious; he was at half strength and in hostile lands with limited access to supplies. Pompey knew that **delaying a battle** would make Caesar weaker and allow himself to grow stronger. Over the coming months, Caesar made several attempts to engage with Pompey and seek peace, but Pompey refused.

Eventually, however, Pompey's delaying tactics backfired: Mark Antony successfully crossed the Adriatic with the other half of Caesar's army and joined his commander.

The end of the civil war: the Battle of Pharsalus

Caesar now believed he was in a position to take **direct action against Pompey**. He attacked by laying siege to Pompey's camp in **Dyrrhachium** in modern-day Albania. Pompey maintained a defensive position for a few weeks and then launched a successful attack, **forcing Caesar to retreat**. Instead of pursuing him immediately, however, as many of his allies urged, Pompey ordered his army to remain where it was. Plutarch records that Caesar remarked that 'today victory would have been with the enemy, if they had a winner in command'. Caesar had suffered his first significant defeat of the civil war but Pompey's caution meant that Caesar lived to fight another day.

> The Latin noun *signum* means *sign* or *signal* and the Latin verb *facio* means *make*. Explain the meaning of *significant*.

In due course, Pompey pursued Caesar across northern Greece and the two armies fought each other near **Pharsalus**. Caesar's victory in this battle proved to be a turning point in the civil war. In *scripta* **13.7** you can read about the end of this battle, Caesar's decisive attack on Pompey's camp and Pompey's night-time escape.

What happened next?

Caesar's success in the Battle of Pharsalus tipped the balance of power firmly in his favour. **Pompey** attempted to continue the war, fleeing to **Egypt** where he hoped that his ties with the previous Egyptian king Ptolemy XII would be enough to earn the support of his son

> The Latin verb *teneo* means *hold, keep*. Explain the meaning of *continue*.

FIGURE 13.4 Coin of Pompeius Magnus

After the death of Pompey the Great in 48 BC, his sons used his image to capitalise on his fame. This denarius, minted in 44–43 BC, combines the image of Pompey along with symbols of Neptune (a trident and a dolphin) on the obverse, and a ship in full sail on the reverse. These images were employed by Pompey the Great's son to promote his own naval abilities.

Chapter 13 Cicero and Caesar – Eye-Witness Accounts of Civil War

> The Latin verb *resisto* means *stand against*. Explain the meaning of *resistance*.

Ptolemy XIII, brother of Cleopatra. These hopes soon proved false; as you read in Chapter 10, the treacherous boy-king Ptolemy XIII had Pompey killed in an attempt to earn the approval and respect of Caesar. Although the outcome of the Civil War was now clear, **Caesar** still spent the following years campaigning. In Egypt, he supported Cleopatra's claim to the throne against her brother before marching north to defeat the King of Pontus. Finally, he tackled the last pockets of Roman resistance in Africa and Spain before he returned to Rome triumphant.

In 49 BC, **Caesar was elected dictator** for the first time; each year the appointment was renewed until 44 BC when he was declared dictator for life. This was too much for some of the senators and a month or so later **Caesar was assassinated** on the grounds that he had become too much like a king. As you read in Chapter 11, Caesar's death set in motion a chain of events that led to another triumvirate which in turn collapsed into another civil war, this time between Mark Antony and Caesar's adopted son Octavian. Octavian would eventually defeat Mark Antony and Cleopatra at the Battle of Actium in 31 BC, end the decades of civil war, establish a long-lasting period of Roman peace and become the first Roman emperor, Augustus. In Chapter 15 you will read about how rule-by-emperor changed Rome.

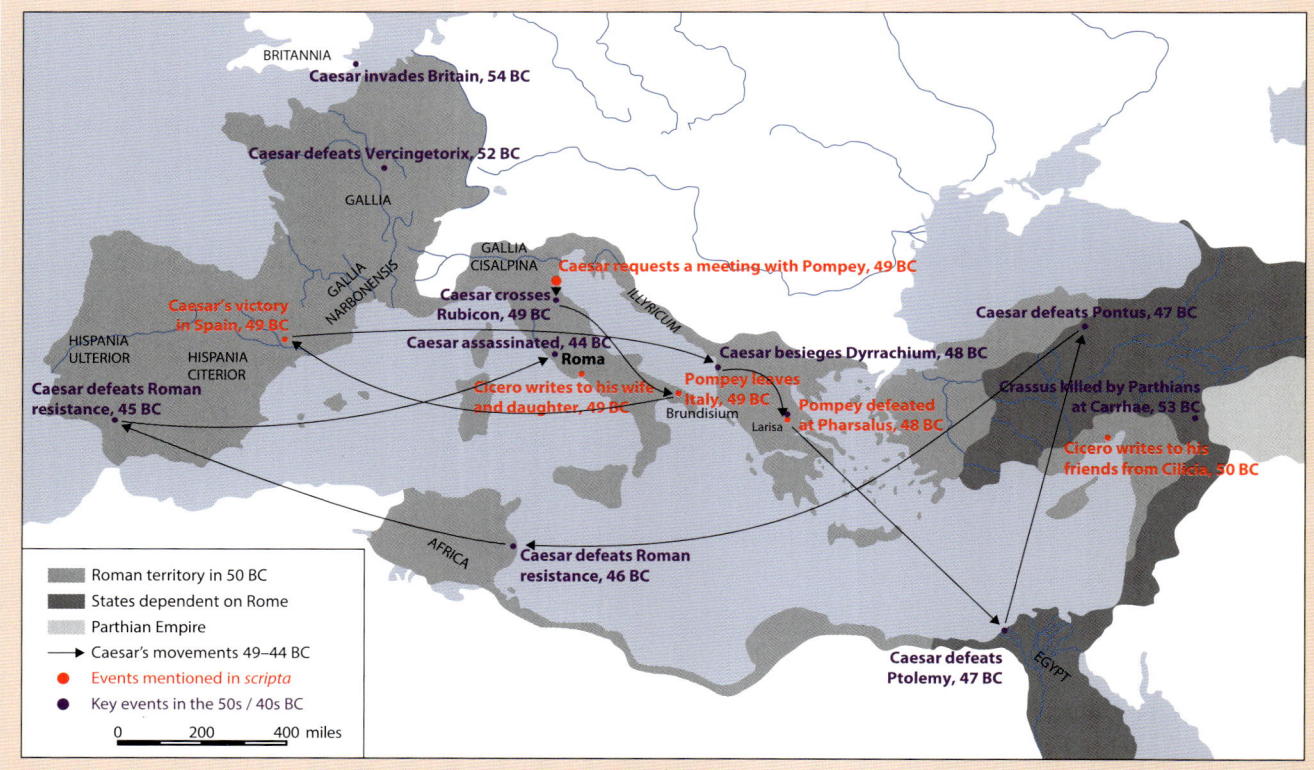

FIGURE 13.5 Map of Julius Caesar's movements 49–44 BC

This map tracks Julius Caesar's movements during this period; it shows the vast geographical scale of his campaigns. The arrows will help you follow him, starting from his request to meet with Pompey in 49 BC. The arrows depict the sequence of Caesar's movements, they do not represent his route from one place to another. A bigger version of this map is available on the Companion Website.

CHAPTER 13: READ THE *SCRIPTA* IN ENGLISH

The texts for each scripta *are printed in this book in Latin and English. These texts can be read in English, Latin or a combination of the two. The* scripta *texts for this chapter start on p19. They follow the Core Language section because their Latin versions contain new grammar and vocabulary from this chapter.*

The questions below can be answered by reading the scripta *in English. Available on the Companion Website are copies of the English version of each* scripta *along with the questions for each text.*

scripta 13.1 in English (p21): Caelius Rufus fears the outbreak of civil war

1. Why does Cicero's friend – Caelius Rufus – believe that civil war is inevitable?
2. Explain why Caelius Rufus finds it difficult to work out whether he should support Pompey or Caesar.
3. Caelius Rufus is worried about the prospect of civil war. Find as many details as you can from this letter which suggest that there are difficult times ahead.
4. Do you think Caelius Rufus' letter is likely to be honest? What do you think are the factors which may have influenced what he chose to write?

scripta 13.2 in English (p23): Cicero's loyalty to Pompey

1. Cicero says that Caesar's demands are outrageous; do you think Cicero believes that the Romans will stand up to Caesar or give him what he wants? Explain your answer.
2. What reasons does Cicero give for choosing to support Pompey publicly? How do his private thoughts differ from his public position?
3. What evidence is there in this letter that Cicero thinks war should be avoided?
4. What impression do you get of Cicero's character from this letter?

scripta 13.3 in English (p25): Caesar requests a meeting with Pompey

1. What does Caesar say about his relationship with the Republic?
2. What does Caesar say which suggests he is keen to avoid civil war?
3. How does Caesar create the impression that Pompey is aiming for war rather than peace?
4. Based on your knowledge of Caesar's life-story, are you surprised by how Caesar presents himself in this text? Explain your answer with reference to details from this letter and from what you know about Caesar's career.

Chapter 13 Cicero and Caesar – Eye-Witness Accounts of Civil War

scripta 13.4 in English (p27): Cicero urges his wife and daughter to think of their safety

1. What does Cicero say are the benefits and the risks if his wife and daughter stay in Rome?
2. What does Cicero tell his wife and daughter to do if they stay in Rome?
3. What does this letter show us about Cicero's relationship with his wife and daughter?

scripta 13.5 in English (p29): Cicero is angry at Pompey's decision to leave Italy

1. Cicero believes that Pompey helped Caesar become more powerful: use bullet points to list all the ways in which, according to Cicero, Pompey increased Caesar's power.
2. What does Cicero believe is the worst thing that Pompey has done? Why do you think he is most angry about this?
3. How does Cicero convey his anger towards Pompey in this letter? What does this anger show about Cicero's values?

scripta 13.6 in English (p31): Caesar's victory in Spain

1. At the start of this extract Caesar says that he and his army have acted correctly; what does he mean by this? Explain his reasons in your own words.
2. How does Caesar criticise Pompey in this extract?
3. At the end of the extract what terms does Caesar offer for peace in Spain?
4. Caesar was able to inspire great loyalty from his troops: what picture does this text create of Caesar as a military leader?

scripta 13.7 in English (p34): Caesar wins the civil war

1. How does Caesar create the impression of a dramatic end to the Battle of Pharsalus?
2. What does Caesar do to create a negative impression of Pompey's army?
3. Caesar creates a dramatic image of Pompey's escape: how is Pompey characterised here? Do you think we should take this text as an accurate characterisation of Pompey? Explain your answer.

Chapter 13: Core Language Vocabulary List

Some of the words listed here look very different from those you have met so far. This will be explained later in the chapter.

conor	conari, conatus sum	try
miror	mirari, miratus sum	wonder at; admire
videor	videri, visus sum	seem; appear
loquor	loqui, locutus sum	speak; talk
egredior	egredi, egressus sum	go out
ingredior	ingredi, ingressus sum	enter
morior	mori, mortuus sum	die
patior	pati, passus sum	suffer; endure
progredior	progredi, progressus sum	advance
proficiscor	proficisci, profectus sum	set out
regredior	regredi, regressus sum	go back; return
sequor	sequi, secutus sum	follow
tollo	tollere, sustuli, sublatum	raise; lift up; hold up
aufero	auferre, abstuli, ablatum	take away; carry off; steal
offero	offerre, obtuli, oblatum	offer
refero	referre, rettuli, relatum	bring / carry back; report; tell
coepi	coepisse	began
malo	malle, malui	prefer
domus	domus, f	home
domi		at home
exercitus	exercitus, m	army
manus	manus, f	hand; group of people
dies	diei, m	day
res	rei, f	thing; matter; event
spes	spei, f	hope
alter	altera, alterum	the other; another; one (of two); the second (of two)
nonnulli	nonnullae, nonnulla	some; several
solus	sola, solum	alone; lonely; only; on one's own

Chapter 13 Cicero and Caesar – Eye-Witness Accounts of Civil War

totus	tota, totum	whole
idem	eadem, idem	the same
ipse	ipsa, ipsum	myself, yourself, himself, herself, itself etc.
quidam	quaedam, quoddam	one; a certain; some
sine	+ ablative	without
sub	+ accusative / ablative	under; beneath

4th and 5th declension nouns

So far, you have met case endings for the 1st, 2nd and 3rd declensions.

Latin also has a 4th and a 5th declension. You can recognise a 4th or 5th declension noun as follows:

exercitus, exercitus, m   **4th** declension, stem = **exercit-**
res, rei, f   **5th** declension, stem = **r-**

There are no 4th or 5th declension adjectives; the endings from the 4th and 5th declensions are used only for nouns.

The endings for the 4th and 5th declensions are as follows:

	4th declension	5th declension
nominative sg	exercit-us	r-es
accusative sg	exercit-um	r-em
genitive sg	exercit-us	r-ei
dative sg	exercit-ui	r-ei
ablative sg	exercit-u	r-e
nominative pl	exercit-us	r-es
accusative pl	exercit-us	r-es
genitive pl	exercit-uum	r-erum
dative pl	exercit-ibus	r-ebus
ablative pl	exercit-ibus	r-ebus

Both the 4th and the 5th declension contain masculine and feminine nouns, but there are no neuter nouns in the 5th declension. Only a small number of 4th declension neuter nouns exist; their endings are given in the Reference Grammar, on p220.

The noun *domus, domus, f* has unusual endings; see the Reference Grammar, p255.

Remember, masculine and feminine nouns within a declension share the same endings.

Consolidation: case endings

Case endings are a difficult part of Latin grammar: the same spellings appear for different cases and it is easy to get confused. It is helpful to learn the endings grouped together by case so that the patterns within a set of endings are clear. For example:

	1st	2nd	3rd	4th	5th
accusative sg	-am	-um	-em	-um	-em
accusative pl	-as	-os	-es	-us	-es

Remember, neuter nouns have different accusative endings. See the Reference Grammar, pp219–220.

	1st	2nd	3rd	4th	5th
ablative sg	-a	-o	-e / -i	-u	-e
ablative pl	-is	-is	-ibus	-ibus	-ebus

Remember, in the 3rd declension, *-e* is the ablative sg ending typically used by **nouns** and *-i* is the ending typically used by **adjectives**.

The accusative and ablative case endings are the most important to know well because:

- **prepositions** are followed by the accusative or ablative case; it is important to recognise the accusative or ablative words which are working with a preposition and group them together as a phrase
- Latin typically puts the **accusative object** before its verb, but in English you will need to **translate the verb first**
- you will need to be able to recognise an accusative noun in order to identify an **accusative + infinitive indirect statement**, and you will need to recognise an ablative noun + participle in order to identify the **ablative absolute construction**. These constructions are very common and they will be practised further in Chapter 14.

Chapter 13 Cicero and Caesar – Eye-Witness Accounts of Civil War

> The nouns in bold are either **accusative** or **ablative** case. Identify the **case** of each one.

> **Note that** no prepositions are used with *domus* when the meaning is *towards / away from / at home*; instead the forms *domum*, *domo* and *domi* are used (see p225).

EXERCISE 13.1

1. dux **exercitum** iussit **oppidum** incendere.
2. diu in **agris** laboravi; nunc manus meae fessae sunt.
3. tres **dies** senatores ab **urbe** aberant; quarto **die** redierunt.
4. 'perterriti sumus!' inquiunt liberi, 'nam nullam **spem** habemus.'
5. in **foro** cives de **rebus** magnis audiverunt.
6. 'cur domi manebas?' rogavit mulier irata. 'cur ad **oppidum** non festinavisti?'
7. diutissime milites huius exercitus fortiter pugnabant.
8. incolae fortissime pugnabant sed sine **spe**.
9. postquam rex ab **urbe** missus est, cives **spem** rerum meliorum habebant.
10. duces illius exercitus audaciores sunt quam huius exercitus.

scripta in Latin you could now look at the Latin version of *scripta* 13.1

Deponent verbs

In the vocabulary for this chapter, there are verbs of the following types:

conor	conari, conatus sum	try
videor	videri, visus sum	seem; appear
loquor	loqui, locutus sum	speak; talk
egredior	egredi, egressus sum	go out

These verbs look passive in form but their translations are active in meaning. They are known as **deponent verbs**. Because they use passive rather than active forms, they have no perfect active stem. This means that they only have three principal parts: the present tense, the infinitive and the perfect tense.

   conor (I try), conari (to try), conatus sum (I tried)

The **infinitives** for deponent verbs look different from the infinitives you have met so far. This is because they are the passive form of the infinitive. You will learn more about passive infinitives in Chapter 14.

There are deponent verbs in each conjugation. You can recognise the conjugation from the deponent verb's principal parts.

con**or**, con**ari**	1st conjugation
vid**eor**, vid**eri**	2nd conjugation
loqu**or**, loqu**i**	3rd conjugation
egred**ior**, egred**i**	mixed conjugation
4th conjugation deponent verbs are very rare; see Reference Grammar p233.	

Deponent verbs change their forms in line with other verbs in their conjugation; the only difference is that their form will be passive, but their meaning active.

Examples are given below.

conantur	they try
videbitur	he / she / it will seem
loquebamur	we were speaking
locutus es	you (sg) spoke
egressi erant	they had gone out

EXERCISE 13.2: DEPONENT VERBS ONLY

1. **conabamur** patrem matremque invenire.
2. puellae magnum templum **miratae sunt**.
3. cras ex urbe **regrediar** et ducem alterum **sequar**.
4. fratres sororesque cum parentibus **profecti sunt**.
5. cur haec pessima in bello **passus es**? hostesne saevi erant?
6. nonne cum duce huius exercitus **locutus es**?
7. multi prope flumen **moriuntur**; nunc magnopere lacrimamus.
8. quamquam in nave solus eram, fortiter ad insulam **profectus sum**.
9. hi socii audaciores **videbantur** quam illi.
10. numquam Romani ducem meliorem **secuti erant**; spem enim pacis eis dedit.

The **deponent** verbs are in bold. Identify the **tense** and **person** of each one.

Chapter 13 Cicero and Caesar – Eye-Witness Accounts of Civil War

> Look at the verbs in bold: which are **deponent** verbs? Which are **passive** forms of **non-deponent** verbs?

EXERCISE 13.3: DEPONENT VERBS AND PASSIVE VERBS

1. omnia de periculo **narrata sunt** quod nuntius diu **loquebatur**.
2. ubi navis **conspecta est**, nautae ad mare **profecti sunt**.
3. omnes aurum **mirabuntur** quod nunc in templum **portatur**.
4. postquam urbem **ingressi sumus**, prope portas convenimus.
5. ubi pax **nuntiata est**, coniunx maritum invenire **conata est**.
6. cives, qui graviter **vulnerati sunt**, mortem pessimam **patientur**.
7. quamquam parentes **servati sunt**, soror vestra de fratre desperare **videbatur**.
8. prima luce **progressus es** sed mox **interficieris**.
9. tandem loqui de consilio constituerunt quod servi **venditi erant**.
10. quamquam domum regredi volebat, poeta in forum **tractus est**.

| *scripta* in Latin | you could now look at the Latin version of *scripta* 13.2 |

Consolidation: *fero*

fero is one of Latin's most important **irregular verbs**. Its forms are listed in full in the Reference Grammar on p252.

Like most irregular verbs, *fero* only has unusual forms for its present tense, imperative and infinitive; all its other forms have the usual endings for a 3rd conjugation verb.

Its principal parts, however, can be easy to forget because its stems are very different from each other. It is important to learn these carefully.

fero, ferre, tuli, latum – bring, carry, bear

Compounds of *fero*

Like other very common verbs such as *eo, ire, ivi / ii, itum*, prepositions are often combined with *fero* to form a **compound verb**.

In the vocabulary for this chapter there are three of these compound verbs.

aufero	auferre, abstuli, ablatum	take away; carry off; steal
offero	offerre, obtuli, oblatum	offer
refero	referre, rettuli, relatum	bring / carry back; report; tell

Notice how the spelling of the preposition prefix changes along with the stem of *fero*.

tollo

tollo is a regular 3rd conjugation verb, but its stems look very different from each other and it can be easily confused with **fero**. It is worth learning these verbs as a pair in order to avoid confusing them.

tollo	tollere, sustuli, sublatum	raise; lift up; hold up
fero	ferre, tuli, latum	bring; carry; bear

EXERCISE 13.4

1. quamquam omnes cenam consumere volebant, nauta crudelis cibum **abstulit**.
2. cur his poetis praemia non **obtulisti**?
3. ubi per flumen currebat, mater audax liberos parvos **sustulit**.
4. socii pecuniam duci **rettulerunt**.
5. 'quando,' inquiunt cives, 'consilium nobis **offeres**? periculum magnum adest et perterriti sumus.'
6. fratres sororesque aurum e templo **auferre** nolebant; nam iram deorum timebant.
7. tandem nuntius **rettulit** Romanos pacem habere.
8. coniunx, quamquam irata erat, cibum marito **obtulit**.
9. mulieres nonnullae a militibus saevis **auferuntur**.
10. ad portas urbis clamores a turba civium iratorum **tollebantur**.

Look at each of the verbs in bold: is it from **tollo**, **ferro** or from a **compound** of **ferro**?

scripta in Latin	you could now look at the Latin version of *scripta* 13.3 and 13.4

Chapter 13 Cicero and Caesar – Eye-Witness Accounts of Civil War

> **New irregular verbs: *malo*, *coepi***
>
> ***malo*** is an irregular verb whose present tense forms are very similar to ***volo***.
>
> | I prefer | malo |
> |---|---|
> | you (sg) prefer | mavis |
> | he / she / it prefers | mavult |
> | we prefer | malumus |
> | you (pl) prefer | mavultis |
> | they prefer | malunt |
>
> The forms of ***malo*** are listed in full in the Reference Grammar on p251.
>
> ***coepi*** is known as a **defective verb**; this is because it only exists in certain forms. It has no present stem. ***coepi*** is its perfect tense; its endings are like all other perfect tense verbs.
>
> | I began | coep-**i** |
> |---|---|
> | you (sg) began | coep-**isti** |
> | etc. | |
>
> Its **infinitive** – ***coepisse*** – means 'to have begun'. This is a perfect tense infinitive. You will meet other examples of these in Chapter 14.

EXERCISE 13.5

The verbs in bold are from ***malo*** and ***coepi***. Translate each one.

1. 'cur maritum meum amare **mavis**?' rogavit mulier irata.
2. non **malumus** pugnare quam domum redire.
3. ubi de exercitu audiverunt, incolae fugere **coeperunt**.
4. quod cives multi iam in foro aderant, poeta tacere **malebat**.
5. nautae, ubi navis progredi **coepit**, laetissimi erant.
6. milites in illo bello multa passi sunt sed etiam tum ducem defendere **malebant**.
7. 'o parentes, conati sumus esse boni,' inquiunt liberi, 'sed irati esse **mavultis**.'
8. prima luce milites urbem oppugnare **coeperunt**.
9. socii spem pacis habere **malebant**.
10. 'quam partem libri mei **maluisti**?' rogavit poeta.

scripta in Latin   you could now look at the Latin version of *scripta* 13.5

Pronouns: *idem*, *ipse*, *quidam*

In the vocabulary for this chapter there are three new pronouns.

idem	eadem, idem	the same
ipse	ipsa, ipsum	myself, yourself, himself, herself, itself etc.
quidam	quaedam, quoddam	one; a certain; some

ipse is an emphatic pronoun which often expresses surprise or shock.

Two of these are **compounds**: *idem* is a compound of *is, ea, id* and *quidam* is a compound of *qui, quae, quod*. As a result, it is the **start** of each word which changes.

The forms of all three pronouns are listed in full in the Reference Grammar on pp224–227.

As with the other pronouns, these words can be used with a noun or on their own.

e.g. soror **in eadem insula** habitabat.   My sister lived on the **same island**.

Caesar **gentem quandam** vicit.   Caesar conquered **a certain tribe**.

ipsi prope forum sedebant.   **The men themselves** were sitting near the forum.

EXERCISE 13.6

1. nonne nuntius tibi **eadem** rettulit?
2. milites **quidam** ex hoc exercitu fugere conabantur.
3. soror **ipsa** caput fratris sui vulneravit.
4. 'visne navem **eandem** emere?', rogavit nauta.
5. turba ad portas **ipsas** progrediebatur.
6. magister **quidam** semper **eadem** docebat.
7. die **eodem** multi mortui sunt.
8. cur ducem **ipsum** non secutus es?
9. omnes cives de **eisdem** rebus tacebant.
10. in foro, poeta **quidam** pulcherrime de pace locutus est.

Look at each of the **pronouns** in bold. Is the pronoun a form of *idem*, *ipse* or *quidam*?

scripta in Latin   you could now look at the Latin version of *scripta* 13.6

Chapter 13 Cicero and Caesar – Eye-Witness Accounts of Civil War

Unusual adjectives: *alter, nonnulli, solus, totus*

These four adjectives are part of the vocabulary for this chapter.

alter	altera, alterum	the other; another; one (of two); the second (of two)
nonnulli	nonnullae, nonnulla	some; several
solus	sola, solum	alone; lonely; only; on one's own
totus	tota, totum	whole

They look like 2-1-2 adjectives but notice that they have exceptional genitive and dative sg endings.

	alter	nonnulli	solus	totus
genitive sg	alterius	nonnullius	solius	totius
dative sg	alteri	nonnulli	soli	toti

The same ending is used for **all genders**.

The endings for these adjectives are listed in full in the Reference Grammar on p254 and p256.

EXERCISE 13.7

> Look at each of the **adjectives** in bold. Which **noun** does it describe?

1. prope oppidum illud, exercitus **totus** deletus est.
2. mulier **sola** ad urbem progrediebatur.
3. 'num de gente **altera** audivisti?' rogaverunt incolae.
4. heri **nonnullae** naves a nautis iratissimis incensae sunt.
5. cur senator praemia poetae **alteri** non dedit?
6. uxor mariti **alterius** desperabat quod pecuniam invenire non poterat.
7. domi frater erat **solus** quod parentes aberant.
8. socii **nonnulli** auxilium civibus offerebant.
9. ubi dux interfectus est, milites **nonnulli** magnopere lacrimabant.
10. per insulam **totam** pecunia ex domibus ablata est.

> *domi* means 'at home' – see p9.

scripta in Latin — you could now look at the Latin version of *scripta* 13.7

Chapter 13: *scripta*

For guidance on how to make use of these Latin texts and their English translations, see pp.viii–ix.

On the Companion Website you will find resources to accompany these texts:

- in the **scripta in English** section you will find copies of each text in English only, with questions on each one
- in the **scripta in Latin** section you will find notes for each of the Latin texts: these contain glosses for all words not yet met in a Core Language vocabulary list, explanations to help you understand the Latin and material designed to help you build your appreciation of literary style.

Meet the *scriptores*: Cicero and Caesar

The life-stories of **Marcus Tullius Cicero** and **Gaius Julius Caesar** were central to *de Romanis* Book 2. Chapter 8 discussed Cicero's meteoric rise to power and the dramatic events during his consulship in 63 BC. Cicero's career is a good example of the role that oratory played in creating and wielding power in Rome; Cicero remains famous today partly because a large number of his speeches survive and they are still used as examples of great oratorical skill. Chapter 9 focused on Julius Caesar, his ruthless ambition, and how he used his financial and military power to achieve dominance in Rome.

Both men recorded their own careers in different ways. Many of **Cicero**'s speeches were published in written form during his lifetime. These speeches highlight Cicero's political career and the power struggles of the day, many of which were played out in the law courts as one noble tried to score political points over another by accusing him of some sort of illegal act. In addition, Cicero also wrote a large number of **private letters** which were collected and published after his death; 900 of these still survive today and the collection includes letters written to Cicero by his friends. Some of the *scripta* for this chapter are taken from Cicero's private letters. These letters offer a more personal view of events in Rome at this time and reveal the fear, uncertainty and trauma caused by living in the shadow of ruthless and personal power battles.

FIGURE 13.5 Statue of Julius Caesar

This statue of Julius Caesar is outside the Parliament in Vienna. It dates from the late 19th century. The statue highlights Caesar's military and political roles. Caesar wears a military breastplate with the head of the Gorgon Medusa in the middle; his seated position and the rolled document in his hand indicates political power and importance.

Chapter 13 Cicero and Caesar – Eye-witness Accounts of Civil War

The texts written by **Julius Caesar** are rather different: referred to as **commentaries**, they present a seemingly dispassionate log of events during the Gallic and civil wars. Caesar only refers to himself in the 3rd person, a technique which creates the illusion of an objective account, appearing to be about Julius Caesar rather than by him. As you read the following texts, it will be interesting to think about how Julius Caesar is curating his own image and the choices he makes about how to describe his words, actions and intentions.

> **Idiom** means the quirks of a language which are particular to that language.

Reading original Latin note 1: Getting started

The reading passages in this chapter are lightly adapted versions of original Latin texts. They contain more **idiom** than the Latin you read in *de Romanis* Book 2. It will be useful to bear the following things in mind:

- there will be more words which you do not know and sometimes the words which you do know will have different meanings. Some of the new words are not glossed; this is because you can **work out their meaning** from context, Latin words which are similar or from English derivations.
- **adjectives** are often moved away from their noun **for emphasis**: you will need to look at their endings carefully and only translate them when you reach the noun with which they agree.
- Latin is much more concise than English; English will often need **more words** in order to make the meaning clear or to bring out the emphasis which Latin has achieved by word order.
- sometimes English will use a **different part of speech.** This is particularly common for words which convey actions. Latin might use a noun (e.g. *their departure*), but English is much more likely to use a verb (e.g. *they departed*). You will also find that Latin participles are often translated as finite verbs in English.
- **passive verbs** can be cumbersome in English; it is often better to use an **active verb** instead.
- **emphasis** is often created in Latin by unusual word order or by adding demonstratives like *hic, haec, hoc* or *ille, illa, illud*. English tends to emphasise by adding more words or by reshaping the sentence structure.

Remember that the idiomatic English translation provided may be quite different at times from the most literal translation of the Latin. You may end up thinking that a different translation would be better. If so, this is entirely constructive: critical reflection on how to translate is an excellent way of improving your understanding of both Latin and English.

Further help for a more literal translation of each passage is provided on the Companion Website. The online notes for each Latin text contain full listings of all vocabulary not yet covered by the Core Language Vocabulary Lists and guidance on how to translate.

scripta 13.1: Caelius Rufus fears the outbreak of civil war

In 50 BC, Cicero was away from Rome governing the province of Cilicia in modern-day Turkey. This text is an adapted extract from a letter written to him in August of that year by his friend Caelius Rufus.

Caelius Rufus updates Cicero on the deteriorating political situation in Rome. He fears that the disagreement between Pompey and Caesar is likely to erupt into civil war. The senate, the consuls and Pompey have all decided that Caesar must stand down from his military command in Gaul and return to Rome as a private citizen if he wishes to be elected consul for 49 BC. Caesar has said that he will only give up his military command if Pompey does the same.

In this letter, Caelius Rufus shares his uncertainty about whom to support: personal connections tie him to both men and support for one risks alienating the other.

The Latin text is adapted from Cicero's Ad Familiares *collection, VIII.14.*

Regarding the Republic, I've often written to you that I don't see peace lasting another year and – because this stand-off is getting closer – the danger it poses is getting more obvious. This is what is before us: Pompey has decided that it is necessary for Caesar to hand back his army and provinces; otherwise, he will not be consul. Caesar, however, believes that he cannot be protected if he steps back from his military command. Caesar puts forward the following condition: it is necessary for both of them to hand back their armies.

de re publica saepe tibi scripsi me ad annum pacem non videre, et, quod ea contentio propius appropinquat, clarius id periculum est. propositum hoc est: Cn. Pompeius constituit necesse esse Caesari exercitum et provincias tradere; aliter consul non fiet. Caesar autem credit se tutum esse non posse, si ab exercitu recesserit. fert illam tamen condicionem: necesse ambobus exercitus tradere.

ad annum	'to the end of the year', i.e. peace will not last for another year
contentio, contentionis, f	disagreement
propositus -a -um	(having been) put in front of
aliter	adverb from *alius*
fiet	'will become'
recesserit	'steps back'
ambo (dative = *ambobus*)	both

Chapter 13 Cicero and Caesar – Eye-Witness Accounts of Civil War

And so it is that those best friends of old and their distasteful alliance is breaking down into outright conflict. When it comes to my own situation, I do not know what to do: indeed I think that you too are worried by the same conundrum. I am bound to these men by friendship and old ties: what's more, it's their disagreement I hate, not the men themselves.

sic illi amores et invidiosa coniunctio ad bellum se erumpit. neque mearum rerum consilium invenio – puto quidem te quoque hac deliberatione esse perturbatum. nam mihi cum hominibus his et gratia et necessitudo; tum causam illam, non homines odi.

invidiosus -a -um	distasteful
coniunctio, coniunctionis, f	union, partnership
consilium, consilii, n	plan
gratia, gratiae, f	influence, friendship
necessitudo, necessitudinis, f	connection, association
odi	'I hate'

In this conflict, I see that Pompey has with him on his side the senate, and also the men who make the laws. Caesar will gather up all those who are either living in fear or in false confidence. I see that large-scale disagreements hang over us, in which fighting and violence will give the verdict. Each of these two men is ready in their resolve and with their armies. Fortune puts before you a remarkable show, but not one without its own risk.

in hac discordia video Cn. Pompeium secum habere senatum eosque qui res iudicant; ad Caesarem adibunt omnes, qui cum timore aut mala spe vivunt. video magnas impendere discordias, quas ferrum et vis iudicabit; uterque et animo et copiis est paratus. magnum tibi Fortuna spectaculum parat; nec tamen sine suo periculo.

iudico, iudicare	judge, act as a judge in a law court
impendeo, impendere	hang over
ferrum, ferri, n	iron
vis, f	force, violence (this noun is highly irregular; *vis* is its nominative sg)
uterque, utraque, utrumque	each of two, both

DERIVATIONS

This task builds skills in deducing the meaning of one word by using a related word.

The words below derive from words in the passages above which have not been glossed.

Can you find the Latin words from which these English words derive? Can you use either the Latin or the English word to help you explain the meaning of the other?

Remember that you will need to think about the part of speech of both the Latin and English words and – if they are different – you will need to consider how to adjust the meaning to move from one part of speech to the other.

inscription, pacify, necessity, condition, eruption, deliberate, perturbed, cause, discordant, timorous, spectacular

scripta 13.2: Cicero's loyalty to Pompey

This text is an adapted extract from one of Cicero's many letters to his close friend Atticus in December, 50 BC. Although Cicero would not return to Rome from his province until January 49 BC, he was well aware of the perilous situation. He writes that he fears for the Republic and thinks that his fellow citizens will give Caesar all that he wants in order to avoid a civil war.

Cicero expresses regret that he and the other senators did not realise the threat posed by Caesar sooner and even helped him increase his power. Cicero feels that he has to honour his loyalty to Pompey and speak in support of what Pompey wants, even though his personal preference is to avoid war at all costs.

The Latin text is adapted from Cicero's Ad Atticum collection, VII.6.

I am really worried about the Republic: nearly everyone now prefers to hand over to Caesar everything he has asked for rather than fight it out. Indeed, his demands are outrageous, but their traction is greater than was expected. Why, then, is this the moment to stand up to him for the first time? To quote Homer, *this is no greater evil* than when we extended his five year command in Gaul. Did we hand over that military power to him then so that now we could fight with a man who is battle-ready for sure?

de re publica magnopere timeo. <u>fere</u> omnes malunt concedere Caesari ea quae <u>postulavit</u> quam pugnare. est illa <u>quidem</u> impudens postulatio, sed opinione <u>valentior</u>. cur autem nunc primum ei resistimus? **οὐ γὰρ δὴ τόδε μεῖζον ἔπι κακόν** quam ubi <u>quinquennium</u> <u>prorogabamus</u>. dedimusne haec illi tum arma <u>ut</u> nunc cum bene parato <u>pugnaremus</u>?

fere	almost
postulo, postulare	demand
quidem	indeed
postulatio, postulationis, f	demand
valentior, valentioris	stronger, more powerful
οὐ γὰρ δὴ τόδε μεῖζον ἔπι κακόν	a quotation from Homer's *Odyssey* – 'Indeed, this thing isn't a greater evil'
quinquennium, quinquennii, n	Julius Caesar's 5-year command in Gaul
prorogo, prorogare	prolong
ut . . . pugnaremus	'so that we could fight'

Note that Roman authors often quoted famous Greek texts as a way to demonstrate their erudition and status.

Chapter 13 Cicero and Caesar – Eye-Witness Accounts of Civil War

You'll say to me, 'What are you going to do then?' I'm not going to say to you privately the same thing that I'll say publicly in the senate: personally, I think that it is necessary to do everything we can to avoid armed combat, but publicly I'll say the same as Pompey – and I won't do this in a downtrodden manner. The fact is that – even though this war is the greatest harm facing the Republic – it isn't appropriate for me to disagree with Pompey in matters of this importance.

dices, 'quid tu igitur senties?' non idem quod in senatu dicam; sentio enim necesse esse omnia facere ne armis pugnent sed in senatu dicam idem quod Pompeius neque id faciam humili animo. sed quamquam hoc maximum rei publicae malum est, mihi non rectum me in magnis rebus a Pompeio dissidere.

sentio, sentire	think, decide
senatus, senatus, m	senate
ne . . . pugnent	'so that they do not fight'
humilis, humile	abject, downtrodden
rectus -a -um	right
dissideo, dissidere	dissent, disagree

DERIVATIONS

This task builds skills in deducing the meaning of one word by using a related word.

The words below derive from words in the passages above which have not been glossed.

Can you find the Latin words from which these English words derive? Can you use either the Latin or the English word to help you explain the meaning of the other?

Remember that you will need to think about the part of speech of both the Latin and English words and – if they are different – you will need to consider how to adjust the meaning to move from one part of speech to the other.

concession, pugnacious, impudent, opinionated, animated, malevolent, magnificent

scripta 13.3: Caesar requests a meeting with Pompey

This text is an adapted extract from Julius Caesar's account of the civil war.

Caesar gained permission in 52 BC to stand in absentia *for election as consul. This was an important concession because it protected him from the risk of prosecution if he returned to Rome as a private citizen. By 50 BC this decision had been revoked and prominent senators were calling for Caesar to disband the army he had commanded in Gaul.*

On 1st January 49 BC, Caesar sent an ultimatum to the senate: he would disband his army only if Pompey did the same. The senate decreed that Julius Caesar had to stand down from his military command or be declared a public enemy.

Caesar advanced to gather his troops at Ariminum, a town in northeast Italy. From there, Caesar sent the following message to Pompey. Caesar's account claims that his first priority is to avoid war and re-establish peaceful political rule within Republican power structures; the reality of events, however, suggests otherwise.

The Latin text is adapted from Caesar's Bellum Civile, *1.9.*

For my part, I have always believed that the importance of the Republic comes first and that this is more important than life. I am really pained because my enemies have insulted me by taking away the Roman people's kindness to me. What's more – now that my military command has been removed – I am being dragged back to Rome, even though the people had ordered that I could stand **in absentia** at the next elections.

ego credo semper primam rei republicae esse dignitatem vitaque potiorem. maxime doleo quod beneficium mihi populi Romani per contumeliam ab inimicis raptum est, ereptoque imperio in urbem retrahor quamquam mei absentis rationem haberi proximis comitiis populus iusserat.

Note that sometimes our most idiomatic English equivalent is an inherited Latin phrase!

potior, potius	preferable, more important
doleo, dolere	grieve, feel pain
beneficium, beneficii, n	kindness
contumelia, contumeliae, f	insult
eripio, eripere, eripui, ereptum = e+rapio	
imperium, imperii, n	military command
rationem haberi	'[that my] candidacy be considered'
comitia, comitiorum, n pl	elections

But even so, for the sake of the Republic I have been level-headed and I have put up with this loss of respect. When I sent letters to the senate to say that everyone should stand down from their armies, I did not even get this agreed.

tamen hanc iacturam honoris mei rei publicae causa aequo animo tuli. ubi epistulas ad senatum misi ut omnes ab exercitibus discederent, ne id quidem impetravi.

iactura, iacturae, f	loss
(genitive +) causa	for the sake of
ut . . . discederent	'[asking] that they should stand down from'
ne . . . quidem	not even
impetro, impetrare, impetravi	obtain (a request)

Chapter 13 Cicero and Caesar – Eye-Witness Accounts of Civil War

All through Italy soldiers have been recruited; Pompey has two legions which were commandeered by him under the pretence of the **Parthian war**; Roman citizens are armed. How will this end? Everything is on course to destroy itself.

per totam Italiam milites collecti sunt; Pompeius legiones II tenet quae ab eo simulatione **Parthici belli** sunt abductae; cives sunt in armis. quis finis erit? omnia ad suam perniciem pertinent.

> In 53 BC Crassus had suffered a crushing defeat in **Parthia** and conflict in this region was ongoing.

simulatio, simulationis, f	pretence
pernicies, perniciei, f	destruction
pertineo, pertinere	pertain, lead to

Nevertheless, I am prepared to endure any sort of degradation and I am ready to put up with it all for the sake of the Republic. But I do want Pompey to go to his own provinces, I want him to dismiss his troops, and I want everyone in Italy to stand down from their weapons. I want to release the citizens from fear, I want the elections to be unrestricted and I want to let the whole Republic be in the hands of the senate and the Roman people.

sed tamen ego paratus sum ad omnia descendere atque omnia pati rei publicae causa. volo Pompeium proficisci in suas provincias, exercitus dimittere, omnes in Italia ab armis discedere. volo timorem e civibus tollere, libera esse comitia atque omnem rem publicam senatui populoque Romano permittere.

As for Pompey: he should come closer in person or allow me to go to him: in face-to face discussions, all disagreements can be settled.

Pompeius ipse debet propius progredi aut pati me ad se appropinquare: per colloquia omnes controversiae componuntur.

aut	or
colloquium, colloquii, n	conversation

DERIVATIONS

This task builds skills in deducing the meaning of one word by using a related word.

The words below derive from words in the passages above which have not been glossed.

Can you find the Latin words from which these English words derive? Can you use either the Latin or the English word to help you explain the meaning of the other?

Remember that you will need to think about the part of speech of both the Latin and English words and – if they are different – you will need to consider how to adjust the meaning to move from one part of speech to the other.

inimical, retraction, absence, approximately, population, honourable, equanimity, epistle, collection, tenacious, abduction, dismissal, liberally, permitted, controversy.

scripta 13.4: Cicero urges his wife and daughter to think of their safety

This text is an adapted extract from a letter written by Cicero in January 49 BC, just after Caesar's ultimatum had been refused by the senate. Cicero was in Formiae, a coastal town to the south of Rome. In this letter he writes to his wife Terentia and their daughter Tullia urging them to give careful thought to their safety. He refers to the protection available from Dolabella, a prominent supporter of Caesar.

Cicero is worried about the risks of remaining in the city. Balanced against this are fears for their property and the need to take measures to protect it from looting.

The Latin text is adapted from Cicero's Ad Familiares collection, XIV.18.

My darlings, it is essential for you to think about this carefully again and again. What are you going to do? Will you stay in Rome or will you stay with me or in some other safe place? This is not only for me to think about; it is also for you to decide. The following things occur to me: in Rome, you can be safe because of **Dolabella**'s influence and this option can benefit us, for I am worried about violence and theft. But I am concerned because I see that all the good men are now gone from Rome and that they have taken their women with them. What's more, this area, where I am, is in reach of friendly towns and even our country estates: here you will be able to be with me to a great extent and on our own property.

considerare necesse est vobis etiam atque etiam, animae meae, diligenter. quid facietis? Romaene eritis an mecum an aliquo tuto loco? id non solum meum consilium est, sed etiam vestrum. mihi veniunt in mentem haec: Romae vos esse tutae potestis per **Dolabellam**; ea res potest nos adiuvare, nam t meo vim et rapinas; sed moveor quod video omnes bonos abesse Roma et eos mulieres suas secum habere. haec autem regio, in qua ego sum, et nostrorum est oppidorum et etiam praediorum: hic poteritis multum esse mecum et in nostris praediis esse.

Dolabella was a prominent Roman noble; he had married Cicero's daughter in 50 BC.

atque	again
an	or
aliquis, aliquid	some (other)
mens, mentis, f	mind
adiuvo, adiuvare	help
vis (accusative sg – vim), f	violence
rapinae, rapinarum, f pl	looting
secum = cum se	
praedia, praediorum, n pl	country estates
multum (adverb)	to a great extent

Chapter 13 Cicero and Caesar – Eye-Witness Accounts of Civil War

I just do not know well enough what will be better: what will the other women do where you are? If you stay, I fear that it will not be possible for you to leave. I want you to go through this carefully again and again with yourselves and also with your friends. Tell **Philotimus** to prepare barriers and protection for our house; I want you also to find trustworthy messengers because I want to receive letters from you on a daily basis. Most of all, though, take care that you stay safe, if you want me to be in good spirits too.

ego non satis scio utrum sit melius: quid aliae facient illo loco feminae? si manebitis, timeo ne exire non liceat. id volo diligenter vos etiam atque etiam vobiscum et cum amicis considerare. domui propugnacula et praesidium parare **Philotimum** iubete; et volo vos tabellarios parare certos quod quotidie a vobis epistulas accipere volo. maxime autem date operam, ut valeatis, si nos vultis valere.

> **Philotimus** was one of Cicero's wife's freedmen, trusted with managing their property.

utrum sit	'which would be . . .'
si	if
ne . . . non liceat	'that it will not be allowed'
propugnaculum, propugnaculi, n	fortification
praesidium, praesidii, n	defence
tabellarius, tabellarii, m	letter-carrier
certus -a -um	reliable, fixed
quotidie	every day
date operam	'focus your energy'
ut valeatis	'so that you stay well'
valeo, valere	be healthy, thrive

DERIVATIONS

This task builds skills in deducing the meaning of one word by using a related word.

The words below derive from words in the passages above which have not been glossed.

Can you find the Latin words from which these English words derive? Can you use either the Latin or the English word to help you explain the meaning of the other?

Remember that you will need to think about the part of speech of both the Latin and English words and – if they are different – you will need to consider how to adjust the meaning to move from one part of speech to the other.

consideration, diligent, regional, science, location, domestic, acceptance

Reading original Latin note 2: Cognate nouns

When translating Latin it is really important to think about **parts of speech**. This can be difficult because idiomatic English and Latin may end up using different parts of speech to convey the same meaning.

It is particularly important to think about parts of speech when you meet words which resemble words you already know.

You will often meet Latin nouns which are **cognates** of verbs, i.e. they share a similar stem. These cognate nouns usually fall into one of four categories; examples of each of these below are taken from *scripta* 13.5.

- 1st declension feminine nouns

    fuga, fugae, f   flight
    (related to the verb *fugio, fugere, fugi* – *flee*)

- 3rd declension masculine nouns

    propagator, propagatoris, m   prolonger
    (related to the verb *propago, propagare* – *prolong*)

    Cognate nouns of this **-or, -oris** type (e.g. *pugnator* – a fighter) usually mean the person who does the action; Feminine cognate nouns also exist, e.g. *bellatrix, bellatricis*, f – a (female) warrior.

- 3rd declension feminine nouns

    ratio, rationis, f   thought, consideration
    (related to the verb *reor, reri, ratus sum* – *think*)

- 4th declension masculine nouns

    discessus, discessus, m   departure
    (related to the verb *discedo, discedere, discessi, discessum* – *depart*)

    It is worth watching out for 4th declension nouns of this type because they can be easily confused with a perfect passive or deponent participle.

scripta 13.5: Cicero is angry at Pompey's decision to leave Italy

This text is an adapted extract from a letter written by Cicero to his friend Atticus in February, 49 BC. Pompey is about to withdraw from Italy, and Cicero writes of his dismay that Rome is about to fall into the hands of Julius Caesar.

In this letter Cicero expresses his anger at Pompey's actions so far. He thinks that Pompey was wrong to support Caesar for so long and to allow his power to build. Cicero thinks that it is shameful that Pompey is now about to desert Rome.

The Latin text is adapted from Cicero's Ad Atticum collection, VIII.3.

Our man Pompey has done nothing wisely, he has done nothing bravely, indeed I'd go as far as saying that he has done nothing other than go against my advice and my influence. That's without

nihil actum est a Pompeio nostro sapienter, nihil fortiter, addo etiam nihil <u>nisi</u> contra consilium auctoritatemque meam. omitto illa

Chapter 13 Cicero and Caesar – Eye-Witness Accounts of Civil War

mentioning the things from before: Pompey nurtured Caesar for public life, he boosted him, he gave him military power, he got laws passed through violence and against the **auspices**, he added to Caesar's power the command over Further Gaul, he married Caesar's daughter, he cared more about bringing me back to Rome than about preventing my exile in the first place, he was the man who extended Caesar's provincial command, and – when Caesar was away – he was his assistant in all matters and even in his bid for his third consulship; after he began to defend the Republic, Pompey still wanted Caesar to stand for election *in absentia*. But, what is more shameful, what is more disturbing than leaving the city like this or fleeing so utterly disgracefully? Surely all Caesar's terms were better for Pompey than the option of abandoning his country? Caesar's terms were bad – I don't deny it – but what is worse than this?

vetera: Caesarem in rem publicam ille aluit, auxit, armavit, ille leges per vim et contra **auspicia** tulit, ille Galliae Ulterioris imperium adiunxit, ille gener factus est, ille magis cupiebat restituere me quam retinere, ille provinciae propagator, ille – ubi Caesar aberat – in omnibus erat adiutor et etiam tertio consulatu, postquam defendere rem publicam coepit, volebat absentis rationem haberi. sed quid foedius, quid perturbatius est quam hic ab urbe discessus sive turpissima fuga? nonne omnes condiciones meliores erant quam patriam relinquere? Caesaris malae condiciones erant, fateor, sed quid est peius quam hoc?

> The Romans took the **auspices** before major undertakings to look for signs of divine favour or disapproval (see Chapter 5).

nisi	if not, unless
vetus, veteris	old, from long ago
alo, alere, alui	nourish
augeo, augere, auxi	increase
per vim	'through violence'
adiungo, adiungere, adiunxi	add to, join
gener, generis, m	son-in-law
restituo, restituere	restore (i.e. bring back to Rome from exile)
retineo, retinere	keep
propagator, propagatoris, m	prolonger
adiutor, adiutoris, m	helper
absentis rationem haberi	'[Caesar] to stand for election while absent'
foedus -a -um	foul, shameful
discessus, discessus, m	departure
sive	or
turpis, turpe	ugly
fuga, fugae, f	flight
fateor, fateri	confess, admit

DERIVATIONS

This task builds skills in deducing the meaning of one word by using a related word.

The words below derive from words in the passages above which have not been glossed.

Can you find the Latin words from which these English words derive? Can you use either the Latin or the English word to help you explain the meaning of the other?

Remember that you will need to think about the part of speech of both the Latin and English words and – if they are different – you will need to consider how to adjust the meaning to move from one part of speech to the other.

homo sapiens, authority, omission, auspicious, tertiary, defensive, volition, perturbed, ameliorate, pejorative

scripta 13.6: Caesar's victory in Spain

In February 49 BC, Pompey had decided to leave Rome in order to build an army in the east. Caesar chose not to pursue him, but he went instead to Spain to confront the Republican armies there, led by Marcus Petreius and Lucius Afranius. The initial skirmishes between the two sides were inconclusive and, instead of fighting a decisive battle, each manoeuvred around the terrain, trying to prevent the other from accessing food and water.

Due to the close proximity of the armies, there began to be a certain degree of fraternisation between both sides. Caesar's men would visit the Pompeian camp to drink and socialise with their fellow Romans and vice versa. When Petreius and Afranius learnt of this intermingling, they stamped it out, demanding that any soldier of Caesar's in their camp should be brought forward and executed. Caesar, on the other hand, ordered that the Republican soldiers in his camp should be returned unharmed.

Eventually, the Republican forces were severely deprived of supplies, and Afranius was forced to request an audience with Caesar, who granted it on the condition that it was in front of the soldiers. In public, Afranius admitted that they were defeated; he begged Caesar not to punish them for remaining loyal to Pompey and he asked for mercy.

This text is an adapted extract from Caesar's bruising reply to Afranius. In it he says that the only people at fault are leaders like Pompey, Petreius and Afranius, whose actions have caused Roman deaths. Caesar, on the other hand, deliberately chose not to fight even when the conditions suited him. Caesar demands that Afranius and Petreius disband their legions. He says that there is no need for so many troops to pacify a province like Spain; the Pompeian legions were there solely to oppose him.

The Latin text is adapted from Caesar's *Bellum Civile*, 1.85ff.

All of us have acted as we should: I have acted correctly because I am someone who does not want to fight even when the conditions are good and the ground and the time are in my favour; this is because I wanted everything to be as unspoilt as possible for peace. My army has acted correctly because they are men who, even though they received injuries and their own men were killed, spared those soldiers who came under their control. The soldiers of Pompey's army have also acted correctly, because they are men who wanted peace. So it is that the sections of every rank have placed themselves at my mercy. It is only the leaders who have shrunk from peace and who have caused men to die most cruelly.

omnes nos officium nostrum praestitimus: ego, qui etiam bona condicione et loco et tempore aequo pugnare nolo – nam volui quam integerrima esse ad pacem omnia; exercitus meus, qui iniuria etiam accepta suisque interfectis, eos, quos in sua potestate habuit, conservavit; illius etiam exercitus milites, qui pacem voluerunt. sic omnium ordinum partes in misericordia constiterunt: ipsi duces a pace abhorruerunt et homines crudelissime interfecerunt.

praesto, praestare, praestiti	show, perform
integer, integra, integrum	whole, unspoilt
iniuria, iniuriae, f	injury
ordo, ordinis, m	rank, order, group
misericordia, misericordiae, f	pity
consisto, consistere, constiti	place oneself
abhorreo, abhorrere, abhorrui	shrink back from, be opposed to

Chapter 13 Cicero and Caesar – Eye-Witness Accounts of Civil War

I have not – even though the other side is now obviously the weaker – asked for those things which would make me personally richer, but I do want those armies, which Pompey has maintained now for many years against me, to be disbanded. It was for no other reason that six legions were sent to Spain and a seventh conscripted there, and the fleets made ready and commanders sent in support. None of these things was for the sake of pacifying **Spain**, none of them was done for the benefit of a province which, because of its long-lasting peace, had no need for any reinforcements. All these things were prepared against me; Pompey established these commands with his eyes on me. Pompey wanted to hold sway over affairs in the city and – without leaving Rome – to get hold of the two provinces which were best resourced for war.

> **Spain** at this time was divided into two provinces.

neque nunc illorum humilitate postulavi ea quibus opes meae augebunt; sed illos exercitus, quos Pompeius contra me multos iam annos aluit, volo dimitti. neque enim sex legiones alia de causa missae sunt in Hispaniam septimaque ibi conscripta est neque classes paratae neque submissi duces. nihil horum erat ad pacandas **Hispanias**, nihil ad usum provinciae factum est, quae propter diuturnitatem pacis nullum auxilium desideravit. omnia haec contra me parata sunt; in me Pompeius imperia constituit; ille volebat urbanis praesidere rebus et duas bellicosissimas provincias absens obtinere.

postulo, postulare, postulavi	demand
opes, opum, f pl	wealth
augeo, augere	increase
alo, alere, alui	nourish
dimitti	'to be dismissed'
causa, causae, f	reason
classis, classis, f	fleet (of boats)
submitto, submittere, submisi, submissum	sent (to help)
ad pacandas Hispanias	'for the purpose of pacifying Spain'
usus, usus, m	use, benefit
diuturnitas, diuturnitatis, f	long duration

Even so, I have put up with all these things patiently and I will continue to do so; I do not want now to take your army from you and keep it, but I also do not want you to keep hold of an army against me. As I have already said, you must now leave the province and disband your army. If you do this, I won't harm anyone. This is my only – and final – condition for peace.

omnia tamen haec tuli patienter et feram; neque nunc ab vobis abductum exercitum tenere volo neque volo vos exercitum contra me tenere. nunc, <u>ut</u> iam dixi, debetis provinciis exire et exercitum dimittere. <u>si</u> hoc <u>feceritis</u>, nemini <u>nocebo</u>. haec una atque <u>extrema</u> est pacis condicio.

ut	as
si . . . feceritis	'if you do this'
noceo, nocere (+ dative)	harm
extremus -a -um	last, final

DERIVATIONS

This task builds skills in deducing the meaning of one word by using a word.

The words below derive from words in the passages above which have not been glossed.

Can you find the Latin words from which these English words derive? Can you use either the Latin or the English word to help you explain the meaning of the other?

Remember that you will need to think about the part of speech of both the Latin and English words and – if they are different – you will need to consider how to adjust the meaning to move from one part of speech to the other.

official, exercise, conservation, humiliate, sextet, conscription, imperiousness, president, bellicose, patiently

Chapter 13 Cicero and Caesar – Eye-Witness Accounts of Civil War

> ### *scripta* 13.7: Caesar wins the civil war
>
> The text below is an adapted extract from Julius Caesar's account of the end of the Battle of Pharsalus in 48 BC. This was the decisive battle of the civil war.
>
> This text focuses on the moment at the very end of the battle when Caesar ordered his soldiers to assault Pompey's camp, probably hoping to capture Pompey and thus end the war. The defenders fought bravely but were overrun by Caesar's men. Realising it was a lost cause, Pompey abandoned his camp to avoid capture. He rode north to the city of Larisa before heading to the coast and boarding a grain ship to escape.
>
> The Latin text is adapted from Caesar's *Bellum Civile*, 3.95.

Pompey's soldiers had taken flight and had been driven back inside their rampart; Caesar urged his troops on and ordered them to be the ones to attack the camp. The battle had kept going until midday and, although his men were exhausted by the great heat, nevertheless they were ready in their resolve to face every task and obeyed Caesar's command.

Caesar Pompeianis ex fuga intra vallum compulsis milites cohortatus est et iussit ipsos castra oppugnare. illi, quamquam magno aestu fessi (nam ad meridiem res erat perducta), tamen ad omnem laborem animo parati imperio paruerunt.

The soldiers on Pompey's side who had fled were shaken to the core and worn out by exhaustion; they threw down their weapons and the military standards and gave more thought to completing their escape than to guarding the camp. The men who had taken a stand on the rampart were not able to withstand the quantity of missiles any longer; wounded and worn out, they abandoned their position. Immediately, they all fled as one to the high mountain range which was near to the camp.

Pompeiani milites qui refugerant, et animo perterriti et lassitudine confecti, missis armis signisque militaribus, magis de reliqua fuga quam de castrorum defensione cogitabant. neque diutius ei, qui in vallo steterant, multitudinem telorum sustinere potuerunt, sed confecti vulneribus locum reliquerunt, statimque omnes in altissimos montes, qui prope castra erant, confugerunt.

vallum, valli, n	rampart
compello, compellere, compuli, compulsum	drive together
cohortor, cohortari, cohortatus sum	urge on
castra, castrorum, n pl	camp
aestus, aestus, m	heat
pareo, parere, parui (+ dative)	obey
lassitudo, lassitudinis, f	weariness, exhaustion
confectus -a -um	weakened, worn out, finished off
signa, signorum, n pl	(military) standards, emblems
cogito, cogitare	think
tela, telorum, n pl	missiles

Now that our men had gained entry through the rampart, Pompey dashed out from the camp through the rear gate and – right away – rode off at a gallop for Larisa. He did not linger there, but – at the same speed and without pausing his journey during the night – he reached the sea and boarded a grain ship, crying out repeatedly about the scale of his defeat.

Pompeius, iam ubi intra vallum nostri progressi sunt, <u>decumana</u> porta se ex castris eiecit <u>protinusque</u> <u>equo citato</u> <u>Larisam</u> contendit. neque ibi manebat, sed eadem celeritate, nocturno itinere non intermisso ad mare advenit navemque <u>frumentariam</u> ascendit, saepe <u>querens</u> de maxima <u>clade</u>.

decumanus -a -um	rear (gate of a camp)
protinus	immediately
equo citato	'with his horse at full gallop'
Larisa, Larisae, f	Larisa
frumentarius -a -um	grain, granary
queror, quereri	complain, lament
clades, cladis, f	defeat, disaster

DERIVATIONS

This task builds skills in deducing the meaning of one word by using a related word.

The words below derive from words in the passages above which have not been glossed.

Can you find the Latin words from which these English words derive? Can you use either the Latin or the English word to help you explain the meaning of the other?

Remember that you will need to think about the part of speech of both the Latin and English words and – if they are different – you will need to consider how to adjust the meaning to move from one part of speech to the other.

fugitive, ante meridiem, laborious, military, multitudinous, sustain, vulnerable, mountainous, intravenous, progressive, eject, nocturnal, itinerary

QUESTIONS FOR DISCUSSION

1 What do you think are the pros and cons of using eye-witness texts as evidence for this period in history? What types of insight do they offer into the civil war? How does the risk of personal bias impact their usefulness to us as sources?

2 Cicero's letters offer us a personal viewpoint into his life: what impression do you get of him as a person from these texts?

3 Caesar's decision to refer to himself only in the 3rd person seems designed to create a more objective tone to his narrative, but his commentary on the civil war reads as personal propaganda nonetheless. In the texts in this chapter, where and how does he create a positive impression of his actions in the civil war?

4 Human experience is as much about feelings as it is about facts: discuss this with reference to the texts in this chapter.

5 Emphasis is the life-blood of literary style: choose one text and explore how Latin uses word order, word choice or grammatical shape to focus attention on key details within the text.

Chapter 13: Additional Language

SECTION A13: CHAPTER 13 VOCABULARY

Exercise A13.1: Derivations

This exercise explores derivations from the vocabulary list for Chapter 13.

Each of the words below derives from a Latin word. Find this Latin word and use it to help you explain the meaning of the English word. You may not know some of these words; think about what part of speech they might be and see if you can work out their meaning based on the Latin.

	derivation	Latin word and translation	meaning of the English derivation
1	manual		
2	relate		
3	consecutive		
4	loquacious		
5	regression		
6	admiration		
7	conative		
8	passive		
9	alternate		
10	domestic		

Exercise A13.2: Parts of speech

Sort the following words from the vocabulary list for Chapter 13 into the correct categories and write the meaning next to each word.

alter   loquor   quidam   coepi   res   proficiscor
    sub   manus   nonnulli   sine   malo   idem

noun	verb	adjective	pronoun	preposition

Chapter 13 Cicero and Caesar – Eye-Witness Accounts of Civil War

Exercise A13.3: *fero* compounds

Below are the principal parts of *fero* and its compounds.

fero	ferre, tuli, latum	bring; carry; bear
aufero	auferre, abstuli, ablatum	take away; carry off; steal
offero	offerre, obtuli, oblatum	offer
refero	referre, rettuli, relatum	bring / carry back; report; tell

For each of the verb forms given in the table below, name the tense, state whether it is active or passive, and translate it.

You may find it helpful to look at the forms of *fero* listed in the Reference Grammar on pp252–253.

		tense	voice	translation
1	offerimus			
2	referunt			
3	abstulistis			
4	oblati sunt			
5	offerebatur			
6	refereris			
7	abstulerant			
8	relata sunt			
9	ablatae sumus			
10	tollebar			

Exercise A13.4: Cognates

In the table below are pairs of words: the first in each pair is a word from the vocabulary list for Chapter 13 and below it is a cognate word, i.e. a word which is related to it. You may not have met the cognate word before and it will not be listed in the vocabulary list at the back of this book.

Identify the part of speech of each Latin word and then give the meaning; you will have to work out the meaning of the second word by thinking about its part of speech and how it relates in meaning to the first word in each pair.

	Latin	part of speech	meaning
1	spes, spei, f		
	spero, sperare, speravi, speratum		
2	exercitus, exercitus, m		
	exerceo, exercere, exercui, exercitum		
3	aufero, auferre, abstuli, ablatum		
	ablatio, ablationis, f		
4	loquor, loqui, locutus sum		
	loquax, loquacis		
5	miror, mirari, miratus sum		
	mirabilis, mirabile		

Chapter 13 Cicero and Caesar – Eye-Witness Accounts of Civil War

SECTION B13: WORD ENDINGS

Exercise B13.1: 4th and 5th declension nouns – English into Latin

This exercise focuses on the 4th and 5th declension nouns from the vocabulary list for Chapter 13. For each noun, give its meaning and declension. Then put each of them into the forms requested. It may be helpful to refer to the table of endings in the Reference Grammar on pp220–221.

		meaning	declension		
1	dies, diei, m			accusative sg =	accusative pl =
2	res, rei, f			dative sg =	nominative pl =
3	exercitus, exercitus, m			genitive sg =	ablative pl =
4	manus, manus, f			accusative sg =	genitive pl =
5	spes, spei, f			ablative sg =	accusative pl =

Exercise B13.2: 4th and 5th declension nouns – Latin into English

This exercise focuses on the 4th and 5th declension nouns from the vocabulary list for Chapter 13. List the case and number of each form given. Remember that the same endings are sometimes used for more than one case; give all the possible cases for each word.

You may find it useful to look at the Reference Grammar on pp220–221.

		case and number
1	diei	
2	manus	
3	res	
4	exercitum	
5	manibus	

Exercise B13.3: Nouns of all declensions in the accusative and ablative cases

This exercise focuses on the accusative and ablative forms of nouns from the vocabulary lists for Chapters 12 and 13.

Here is a reminder of the accusative and ablative case endings for nouns in each of the 5 declensions. The neuter endings for the 2nd and 3rd declensions are shown in brackets.

	1st	2nd	3rd	4th	5th
accusative sg	-am	-um (-um)	-em (--)	-um	-em
accusative pl	-as	-os (-a)	-es (-a)	-us	-es

	1st	2nd	3rd	4th	5th
ablative sg	-a	-o	-e	-u	-e
ablative pl	-is	-is	-ibus	-ibus	-ebus

Identify the declension of each of the following nouns, and give the new forms requested.

		declension	accusative sg	accusative pl	ablative sg	ablative pl
1	gens, gentis, f					
2	dies, diei, m					
3	insula, insulae, f					
4	exercitus, exercitus, m					
5	ventus, venti, m					
6	res, rei, f					
7	manus, manus, f					
8	soror, sororis, f					
9	regnum, regni, n					
10	caput, capitis, n					

Chapter 13 Cicero and Caesar – Eye-Witness Accounts of Civil War

Exercise B13.4: Deponent verbs in the perfect tense

This exercise focuses on recognising deponent verbs in the perfect tense. The verbs are from the vocabulary list for Chapter 13.

Give the principal parts for each verb and then translate the form given.

	tense	principal parts	translation
1	locuti sumus		
2	passa sum		
3	secutae sunt		
4	visum est		
5	mortui sunt		
6	profecta est		
7	egressi estis		
8	miratus es		
9	regressa es		
10	progressi sumus		

Exercise B13.5: Recognising voice (active, passive and deponent verbs)

This exercise uses verbs from the vocabulary lists for Chapters 12 and 13. Some of the verbs are active, some are passive and some are deponent.

Write out the principal parts for each verb and use these to identify if the form given is active, passive or deponent; then translate each one.

		principal parts	active, passive or deponent	translation
1	collectae estis			
2	morietur			
3	malebamus			
4	ceciderant			
5	ablatum est			
6	proficiscebantur			
7	constituit			
8	coepisti			
9	tollit			
10	conabar			

Chapter 13 Additional Language

Exercise B13.6: Deponent verbs in perfect and pluperfect tenses

This exercise practises the perfect and pluperfect tenses of the deponent verbs from Chapter 13.

Using the principal parts given below, write out the Latin for each English form given.

Remember that the deponent verb's perfect participle will need to agree with the nominative subject of the verb; this is why the gender of the subject is specified each time.

			Latin form
1	proficiscor, proficisci, profectus sum	we had set out (masculine)	
2	patior, pati, passus sum	they suffered (feminine)	
3	videor, videri, visus sum	it seemed	
4	sequor, sequi, secutus sum	we had followed (masculine)	
5	loquor, loqui, locutus sum	you (sg) spoke (feminine)	
6	miror, mirari, miratus sum	they wondered at (masculine)	
7	ingredior, ingredi, ingressus sum	you (pl) had entered (feminine)	
8	conor, conari, conatus sum	we had tried (masculine)	
9	ingredior, ingredi, ingressus sum	I entered (feminine)	
10	progredior, progredi, progressus sum	he had advanced	

Chapter 13 Cicero and Caesar – Eye-Witness Accounts of Civil War

Exercise B13.7: Deponent verbs in present, future and imperfect tenses

Identify the conjugation of each of the deponent verbs from Chapter 13 listed below. Then give the 3rd person sg form of the future and imperfect tenses.

		conjugation	future	imperfect
1	progredior, progredi, progressus sum			
2	sequor, sequi, secutus sum			
3	morior, mori, mortuus sum			
4	ingredior, ingredi, ingressus sum			
5	loquor, loqui, locutus sum			
6	miror, mirari, miratus sum			
7	videor, videri, visus sum			
8	regredior, regredi, regressus sum			
9	proficiscor, proficisci, profectus sum			
10	egredior, egredi, egressus sum			

Exercise B13.8: Recognising deponent verbs in present, future and imperfect tenses

Write out the principal parts for the Chapter 13 verbs listed below. Then identify the tense and translate the form given into English.

		principal parts	tense	translate
1	progreditur			
2	sequemur			
3	egrediebamur			
4	conabuntur			
5	patitur			
6	proficiscebaris			
7	regrediemur			
8	videtur			
9	loquebar			
10	mirabimini			
11	ingrediuntur			
12	moriebaris			

Exercise B13.9: Case endings (nouns, adjectives and pronouns)

The table below contains adjectives and pronouns from the vocabulary list for Chapter 13. Remember, each of these words has a genitive sg form ending in *-ius* and a dative sg form ending in *-i*.

Give the meaning of each word and write out the form requested. You may find it helpful to look at the Reference Grammar on pp224–227 and pp253–256.

	Latin	meaning	
1	nonnulli, nonnullae, nonnulla		accusative masculine pl =
2	alter, altera, alterum		dative feminine sg =
3	solus, sola, solum		nominative masculine pl =
4	totus, tota, totum		genitive masculine sg =
5	idem, eadem, idem		dative feminine sg =
6	ipse, ipsa, ipsum		genitive neuter sg =
7	quidam, quaedam, quoddam		ablative masculine pl =

SECTION C13: ENGLISH TO LATIN SENTENCES

Exercise C13.1: 4th and 5th declension nouns

This exercise focuses on the 4th and 5th declension nouns from the vocabulary list for Chapter 13. Given below are the Latin translations of the words in bold in the sentences; match these up with the English and identify the case of each.

spem   dies   rem   exercitui   domi   manu
  rebus   spes   spem   manu   diebus   exercitu

1. No **hope** of victory remained.
2. We tried to stay **at home**.
3. The **day** was very long.
4. Within a few **days** they were dead.
5. We wondered at **the matter**.
6. He was the general of the greatest **army**.
7. The new leader gave great **hope** to the tired **army**.
8. The messenger reported many things about the **events**.
9. A man went out from the **group of people**, raising a sword with his **hand**.
10. Offer them **hope**!

Remember: no prepositions are used with **domus** when the meaning is *towards / away from / at home* (see p9).

Exercise C13.2: Nouns in accusative and ablative cases

Each of the nouns in bold in the sentences below would take either the accusative or ablative form. Identify the case of each and then translate the noun into Latin. Remember, the accusative and ablative cases are used as follows:

accusative case
- direct object
- after certain prepositions
- in time phrases denoting 'how long' something lasted for
- in an accusative + infinitive indirect statement

ablative case
- to mean 'by / with / from / than / in'
- after certain prepositions
- in time phrases denoting 'when' or 'within which' time period an action took place
- as part of a noun + participle ablative absolute

1. For several **days** they suffered very greatly.
2. Although the enemy had left behind no **hope** of peace, some still did not despair.
3. They reported that the **same women** were stealing food.
4. A certain soldier, who had returned from the **army,** began to speak about the **matters**.
5. Within ten **days** he was dead.
6. They boldly carried off many things from the **homes** of citizens.
7. Because they admired their leader, they had **hope**.
8. Without a **leader** we shall suffer.
9. For the **whole day** you followed the army.
10. He reported the **event** to the army.

Exercise C13.3: Sentences to translate into Latin

1. Several men began to destroy things brought back from the homes of the enemy.
2. Raising their hands towards the sky, the women spoke words without hope.
3. The weeping girl followed her mother and said, 'Pick me up!' Then the mother herself lifted up her daughter.
4. 'There is great hope of peace for us!' shouted the inhabitants.
5. The whole crowd returned home, after they had seen very bad things.
6. I wonder at the bad things which you have endured at the enemy's hands.
7. Certain senators, who seemed to offer hope to our citizens, stole that very hope.
8. With several from my group of men dead, I set out alone.
9. One leader is reporting in the forum that the other leader is dead.
10. Although he desired peace, he understood that he ought to set out for the battle.

CHAPTER 14
VIRGIL AND OVID – EPIC POETRY

Chapter 14: Introduction

The influence of Greek literature on Roman writers

Rome was in many ways a very conservative society, often looking to the past for a rationale for decisions in the present. This conservatism also applied to literature and Roman texts, which were often modelled on the works of respected authors. The Romans acknowledged the pre-eminence of the greatest of the Greek texts and believed that a good knowledge of Greek literature was a mark of a well-educated Roman. References to Greek texts and an **imitation of Greek style** can be found frequently in the works of later Roman writers. You saw an example of this in *scripta* **13.2**, when Cicero quoted from the *Odyssey* in his letter to Atticus.

Epic poetry

The influence of Greek texts upon Roman literature is perhaps most obvious in the genre of **epic poetry**. Western literature began with the epic poetry of the Greeks. The epic poems attributed to **Homer**, the ***Iliad*** and the ***Odyssey***, are among western Europe's oldest written texts. They date from so long ago that it is impossible to know much about their composition, but it is generally believed that they were originally **composed orally**, perhaps in sections by multiple poets, recited for entertainment at feasts and eventually written down. Homer's poetry was revered by both the Greeks and the Romans and it had a profound influence in shaping the literature which followed.

Epic poetry was seen as the greatest of all the literary genres, and the adjective 'epic' still carries connotations today of **grandeur**, **importance** and **length**. Many epic poems are so long that they are subdivided into sections, known as 'books', similar to a modern-day chapter. Epic poetry is typically characterised by its length and grand content, but the formal requirement for a poem to be classed as epic poetry was the metre – **rhythm** – that the poem was written in. All epic poetry was composed in a rhythm known as **hexameter**. You can read more about this metre in the *Reading original Latin* box on p85 and in Appendix 2: Latin Metre on p215.

The content of Classical epic poems varied significantly. Homer's two epic poems are very different. The ***Iliad*** is more than 15,000 lines long and offers a tragic exploration of the **Trojan war**; it focuses on the rage of Achilles, a Greek warrior who fought against the Trojans, and the damage this rage wrought upon Achilles, the Greeks and the Trojans. At just over 12,000 lines long, the ***Odyssey*** is a slightly shorter and more humorous epic which chronicles the lengthy adventures of the **resourceful hero Odysseus** as he made his way home after the Trojan War.

> The Latin verb *servo* means *keep safe, preserve*. Explain the meaning of *conservative*.

> The Latin noun *ratio* means *account, reason*. Explain the meaning of *rationale*.

> The Latin pariticiple *positus* means *placed, put*. Explain the meaning of *composition*.

> The Latin adjective *profundus* means *deep*. Explain the meaning of *profound*.

FIGURE 14.1 Odysseus and the Sirens

This mosaic depicts one of the fantastical moments from the stories of Odysseus' journey home from Troy. Odysseus has to sail past the Sirens, the mythical creatures who lured sailors to their death by their captivating singing. Odysseus has been tied to the mast at his own request so that he can hear the song of the Sirens yet resist it. His crew have plugged their ears with wax. This mosaic dates from the 3rd century AD and was found in northern Tunisia.

Didactic epic

Both the *Iliad* and the *Odyssey* tell stories from the realm of myth and feature great heroes who were capable of extraordinary actions in a fantastical world where the human and divine spheres often interconnected. There was, however, another type of epic poetry, known as **didactic epic**, which aimed to educate its reader about aspects of the divine or natural world. Didactic epic also dates from roughly the same period as Homer and the earliest known writer of didactic epic was the Greek poet, **Hesiod**. His first poem, the **Theogony**, describes the origin of the universe and offers a family tree of the gods in just over 1,000 lines. In tracing the mind-boggling interconnectedness and hierarchies of the relationships between the gods, Hesiod includes a number of myths which resurface throughout later Greek and Latin literature. His later poem, **Works and Days**, is just over 800 lines. It was written as a guide for Hesiod's brother on how to run a successful farm. The main

> The Latin verb *necto* means *bind, tie*. Explain the meaning of *interconnected*.

FIGURE 14.2 Portrait of Hesiod

The Monnus Mosaic in Trier, Germany, is an elaborate and beautifully detailed mosaic from the 3rd century AD. It includes nine octagons, each with one of the nine muses and the names and images of humans who have been inspired by them. In this section of the mosaic you can see Hesiod.

theme is not the glory of battle and overcoming otherworldly beasts; instead it sets out how to have a prosperous life.

Roman epic

> The Latin noun *genus* means *type, category*. Explain the meaning of *genre*.

Roman literature was greatly influenced by Greek literature and many Roman poets tried to create a Latin version of the literary success of Homer and Hesiod. As you read in Chapter 2, the Romans included heroes from their own history within their favourite stories. It is probably no surprise, therefore, that the earliest Roman epic poets thought that the epic genre was a good way to retell their own **history**. As far as we know, the first Roman poet to attempt the genre of epic was the 3rd-century-BC poet, **Gnaeus Naevius**. He wrote an account of the Punic War with Carthage, but his poem survives only in fragments. Gnaeus Naevius was followed by the poet **Ennius** (3rd–2nd century BC) who wrote an epic poem about the history of Rome. In the 1st century BC, **Lucretius** wrote a famous **didactic epic** about the nature of the soul and the universe. Later that century came the two most famous Roman epic poets of all: **Virgil** and **Ovid**. The *scripta* for this chapter are taken from Virgil and Ovid's most famous poems: the *Aeneid* and the *Metamorphoses*.

Virgil: love and war

> The Latin verb *reflecto* means *bend back*. Explain the meaning of *reflected*.

Several of the stories you read in Chapters 1–12 came from Virgil's great epic poem, the *Aeneid*. In style and composition, Homer's influence on Virgil's *Aeneid* is clear. The first half of the *Aeneid's* twelve books tell of the **wanderings of Aeneas** as he searches for a new home; these six books strongly echo the wanderings of Odysseus in Homer's *Odyssey*. The second half of the *Aeneid* chronicles **the war that Aeneas has to fight** when he reaches his new homeland; the military theme reminds the reader of Homer's descriptions of the horror of battle in the *Iliad*.

Though the works of Homer are clearly reflected in the *Aeneid*, Virgil added his own, uniquely Roman twist to the genre. While Homer looks back to a glorious and heroic past, Virgil's *Aeneid* includes prophecies which chart major events in Roman history, right up to **Virgil's contemporary present-day**. The poem looks forward to the **Augustan era**, predicting a time when the horrors of war will be over, and peace, stability and prosperity will take their place. Virgil explores what it means to be a Roman by linking the virtues and actions of characters from Rome's past to the qualities and lives of his contemporaries. As we read in Chapter 11, Virgil uses the struggles of Aeneas to explore questions about the **ideal Roman character** during the time of Augustus.

The extracts from the *Aeneid* included in the *scripta* texts for this chapter highlight Virgil's great skill in exploring themes of love and war. *scripta* **14.1** focuses on the tumultuously painful experience of **Dido, queen of Carthage**, when she falls in love with Aeneas and the conflict she feels between this new passion and her loyalty to her dead husband, Sychaeus. *scripta* **14.2** is taken from the very end of the *Aeneid* and presents the moment when **Aeneas finally kills his enemy Turnus**. In both these texts Virgil skilfully explores

FIGURE 14.3 **Virgil and the Muses**

This mosaic dates from the 3rd or 4th century AD and was found in a coastal city in modern-day Tunisia. Virgil sits between two muses: Clio, the muse of history, stands behind his right shoulder and Melpomene, the muse of tragedy, stands to his left holding a theatrical mask of tragedy. On his lap is a scroll containing lines from the *Aeneid*. The mosaic highlights the *Aeneid*'s dual identity as an account of Rome's mythical history and an exploration of the tragedy involved in securing Rome's great power.

human emotions, highlighting our powerlessness in the face of feelings that can overwhelm us and the way in which rational decision-making can crumble under the impulses of love, grief or anger.

> The Latin participle *pulsus* means *driven, pushed*. Explain the meaning of *impulses*.

Ovid: mock epic

While Virgil's *Aeneid* shows us the serious side of Roman literature, the Romans also had a love of **humour**. **Ovid**'s poetry is no less ambitious, technically accomplished or influential than Virgil's, but the focus and tone of his poetry is often very different. His most famous

FIGURE 14.4 Apollo and Daphne

Bernini's sculpture dates from the 17th century and it is currently in the Borghese Gallery in Rome. It depicts a moment of transformation from Ovid's *Metamorphoses*. Apollo has fallen in love with beautiful nymph Daphne and has tried to catch her. In the last moments of the chase, Daphne escapes by becoming a tree. In this sculpture, you can see her fingers are becoming twigs and her toes are sprouting roots. Apollo's face bears an expression of desperation as he realises that he has lost what he thought he had captured.

poem, the *Metamorphoses*, reshaped the genre of epic poetry into **mock epic**, where much of its humour comes from stretching the conventions of epic poetry to the point of farce.

Over the course of 15 books, the *Metamorphoses* relates a series of legendary **transformations**. It opens with the very beginning of the universe and the transformation of chaos into an ordered universe and it ends with the transformation of Julius Caesar into a god. In between, Ovid masterfully incorporates human experience, exploring relationships between men and women, mortals and gods, and showing how humans react in extreme circumstances. In a fast-paced series of imaginative and contrasting stories, Ovid describes bizarre and fantastic transformations such as humans becoming trees, flowers or animals. Although these stories of transformation are at times brutal and seemingly tragic, Ovid writes in a much more light-hearted and humorous style than Virgil, often creating exaggerated or farcical moments where the pacing, structure or details of a scene tip tragedy into comedy.

Ovid is a virtuoso poet, able to move between different emotions and styles with ease. In the extracts included in this chapter you will see a dazzling display of poetic bravado as Ovid shows that he can emulate Greek tragedy and material art as well as the more traditional realms of Greek epic poetry. You will encounter passages with atmospheres which range from the **self-indulgently sinister story of Pentheus** in *scripta* 14.3 to the **mock-tragic tale of Pyramus and Thisbe in** *scripta* **14.4**. Ovid also explores painful transformations; the **cautionary tale of Arachne** is told in *scripta* 14.5 and in *scripta* 14.6 you can read about the monumentally monstrous and **blood-curdling death of the hero Hercules**.

> The Latin verb *aemulor* means *rival, copy*. Explain the meaning of *emulate*.

CHAPTER 14: READ THE *SCRIPTA* IN ENGLISH

The texts for each *scripta* are printed in this book in Latin and English. These texts can be read in English, Latin or a combination of the two. The *scripta* texts for this chapter start on p67. They follow the Core Language section because their Latin versions contain new grammar and vocabulary from this chapter.

The questions below can be answered by reading the *scripta* in English. Available on the Companion Website are copies of the English version of each *scripta* along with the questions for each text.

scripta 14.1 in English (p69): Dido's love for Aeneas

1 In Extract 1 Virgil focuses on Dido's pain: find three details which convey her pain and explain your choice.
2 In Extract 2 Virgil tells us that Dido does not want to betray her former husband, Sychaeus. Do you think she is right to feel so guilty?
3 Read Extract 3 and describe in your own words what Dido is doing and why.
4 The story of Dido is often compared to a Greek tragedy; which elements of the Dido and Aeneas story are tragic?

scripta 14.2 in English (p74): Aeneas kills Turnus

1 What does Turnus do and say to try and persuade Aeneas to spare him?
2 Describe in your own words what happens after Turnus' speech: why does Aeneas pause and what does he see that reawakens his anger at Turnus?
3 List the different emotions which Aeneas has in this passage and explain why he feels each one.
4 The *Aeneid* ends here: do you think this is a good ending for a book or not? Why?

scripta 14.3 in English (p77): Pentheus is torn apart by his mother

1 What was Cithaeron? Why do you think the Bacchic rituals are taking place here?
2 Describe in your own words what the Bacchants are doing.
3 Describe in your own words how Pentheus' emotions change as the story progresses.
4 In this extract Ovid creates a fast-paced, intensely dramatic story: how does he do this?

Chapter 14 Virgil and Ovid – Epic Poetry

scripta 14.4 in English (p80): Pyramus and Thisbe

1. In Extract 1 why do Pyramus and Thisbe describe the wall as jealous?
2. Read Extract 2: what makes this scene dramatic?
3. Read Extract 3: imagine that you are creating a scene for a play. What directions would you give to the actor playing Pyramus?
4. In Extract 4 Thisbe kills herself. What is your reaction to this scene? Do you find it funny or sad, or a mixture of the two?
5. The love story of Pyramus and Thisbe is very famous: which bits of the story do you find most memorable and why?

scripta 14.5 in English (p86): Arachne confronts Pallas Athene

1. Why does Arachne say she will not take the old woman's advice?
2. Why does Arachne blush, and why do you think she did not want to?
3. What, if any, do you think are the morals of this story?

scripta 14.6 in English (p88): Hercules dies

1. What is Hercules doing on Mount Oeta? Explain the reference to altars and flames.
2. How does Ovid show Hercules' strength and size?
3. Do you find this scene exaggeratedly dramatic? Explain your answer.

Chapter 14: Core Language Vocabulary List

Some of the words listed here look different from those you have met so far. This will be explained later in the chapter.

celo	celare, celavi, celatum	hide
cogito	cogitare, cogitavi, cogitatum	think; consider
spero	sperare, speravi, speratum	hope; expect
ago	agere, egi, actum	do; act; drive
cognosco	cognoscere, cognovi, cognitum	get to know; find out
procedo	procedere, processi	advance; proceed
promitto	promittere, promisi, promissum	promise
vivo	vivere, vixi	live; be alive
nescio	nescire, nescivi	not know
scio	scire, scivi, scitum	know
sentio	sentire, sensi, sensum	feel; notice
audeo	audere, ausus sum	dare
gaudeo	gaudere, gavisus sum	be pleased; rejoice
soleo	solere, solitus sum	be accustomed
cura	curae, f	care; worry
poena	poenae, f	punishment
poenas do		pay the penalty; be punished
animus	animi, m	spirit; soul; mind
gaudium	gaudii, n	joy; pleasure
ars	artis, f	art; skill
labor	laboris, m	work; toil
pes	pedis, m	foot
sanguis	sanguinis, m	blood
virtus	virtutis, f	courage; virtue
vox	vocis, f	voice; shout
vulnus	vulneris, n	wound
dirus	dira, dirum	dreadful

Chapter 14 Virgil and Ovid – Epic Poetry

brevis	breve	short; brief
fidelis	fidele	faithful; loyal
infelix	infelicis	unlucky; unhappy
ac, atque		and
paene		almost; nearly

Semi-deponent verbs

You have now met verbs of two different types:

- non-deponent verbs (e.g. *amo, terreo, rego, audio*): these usually have four principal parts and can have active and passive forms
- deponent verbs (e.g. *conor, videor, loquor, egredior*): these have passive forms but are active in meaning.

Semi-deponent verbs are a mixture of the two: they are non-deponent for their present-stem tenses but deponent for their perfect-stem tenses. As such, they do not have a perfect active stem and they only have three principal parts.

There are very few semi-deponent verbs in Latin. Three of them are included in the vocabulary for this chapter.

audeo	audere, ausus sum	dare
gaudeo	gaudere, gavisus sum	be pleased; rejoice
soleo	solere, solitus sum	be accustomed

All three of these verbs are in the 2nd conjugation and share the same endings. You can see their endings in the Reference Grammar on pp253–4.

The perfect tense of all three of these verbs is comparatively rare; this is because – like all verbs in Latin that refer to an action which is naturally ongoing – it is more idiomatic to use the imperfect tense for past actions.

Remember: some verbs are **intransitive** and do not have passive forms in the way that other verbs do. See Chapter 9, Book 2, p94.

PRACTISE VERB LABELS!

Look at the principal parts for each of the verbs below: is the verb non-deponent, deponent or semi-deponent?

1. celo, celare, celavi, celatum
2. soleo, solere, solitus sum
3. conor, conari, conatus sum
4. ago, agere, egi, actum
5. loquor, loqui, locutus sum
6. gaudeo, gaudere, gavisus sum

EXERCISE 14.1

1. cives vocem diram dei audire **audebant**.
2. ubi hostes poenas dederunt, exercitus breviter **gavisus est**.
3. milites infelices lacrimare **solebant**.
4. cur heri **gavisus es**? hodie miserrimus lacrimas.
5. dux fortissimus vulnera multa accipere **ausus est**.
6. magnum gaudium habeo; nam semper fortissime pugnare **audes**.
7. liberi multa promittere **solent**, quod volunt parentes se laudare.
8. quando domum regredi **audebis**? nonne perterritus es, quod periculum maximum est?
9. ecce! sanguinem video! pes meus vulneratus est quod per silvas currere **ausus sum**.
10. magnus est labor amici fidelis! propter me amicus meus multa pati **solet**.

> The verbs in bold are from **audeo**, **gaudeo** or **soleo**. Translate each one.

Further notes on tenses: time relative to the main verb

So far in this course, notes on the **tense** of a verb have focussed on **when** an action took place (past, present or future time).

You will now learn, however, that the tenses of different categories of verb forms work in different ways. This chapter will focus on the different tenses of **participles** and **infinitives**.

Participles have tenses which indicate a **time relative to the main verb**. Consider the example below:

Running towards the temple, the girl saw the gold.

Running is a present participle, but it does not have to describe an action in present time; instead it describes an action that is in the present relative to the main verb, i.e. an action **at the same time** as the main verb.

The perfect tense for a participle is used for an action which takes place **before the main verb**.

The future tense for a participle is used for an action which will take place at some time **later than the main verb**.

Chapter 14 Virgil and Ovid – Epic Poetry

Participle tenses: future participles and deponent perfect participles

So far you have met two types of participle:

present active	**reg**ens, **reg**entis	ruling
perfect passive	rect**us**, rect**a**, rect**um**	having been ruled

The endings for these participles are listed in full in the Reference Grammar on p243.

Latin has two further types of participle:

future active	rect**urus**, rect**ura**, rect**urum**	being about to rule
perfect active (deponent verbs only)	secut**us**, secut**a**, secut**um**	having followed

Both of these are 2-1-2 adjectives. The 2-1-2 adjective endings are listed in the Reference Grammar on p221. Like all other adjectives, they have to **agree** with the noun they describe in **case, gender** and **number**.

The **future active** participle uses the supine stem; this is the stem given by the 4th principal part (or, for deponent verbs, the 3rd principal part).

Only **deponent verbs** have a perfect active participle. This is because these verbs have passive forms but are active in meaning. The present and future participles, however, are the same for both deponent and non-deponent verbs.

	non-deponent	deponent
present active	regens, regentis – ruling	sequens, sequentis – following
future active	recturus, rectura, recturum – being about to rule	secuturus, secutura, secuturum – being about to follow
perfect participle	rectus, recta, rectum – having been ruled (**passive**)	secutus, secuta, secutum – having followed (**active**)

EXERCISE 14.2

1. gaudium magnum in animo est quod, **miratus** vocem tuam, te magnopere amo.
2. milites, domum **regressuri**, laetissimi erant.
3. nauta, prima luce **profectus**, ad navem celeriter procedit.
4. rem diram **actura**, filia de poena cogitabat.
5. 'non conspexi,' inquit mater, 'laborem a te **promissum**.'
6. incolae, artem magnam poetae **mirati**, verba iterum audire volebant.
7. conspeximus exercitum ad bellum **profecturum**.
8. sequebamur liberos fugere **conantes**.
9. nunc es **moriturus**: **vulneratus**, non iam vivere potes.
10. invenistine pecuniam prope templum **celatam**?

The words in bold are all **participles**. What **tense** is each one? Is it **active** or **passive**?

morior has a slightly unusual future participle: *moriturus*.

Translating participles into idiomatic English

It is much more idiomatic to use a participle in Latin than in English. In English, perfect and future participles are fairly rare. This is because their form in English is unwieldy.

It is often better in English to use a **subordinate clause** with a **finite verb** instead (i.e. a verb with a person and a tense).

> milites Romani, hostes secuti, ducem invenerunt.
>   The Roman soldiers, having followed the enemy, found their leader.
>   → After they followed the enemy, the Roman soldiers found their leader.
>
> nautae, per noctem navigaturi, perterriti erant.
>   The sailors, being about to sail through the night, were terrified.
>   → The sailors, who were about to sail through the night, were terrified.

Remember: idiom means the quirks of a language which are particular to that language.

Chapter 14 Virgil and Ovid – Epic Poetry

Consolidation: ablative absolute

In Chapter 12 you met the **ablative absolute** construction. This construction is used when a participle describes a noun which is grammatically separate from the rest of the sentence.

> e.g. agris incensis, Romani nullum cibum habebant.
> With the fields having been burned, the Romans had no food.
> → When the fields had been burned, the Romans had no food.

As shown by the example above, it is often best in English to turn the participle into a **subordinate clause** containing a **finite verb**. This subordinate clause could start with the word *when, since, because, although* or perhaps something else. You will need to use the context of the sentence to decide which suits the sentence best.

It is possible to form an ablative absolute with any tense of participle, but it is fairly rare to meet a future participle or a deponent verb's perfect active participle in an ablative absolute.

> Remember, a **finite verb** is a verb with a **person** and a **tense**.

EXERCISE 14.3

> The **ablative absolute** in each sentence is in bold. Translate each one.

1. **cura celata**, dux gaudium militibus ostendere conatus est.
2. **poenis datis**, mulier, quae etiam tum alterum hominem amabat, tristissima erat.
3. **vocibus sensis**, perterriti liberi e silvis fugerunt.
4. **nave deleta**, nautae domum regredi non poterant.
5. **pace promissa**, milites gaudebant.
6. **uxore vivente**, maritus non desperabat; **illa mortua**, spem nullam gaudii habebat.
7. '**pedibus vulneratis**,' inquit frater infelix, 'ad urbem procedere non possum.'
8. **omni labore acto**, servi ancillaeque fessi erant.
9. **virtute illius civis cognita**, senator praemia magna obtulit.
10. **poeta verba mirabilia scribere auso**, omnes cives gaudebant.

scripta in Latin	you could now look at the Latin version of *scripta* 14.1 and 14.2

Consolidation: infinitives

The infinitives you have met so far have all been present tense. Like all present tense forms, they use the present stem of the verb and their vowels vary according to conjugation.

	1st conjugation	2nd conjugation	3rd conjugation	4th conjugation
non-deponent	am**are** – to love	terr**ere** – to terrify	reg**ere** – to rule	aud**ire** – to hear
deponent	con**ari** – to try	vid**eri** – to seem	sequ**i** – to follow	

You have also met some **irregular** infinitives, such as *velle* – to want, *nolle* – to not want, *esse* – to be, *posse* – to be able, *malle* – to prefer, *ferre* – to bring, carry, bear.

You have met infinitives used in three different ways:

- with another verb
  - **nolo pugnare.**   I do not want to fight.
- with a neuter sg adjective
  - **pugnare difficile est.**   It is difficult to fight.
- in the accusative + infinitive indirect statement construction
  - **vidit milites pugnare.**   He saw that the soldiers were fighting.

Watch out! It is very easy to confuse a 3rd conjugation deponent infinitive (e.g. *sequi*) with the perfect tense of an active verb (e.g. *rexi*)

Present passive infinitives

The endings you have met for deponent verb infinitives are also used for passive infinitives for non-deponent verbs.

Like all other verb forms built upon the present stem, the **vowel** used in the ending depends upon **conjugation**.

	1st conjugation	2nd conjugation	3rd conjugation	4th conjugation
present active infinitive	am**are** – to love	terr**ere** – to terrify	reg**ere** – to rule	aud**ire** – to hear
present passive infinitive	am**ari** – to be loved	terr**eri** – to be terrified	reg**i** – to be ruled	aud**iri** – to be heard

The present passive infinitive for the mixed conjugation is listed in the Reference Grammar on p245.

Present passive infinitives can be used in the same ways as present active infinitives. For example,

'nolumus,' inquiunt Romani,   'We do not want to be ruled by kings,'
     'a regibus regi.'   said the Romans.

Watch out! Take care not to confuse the 3rd conjugation present passive infinitive (e.g. *regi*) with the perfect active tense (e.g. *rexi*).

Chapter 14 Virgil and Ovid – Epic Poetry

EXERCISE 14.4

> The **present infinitives** are all in bold. Is each one **active**, **passive** or **deponent**?

1. incolae villas ab hostibus **incendi** nolebant.
2. dirum est in bello multa vulnera **pati**.
3. 'o dux,' inquiunt milites audaces, 'multa a te **agi** volumus!'
4. difficillimum est ad mare **proficisci**.
5. fratres malebant a matre **puniri** quam patre.
6. gens illius insulae a Romanis **regi** nolebat.
7. nonnulli de pace **loqui** volebant.
8. nolebant aurum in agris **celari**.
9. cur hunc senatorem **laudare** conati estis? vir est saevissimus.
10. hi servi domino novo **vendi** nolebant.

scripta in Latin — you could now look at the Latin version of *scripta* 14.3

Indirect statements: present passive infinitives

Present passive infinitives can also be used in indirect statements.

Note that – as with all other indirect statements – an idiomatic English translation will convert the accusative + infinitive into a **subordinate clause** containing a **finite verb** and introduced by the word *that*. The tense of the finite verb will depend on the tense of the main verb in the sentence. This is because **present tense infinitives** are used in indirect statements for actions which take place **at the same time as** the main verb.

> Remember, a **finite verb** is a verb with a **person** and a **tense**.

    dicit **servos** a domino saevo **terreri**.
        He says **the slaves to be terrified** by their savage master.
        → He says **that the slaves are terrified** by their savage master.

    dixit **servos** a domino saevo **terreri**.
        He said **the slaves to be terrified** by their savage master.
        → He said **that the slaves were terrified** by their savage master.

EXERCISE 14.5

> In each sentence, the **accusative + infinitive** is in bold. Is the infinitive **active**, **passive** or **deponent**?

1. cur putavisti **incolas** a militibus **vulnerari**?
2. haec puella nescit **parentes** iam domum **regredi**.
3. duos fratres habeo: alter putat **me** ad templum **progredi**; alter scit **me** cum amico **convenire**.
4. senator sensit **verba** a civibus **non audiri**.
5. agricola sciebat **exercitum** agros suos delere **conari**.
6. cognovi **pecuniam** a servis **rapi**; nunc necesse est mihi eos punire.
7. pater nesciebat **filiam** etiam tum **vivere**; credebat **eam** mortuam **esse**.
8. omnes putabamus **neminem** ad bellum **proficisci**.
9. scivistine **cives** illum senatorem **sequi**? **eum** clarissimum nobilissimumque **esse** cognoverunt.
10. nautae lacrimabant quod sentiebant **navem** vento magno **deleri**.

---

scripta in Latin   you could now look at the Latin version of *scripta* 14.4

Perfect active and perfect passive infinitives

Latin also has perfect tense infinitives; these refer to actions which have taken place **before** the main verb.

Like all other perfect active forms, the **perfect active infinitive** is built upon the **perfect active stem**.

Like all other perfect passive forms, the **perfect passive infinitive** uses the **PPP** and **part of the verb** *to be*.

As is typical for a **deponent verb**, deponent verbs use the **passive form** but are **active in meaning**.

Like all other perfect tense forms, the same endings are used for all conjugations.

perfect active infinitive	rex**isse**	to have ruled
perfect passive infinitive	rect**us esse**	to have been ruled
deponent perfect infinitive	secut**us esse**	to have followed

Chapter 14 Virgil and Ovid – Epic Poetry

> **Indirect statements: perfect active and perfect passive infinitives**
>
> You are most likely to meet a perfect infinitive in an **indirect statement**.
>
> As with all other indirect statements, an idiomatic English translation will convert the accusative + infinitive into a **subordinate clause** containing a **finite verb** and introduced by the word *that*. A **perfect infinitive** refers to an action which took place **before** the main verb; how you translate it will depend on the tense of the main verb.
>
> > cognoscit **regem** nonnullos cives **interfecisse**.
> > > He finds out **the king to have** killed several citizens.
> > > → He finds out **that the king has killed** several citizens.
> >
> > cognovit **regem** cives nonnullos **interfecisse**.
> > > He found out **the king to have** killed several citizens.
> > > → He found out **that the king had killed** several citizens.
>
> Because the **perfect passive infinitive** uses the **PPP**, notice that in an indirect statement, the **PPP** will need to **agree** with the **accusative subject** of the infinitive.
>
> > sciebamus femin**as** interfect**as** esse.   We knew that the women had been killed.
> > sciebamus civ**es** interfect**os** esse.   We knew that the citizens had been killed.

EXERCISE 14.6

> In each sentence, the **accusative + infinitive** is in bold. Is the infinitive **active**, **passive** or **deponent**?

1. cur non mihi dixisti **sororem** iam **interfectam esse**?
2. cives mirantur **templum** pulcherrimum **aedificatum esse**.
3. servi fideles cognoverunt **vinum** a domina **celatum esse**.
4. audivimus **exercitum** prima luce **profectum esse**.
5. poeta nesciebat **libros** suos a senatore clarissimo **lectos esse**.
6. filia poetae sentit **se** tandem artem patris **cognovisse**.
7. dux gentis huius credebat **epistulam** a duce Romano **non scriptam esse**.
8. socii intellegebant **pacem** non diram **esse**; itaque nuntiaverunt **se** oppidum suum Romanis **tradidisse**.
9. in illo bello milites sentiebant **se** virtutem optimam **ostendisse**.
10. senator putat **se** in foro breviter sed optime **locutum esse**.

scripta in Latin   you could now look at the Latin version of *scripta* 14.5

Future infinitives

Latin infinitives are also possible in the future tense. **Future infinitives** are used to refer to actions which are **yet to happen** at the time of the main verb.

Future active infinitives are formed in the same way across all conjugations: they are created by using the **future participle + *esse***.

Deponent verbs form their future infinitive in the same way as non-deponent verbs.

non-deponent future active infinitive	rect**urus esse** to be about to rule
deponent future active infinitive	secut**urus esse** to be about to follow

Future passive infinitives do exist in Latin, but are extremely rare. Their form is listed in the Reference Grammar on p246.

Indirect statements: future active infinitives

You are most likely to meet a future infinitive in an **indirect statement**.

As with all other indirect statements, an idiomatic English translation will convert the accusative + infinitive into a **subordinate clause** containing a **finite verb** and introduced by the word **that**. A **future infinitive** refers to an action which is **yet to happen** at the time of the main verb; how you translate it will depend on the tense of the main verb.

> sentit **liberos tacituros esse**.
> > She realises **the children to be about to be silent**.
> > → She realises **that the children will be silent**.
>
> sentiebat **liberos tacituros esse**.
> > She realised **the children to be about to be silent**.
> > → She realised **that the children would be silent**.

Like the perfect passive infinitive, because the future active infinitive uses a **participle**, the ending of the participle will need to **agree** with the **accusative subject** of the infinitive.

> sentiebat puer**os** tacitur**os** esse.   She realised that the boys would be silent.
> sentiebat mulier**es** tacitur**as** esse.   She realised that the women would be silent.

In Latin, the verbs ***promitto*** and ***spero*** are usually followed by an indirect statement (with a future tense infinitive) even though the English idiom is to use an infinitive only.

> promittebant **se** cras **adventuros esse**.
> > They promised themselves to be about to arrive tomorrow.
> > → They promised **to arrive** tomorrow.

Chapter 14 Virgil and Ovid – Epic Poetry

EXERCISE 14.7

In each sentence the **accusative + infinitive** indirect statement is in bold. Translate each one **literally** and then **idiomatically**.

1. copiae credebant **se** ad mare **adventuros esse**.
2. cur sperabant **ducem** mox pacem **oblaturum esse**?
3. milites promiserunt **se** in bello fortiter **pugnaturos esse**.
4. servi sciebant **se morituros esse**.
5. haec mulier sciebat **maritum** de amore feminae alterius **taciturum esse**.
6. incolae sperabant **exercitum** totum Romam **regressurum esse**.
7. hoc vulnus est minimum. putabasne **te** sanguinem **visurum esse**?
8. cives dixerunt **deos** paene omnes hostes **punituros esse**.
9. solus sentiebam **senatorem** verba dira **dicturum esse**.
10. domina sperabat **villam** tutam **futuram esse**.

futurus esse is the future infinitive of the verb *sum* (see the Reference Grammar p248).

se is used when the subject of the infinitive is the **same** as the main verb; otherwise, *he / she / it* will be expressed by the pronoun *is, ea, id* in the accusative case.

Consolidation: indirect statement

The indirect statement is one of Latin's most important constructions and one of the most difficult to translate into English. This is because Latin and English handle the construction in different ways.

Remember these key principles:

- English uses a **subordinate clause** introduced by the word **that**
- Latin uses the **accusative + infinitive**
  - the tense of the Latin infinitive will depend on whether the action took place at the same time as the main verb, before it or at some point afterwards
  - the accusative subject of the infinitive must be expressed; therefore it is very common to meet a **pronoun** in an indirect statement.

  dixit **se** laetum esse.   He said that **he** was happy.

scripta in Latin   you could now look at the Latin version of *scripta* 14.6

Chapter 14: *scripta*

For guidance on how to make use of these Latin texts and their English translations, see pp.viii–ix.

On the Companion Website you will find resources to accompany these texts:

- *in the **scripta *in English*** *section you will find copies of each text in English only, with questions on each one*
- *in the **scripta *in Latin*** *section you will find notes for each of the Latin texts: these contain glosses for all words not yet met in a Core Language vocabulary list, explanations to help you understand the Latin and material designed to help you build your appreciation of literary style.*

FIGURE 14.5 Statue of Ovid

This statue of Ovid is a copy of one created in 1887, by the Italian sculptor Ettore Ferrari. The original was created to commemorate the poet's time in the city of Tomis, where Ovid spent his exile. It is in modern day Constanţa, a Romanian city on the Black Sea. This duplicate of the statue was created in 1925 and placed in Sulmona, Ovid's birthplace in central Italy. The sculptor has positioned Ovid with one arm across his body and the other arm bent, with his chin on his hand. This pose was often used for sculptures of Roman women; it was designed to denote modesty and chastity. The sculptor is perhaps playfully acknowledging that the traditional format of Ovid's poetry is rather different from his witty – and often scurrilous – content.

Meet the *scriptores*: Virgil and Ovid

The life of the Augustan poet **Publius Vergilius Maro** (70–19 BC) was shaped by war and political change. **Virgil** was a boy when Julius Caesar, Pompey and Crassus came to power. His early 20s were marked by civil war, the assassination of Julius Caesar and the punishments which followed: his family farm was confiscated after the Battle of Philippi. The culmination of Virgil's career, and arguably of Roman epic poetry, came with his final work, the ***Aeneid***. Composed soon after Augustus had brought an end to nearly a century of political instability, the *Aeneid* tells the story of the Trojan prince Aeneas. Aeneas fled Troy after its fall and journeyed as a refugee to his prophesied new home in Italy, where he became the father of the Roman people.

Publius Ovidius Naso (20 BC–AD 17/18) was much younger than Virgil. When he was born, Augustus was already in power. Unlike Virgil, **Ovid** did not experience the upheaval of civil war and his upbringing was both more peaceful and more privileged. Though much of his work was in the form of love poetry, his most famous text is the ***Metamorphoses***, a mythic historical account of the universe which ends with the transformation of Julius Caesar into a god. Much of Ovid's poetry sits at the teasing edge of comedy, where publicly revered customs or material are laughed at for the reader's amusement. It seems that Ovid's irreverent approach became too controversial and in AD 8 he was exiled from Rome to Tomis, a small coastal town on the Black Sea in modern-day Romania, where he died ten years later. Exactly why he was exiled remains a mystery and a topic of lively interest amongst scholars. Ovid himself claimed that his exile was due to *carmen et error* ('a poem and a mistake'), but which poem and which mistake are a matter of ongoing speculation.

LITERARY TERMINOLOGY

In this chapter you will meet literary terminology such as **epic simile, metaphor, imagery**. There are notes about these in the *scripta in Latin* Companion Website resources.

Reading original Latin note 3: Latin verse

Translating Latin verse can be more difficult than translating Latin prose. This is mainly because:

- a **wide range of vocabulary** is used and there will be lots of words you do not yet know.
- the **meaning of words can be stretched**; this means that you may recognise a word but need to translate it differently in order to suit the context.
- lots of **adjectives and participles** are used; this means that there will be many words with case endings and you will have to think carefully about what part of speech they are and which other words they agree with.
- the **word order is often dislocated**: because it is possible to work out the noun–adjective agreement from the word endings, Latin writers had much more flexibility in their poetic word order than is possible in English.
- the influence of Greek literature on Latin poetry means that **Greek names are often used**; sometimes the Greek case endings are used too, transliterated into Latin. This means that there will be some case endings which you do not recognise.
- **words are often missed out** if they can be understood from context; this is particularly common with the verb *to be* and the nouns that adjectives describe.

When you translate, it is important to think about **part of speech** and observe the following principles:

- **nouns**: because of the extra descriptive detail pinned to nouns you will often need to take several words together as a noun-phrase bundle; these words may not be next to each other. A noun phrase can include an adjective, a participle, another noun in the genitive case or a combination of these.
- **adjectives**: do not translate an adjective until you have found its noun; if there is no noun in the same number, gender and case, you will need to understand one from context.
- **prepositions**: when these are followed by a noun phrase rather than just a noun, at least one word from this phrase will be immediately after the preposition. The other words in the noun phrase may be separated and even appear before the preposition. Make sure you have identified the words which are part of the prepositional phrase before you translate the rest of the sentence.
- **verbs**: the subject or object of a verb may need to be understood from context; in addition, verbs are often left out if they can be understood from context or if it is the verb *to be*.

Remember that further help for a more literal translation of each passage is provided in the *scripta* in Latin section of the Companion Website.

Navigating adjectives and participles

One of the main challenges when translating Latin verse is the high number of adjectives (including participles). Latin poets delighted in ornate word order patterns and, as a result of this, adjectives / participles are often not positioned next to their nouns. In addition, the natural concision of verse means that the noun described by the adjective / participle is often not there and you will need to supply it by thinking about the number and gender of the adjective.

To help you with this, all the adjectives / participles in the verse passages in this chapter are in **red**. Remember that for each of these adjectives, you should not translate them until you have found – or supplied – their noun. This is particularly important for participles.

In addition, Latin will often use a participle where it would be more idiomatic in English to have a finite verb; this means that you may need to reshape the structure of the sentence when you translate, creating clauses out of participle phrases.

scripta 14.1: Dido's love for Aeneas

Love is a central theme of epic poetry and the great love affair between Aeneas, the father of the Roman race, and Dido, queen of Carthage, is seen by many as one of the most tragic stories in Western literature.

Virgil uses this love affair to explore themes of powerlessness, pain and conflict. Aeneas and Dido both have a traumatic past: Aeneas is fleeing from Troy after seeing his city destroyed by the Greeks. Dido fled her previous home in Sidon after her brother killed her husband, Sychaeus. Aeneas meets her while she is leading her followers in building a new city, Carthage. Dido has sworn to be loyal to her husband's memory, but when the gods decide to make her fall in love with Aeneas, she is unable to resist.

Virgil focuses on the inner turmoil this causes: Dido tries to deny her love, but it consumes her. Virgil uses fire and wound metaphors as symbols of love's power to destroy and to foreshadow Dido's decision at the end of Aeneid, Book 4, to commit suicide when she realises that Aeneas has left her, compelled by the gods to pursue his destiny in Italy.

Extract 1: Dido is tormented by her love for Aeneas

The text below is taken from the opening lines of Aeneid, Book 4. At the end of Book 1, Venus had sent her son, Cupid, to make Dido fall in love with Aeneas; Book 1 ends with a description of Dido's passion spreading through her body, like a fire.

At Dido's request, Aeneas tells her his life-story and his account of his past fills Books 2 and 3. Aeneas focuses on the fall of Troy and the difficulties he has faced on his voyage since then.

At the start of Book 4 we return to Dido and the pain her love is causing her. Dido had sworn to be faithful to the memory of her dead husband; the passion she feels for Aeneas troubles her and she feels torn between her previous loyalty and the pull of this new love.

But the queen had been hurt for some time now by her heavy love; she kept feeding the wound with her life-blood and she was troubled by her blind passion. Aeneas' great talent and the high status of his family kept coming back in her mind; his face and his words stayed with her, imprinted on her heart, and her love did not allow any peaceful rest for her body.

at regina gravi iamdudum saucia cura
vulnus alit venis et caeco carpitur igni.
multa viri virtus animo multusque recursat
gentis honos; haerent infixi pectore vultus
verbaque nec placidam membris dat cura quietem.

Aeneid 4.1–5

at	but
iamdudum	for some time now
saucius -a -um	wounded
alo, alere	feed, nourish
vena, venae, f	vein
caecus -a -um	blind, hidden
carpo, carpere	pluck at, harass, weaken
recurso, recursare	run back, return
haereo, haerere	stick, cling to
vultus, vultus, m	expression, face
membrum, membri, n	limb

Chapter 14 Virgil and Ovid – Epic Poetry

The next day's dawn was moving over the earth with Phoebus' light and it had removed the damp mist from the sky when Dido – scarcely in her right mind – spoke to her sister, her soulmate, in this way: 'Anna, my sister, oh the bad dreams which terrify me and leave me on edge! Who is this new man who has come into our house as a guest? Oh the look he has on his face! How brave he is in his heart and in battle! Indeed – and this is no empty belief – I think that he is born from the gods.

postera Phoebea lustrabat lampade terras
umentemque Aurora polo dimoverat umbram,
cum sic unanimam adloquitur male sana sororem:
'Anna soror, quae me suspensam insomnia terrent!
quis novus hic nostris successit sedibus hospes,
quem sese ore ferens, quam forti pectore et armis!
credo equidem, nec vana fides, genus esse deorum.

Aeneid 4.6–12

Phoebeus -a -um	of Phoebus Apollo (sun-god)
lustro, lustrare	go round
umens, umentis	moist, damp
Aurora, Aurorae, f	Aurora (goddess of the dawn)
polus, poli, m	sky
umbra, umbrae, f	shadow
cum	when
insomnium, insomnii, n	bad dream
succedo, succedere, successi	go within
hospes, hospitis, m	guest
quem sese . . . ferens	'oh how he bears himself . . .'
os, oris, n	face
equidem	indeed, for my part
vanus -a -um	empty
fides, fidei, f	belief
genus, generis, n	origin, family

Extract 2: Dido confides in her sister

Dido admits her feelings to her sister, Anna, and tells her she is determined to stay faithful to her dead husband Sychaeus.

Anna – I will admit it – after the death of my wretched husband, Sychaeus, and after our household gods were soiled with the murder committed by my brother, this man alone has changed my feelings and sent my heart reeling. I recognise the traces of a passion I felt long ago. But I would wish that the bottom of the earth would gape open for me first or that all-powerful Jupiter would drive me down to the darkness with his thunderbolt, the pale darkness in Erebus, and into the deep night before I violate you, my conscience or before I break your laws. The man who first joined me to him took my love; he should hold it with him and keep it safe in his tomb.' Dido spoke in this way but she filled her heart with tears that had welled up.

Anna (fatebor enim) miseri post fata Sychaei
coniugis et sparsos fraterna caede penates
solus hic inflexit sensus animumque labantem
impulit. agnosco veteris vestigia flammae.
sed mihi vel tellus optem prius ima dehiscat
vel pater omnipotens adigat me fulmine ad umbras,
pallentes umbras Erebo noctemque profundam,
ante, pudor, quam te violo aut tua iura resolvo.
ille meos, primus qui me sibi iunxit, amores
abstulit; ille habeat secum servetque sepulcro.'
sic effata sinum lacrimis implevit obortis.

Aeneid 4.20–30

fateor, fateri	confess
sparsus -a -um	spattered
caedes, caedis, f	slaughter
labor, labi	slip, fall
vetus, veteris	old
vel . . . vel	either . . . or
tellus, telluris, f	earth
optem . . . dehiscat	'I would wish that [the earth] gape open'
prius	beforehand, first
imus -a -um	lowest
fulmen, fulminis, n	thunderbolt, lightning
umbra, umbrae, f	shadow
pallens, pallentis	pale
Erebus, Erebi, m	the Underworld
ante . . . quam = antequam	
pudor, pudoris, m	sense of shame / honour
aut	or
ius, iuris, n	law
iungo, iungere, iunxi	join
habeat	'let him have [my love]'
servet	'may he keep [my love] safe'
effatus -a -um	having spoken
sinus, sinus, m	curve, fold, lap, heart
impleo, implere, implevi	fill
oborior, oboriri, obortus sum	arise

Chapter 14 Virgil and Ovid – Epic Poetry

> ### Extract 3: Dido is wounded by her love
>
> *Virgil continues his description of Dido's love and uses an epic simile to deepen the wound imagery, already established as a metaphor for her love for Aeneas. The epic simile compares Dido to a wounded deer; the details in this simile remind us that Dido did not expect to fall in love and that Aeneas is unaware of what is happening to her.*
>
> *After the simile has finished, Virgil continues the story in Carthage and we see Dido showing Aeneas her city; the implication is that – despite her pledge of loyalty to her former husband – she is trying to persuade Aeneas to stay. She is unable to stop thinking about Aeneas and she feels wretched without him.*

Meanwhile Dido's wound lives silently within her heart. Unhappy Dido burns and wanders all over the city, mad in her passion, just like a deer when an arrow has been fired, when a shepherd, hunting from afar with his arrows, has struck the deer off-guard in the Cretan groves. He has left his flying arrow there, without realising what he has done; the deer roams through the woods and the glades of Mount **Dicte** in flight, but the deadly arrow is embedded in her side. Now Dido leads Aeneas with her through the city and she shows him her **Sidonian** wealth and the city which is ready for him. She begins to speak and then stops in mid voice.

interea et tacitum vivit sub pectore vulnus.
uritur infelix Dido totaque vagatur
urbe furens, qualis coniecta cerva sagitta,
quam procul incautam nemora inter Cresia fixit
pastor agens telis liquitque volatile ferrum
nescius: illa fuga silvas saltusque peragrat
Dictaeos; haeret lateri letalis harundo.
nunc media **Aenean** secum per moenia ducit
Sidoniasque ostentat opes urbemque paratam,
incipit effari mediaque in voce resistit.

Aeneid 4.67–76

Dicte was a mountain in Crete.

Aenean is a Greek accusative sg.

Dido was from **Sidon**; she brought great wealth with her when she fled her former home.

interea = inter ea	
uro, urere	burn
vagor, vagari	wander
furens, furentis	raving, mad [with passion]
qualis	'just like'
cerva, cervae, f	deer
procul	at a distance
incautus -a -um	unaware, off-guard
nemus, nemoris, n	grove, wood
telum, teli, n	missile, weapon
ferrum, ferri, n	iron
saltus, saltus, m	glade, pasture
peragro, peragrare	roam through
haereo, haerere (+ dative)	stick, cling to
latus, lateris, n	side, flank
letalis, letale	deadly
harundo, harundinis, f	arrow
moenia, moenium, n pl	walls
opes, opum, f pl	wealth
effor, effari	speak

Now, as the same day is ending, she calls for banquets, and – not in her right mind – again she begs to hear about his efforts in **Troy**; she clings – again – to every word as he speaks. Afterwards, when her guests have left and when, in turn, the faint moon is withdrawing its light and the falling stars are calling for sleep, she grieves alone in her empty house and lies on the abandoned couches. He is not there and she is not with him, but she hears and sees him still. At other times, she keeps hold of Ascanius in her lap, captivated by his likeness to his father, and tries to deceive the love she will not admit to.

nunc eadem labente die convivia quaerit,
Iliacosque iterum demens audire labores
exposcit pendetque iterum narrantis ab ore.
post ubi digressi, lumenque obscura vicissim
luna premit suadentque cadentia sidera somnos,
sola domo maeret vacua stratisque relictis
incubat. illum absens absentem auditque videtque,
aut gremio Ascanium genitoris imagine capta
detinet, infandum si fallere possit amorem.

Aeneid 4.77–85

> **Ilium** was another name for Troy.

labor, labi	slip, fall away
exposco, exposcere	implore
pendo, pendere	hang
os, oris, n	mouth, voice
post = postea	
vicissim	in turn
premo, premere	press
sidus, sidera, n	star
somnus, somni, m	sleep
maereo, maerere	grieve, lament
stratum, strati, m	couch
incubo, incubare	lie on
aut	or
gremium, gremii, n	lap
genitor, genitoris, m	father
infandus -a -um	unspeakable
si . . . possit	'to see if she could'
fallo, fallere	deceive

DERIVATIONS

This task builds skills in deducing the meaning of one word by using a related word.

The words below derive from words in the passages above which have not been glossed.

Can you find the Latin words from which these English words derive? Can you use either the Latin or the English word to help you explain the meaning of the other?

Remember that you will need to think about the part of speech of both the Latin and English words and – if they are different – you will need to consider how to adjust the meaning to move from one part of speech to the other.

curation, placid, sane, suspense, pectoral muscles, fatal, inflexible, sensitive, impulse, vestiges, omnipotent, profound, violation, resolution, sepulchre, tacitly, convivial, dementia, obscure, imagination, detention

Chapter 14 Virgil and Ovid – Epic Poetry

> ### scripta 14.2: Aeneas kills Turnus
>
> The Aeneid ends with a duel between Aeneas and Turnus, the leader of the Italian forces and Aeneas' rival for marriage to Lavinia, daughter of the king of the Latin people. Aeneas kills Turnus, and the moment is used by Virgil to symbolise the first step towards the foundation of Rome.
>
> Virgil's description conveys the conflicting passions of battle: Turnus asks for mercy, appealing to Aeneas' empathy for the grief Daunus, Turnus' father, will feel if his son dies before him. Aeneas hesitates and seems ready to spare Turnus, but then notices that Turnus is wearing armour taken from Pallas, a young soldier previously killed in battle. Pallas' father, king Evander, had agreed to supply troops to Aeneas and he had asked Aeneas to look after Pallas, his only son. When Aeneas sees Pallas' armour he is reminded of his – and Evander's – grief; ablaze with anger, pain and rage, Aeneas kills Turnus. The Aeneid is in many ways a celebration of the greatness of Rome but Virgil is alert to its cost: the final lines of the poem end in a frenzy of pain and with the darkness of death.
>
> The Aeneid builds on the foundations of the epic tradition and Virgil often echoes moments from Homer's great epics. These echoes add depth to the poem, sometimes by reminding us of contrasting scenes. Turnus' appeal for empathy is very similar to the famous scene at the end of the Iliad, where Priam appeals to Achilles for compassion. In the Iliad, Achilles is moved by the sight of a father's grief and the Iliad ends with a moment of restorative understanding; with this scene in the background, Aeneas' descent into savage revenge at the end of the Aeneid becomes more strikingly bleak.

Turnus was on the ground and, as a supplicant, directing his gaze and stretching out his begging right hand he said, 'Indeed I have deserved to die and I do not ask you not to kill me for my sake; the outcome is yours to use. But if any thought for a wretched father is able to affect you, have pity for Daunus' old age (Anchises was also once such a father for you), I beg you, and give me back to my family – or, if you prefer my body to be stripped of its life, then give them back my corpse. You have won and the Ausonians have seen me, beaten, stretching out my hands to you. Lavinia is yours as your wife; don't go any further in your hatred.'

Aeneas stood in his armour ready to strike, but he was running his eyes over Turnus and he held back his own right hand, and now, now, as he hesitated more, Turnus' speech had begun to change his mind; but then he noticed the ill-omened strap on Turnus' tall shoulder and the sword-belt with its familiar studs glittered, once owned by the young boy, Pallas. Turnus had wounded Pallas, overpowered him and struck him down and now he was wearing his enemy's insignia on his shoulders.

ille humilis supplex oculos dextramque precantem
protendens 'equidem merui nec deprecor' inquit;
'utere sorte tua. miseri te si qua parentis
tangere cura potest, oro (fuit et tibi talis
Anchises genitor) Dauni miserere senectae
et me, seu corpus spoliatum lumine mavis,
redde meis. vicisti et victum tendere palmas
Ausonii videre; tua est Lavinia coniunx,
ulterius ne tende odiis.'

                                   stetit acer in armis
Aeneas volvens oculos dextramque repressit;
et iam iamque magis cunctantem flectere sermo
coeperat, infelix umero cum apparuit alto
balteus et notis fulserunt cingula bullis
Pallantis pueri, victum quem vulnere Turnus
straverat atque umeris inimicum insigne gerebat.

Aeneid 12.930–44

humilis, humile	on the ground
dextra, dextrae, f	right hand
precor, precari	beg, pray
protendo, protendere	stretch out
equidem	indeed, for my part
mereo, merere, merui	deserve
utere (+ ablative)	'use'
sors, sortis, f	fortune destiny
si qua	'if any'
tango, tangere	touch
oro, orare	beg
talis, tale	such, of this sort
miserere (+ genitive)	'have pity for'
seu	or if
reddo, reddere	give back
tendo, tendere	stretch out
videre = viderunt	
ulterius	further
acer, acris, acre	sharp, keen
volvo, volvere	turn, roll
cunctor, cunctari	delay, hesitate
umerus, umeri, m	shoulder
cum	when
balteus, baltei, m	belt
fulgeo, fugere, fulsi	flash, glitter
cingulum, cinguli, n	sword-belt
bulla, bullae, f	stud
sterno, sternere, stravi	strike down
insigne, insignis, n	distinguishing mark, decoration

Chapter 14 Virgil and Ovid – Epic Poetry

Aeneas soaked up with his eyes the reminders and remnants of his wild grief and then, inflamed with fury and terrible in his anger, he said, 'Are you to be taken away from me, from here, dressed in the spoils of my people? Pallas kills you with this wound – it is Pallas who does it – and he exacts your punishment from your polluted blood.'

As he said this, Turnus' chest was in front of him and Aeneas plunged his sword into it, wild with emotion. Turnus' limbs grew limp with the chill of death and his spirit – aggrieved – fled with a groan down into the darkness.

ille, oculis postquam saevi monimenta doloris exuviasque hausit, furiis accensus et ira terribilis: 'tune hinc spoliis indute meorum eripiare mihi? Pallas te hoc vulnere, Pallas immolat et poenam scelerato ex sanguine sumit.' hoc dicens ferrum adverso sub pectore condit fervidus; ast illi solvuntur frigore membra vitaque cum gemitu fugit indignata sub umbras.

Aeneid 12.945–52

dolor, doloris, m	pain
exuviae, exuviarum, f pl	spoils, remnants
haurio, haurire, hausi	drink in
accensus -a -um	inflamed
hinc	from here
indutus -a -um	dressed
eripiare	'are you to be taken away'
immolo, immolare	sacrifice, kill
sceleratus -a -um	polluted with guilt, wicked
sumo, sumere	take
ferrum, ferri, n	iron
condo, condere	bury (a sword in a body), found (a city)
ast	but
membrum, membri, n	limb
gemitus, gemitus, m	groan
indignor, indignari, indignatus sum	consider it unworthy
umbra, umbrae, f	shadow

DERIVATIONS

This task builds skills in deducing the meaning of one word by using a related word.

The words below derive from words in the passages above which have not been glossed.

Can you find the Latin words from which these English words derive? Can you use either the Latin or the English word to help you explain the meaning of the other?

Remember that you will need to think about the part of speech of both the Latin and English words and – if they are different – you will need to consider how to adjust the meaning to move from one part of speech to the other.

supplication, ocular, deprecate, despoiled, odium, repression, sermon, apparition, monument, furious, penalty, adverse, dissolve, refrigerator

scripta 14.3: Pentheus is torn apart by his mother

This text is taken from Ovid's *Metamorphoses* Book 3. Dionysus, the god of wild impulse, is angry because Pentheus, the young king of Thebes, has refused to recognise him as a god. Determined to prove his power, Dionysus has come to Thebes, disguised as a human priest. Under Dionysus' influence, the women of Thebes have been overcome by an ecstatic frenzy; they have left Thebes to worship Dionysis on Cithaeron, a nearby mountain.

In the extract below, Pentheus decides to go to Cithaeron to watch the women and try to regain control over them. His mother, in her maddened state, thinks that Pentheus is a wild boar and calls her sisters to come and hunt him. The women charge at him in a terrifying onrush and rip him apart, limb from limb.

The most famous version of the myth was written by Euripides, a Greek tragedian. Ovid's retelling is less serious and full of comic exaggeration. Ovid fast-forwards to Pentheus' gory death scene, creating humour by Pentheus' farcical attempt to supplicate to his aunt even after his arms have been torn off and to appeal to his aunt via grand literary references which she does not understand.

Echion's son's resolve stands firm: no longer does he order others to go to the mountain; instead, he ventures out himself to the place where Cithaeron, the mountain chosen for the sacred rites, was echoing with song and the distinct cry of the Bacchants. Just the same as when a keen horse neighs when the war trumpeter has given the signal from his resounding bronze trumpet, and he takes on his lust for battle, so too the air, filled with loud shrieking, stirred Pentheus and – now he had heard the cry – his anger grew white-hot.

perstat Echionides, nec iam iubet ire, sed ipse
vadit, ubi electus facienda ad sacra Cithaeron
cantibus et clara bacchantum voce sonabat.
ut fremit acer equus, cum bellicus aere canoro
signa dedit tubicen pugnaeque adsumit amorem,
Penthea sic ictus longis ululatibus aether
movit, et audito clamore recanduit ira.

Metamorphoses 3.701–7

> **Penthea** is a Greek accusative sg.

persto, perstare	stand firm
Echionides (nominative)	the son of Echion (i.e. Pentheus)
vado, vadere	rush, go forth
electus -a -um	chosen (i.e. chosen as the location for the religious rites)
facienda ad sacra	'for performing the religious rites'
cantus, cantus, m	song
Bacchans, Bacchantis, f	Bacchant (i.e. a worshipper of Bacchus / Dionysus)
ut	just as
fremo, fremere	roar, neigh
acer, acris, acre	keen-spirited
cum	when
aere canoro	'with sonorous bronze'
tubicen, tubicinis, m	trumpeter
ictus -a -um	struck
ululatus, ululatus, m	ululation, shriek
aether, aetheris, m	upper air
recandesco, recandescere, recandui	grow white-hot

Chapter 14 Virgil and Ovid – Epic Poetry

Almost in the middle of the mountain, there is a grassy plain. Woods surround its edges but the plain itself is free from trees and offers a good view from all directions. Here, Pentheus' mother was the first to see him as he watched the sacred rites with his uninitiated eyes, she was the first to dash with a mad charge, she was the first to hurl her thyrsus and harm her own son, Pentheus. She shouted, 'Sisters – both of you – come here! Here is an enormous wild boar which is roaming our fields; I must strike down this boar!' The whole, mad crowd rushed as one; the women all united and chased the terrified man, Pentheus, a man terrified now and now no longer offering such combative words.

monte fere medio est, cingentibus ultima silvis,
purus ab arboribus, spectabilis undique, campus:
hic oculis illum cernentem sacra profanis
prima videt, prima est insano concita cursu,
prima suum misso violavit Penthea thyrso
mater et 'o geminae' clamavit 'adeste sorores!
ille aper, in nostris errat qui maximus agris,
ille mihi feriendus aper.' ruit omnis in unum
turba furens; cunctae coeunt trepidumque sequuntur,
iam trepidum, iam verba minus violenta loquentem.

Metamorphoses 3.708–17

fere	almost
cingo, cingere	surround
undique	from all sides
oculus, oculi, m	eye
cerno, cernere	see, notice
profanus -a -um	uninitiated
concieo, conciere, concivi, concitum	excite, set into motion
cursus, cursus, m	run
thyrsus, thyrsi, m	wooden staff (as carried by a Bacchant)
adeste	'Come here!'
aper, apri, m	wild boar
feriendus	'must be struck'
ruo, ruere	rush
furens, furentis	wild (with emotion)
cunctus -a -um	all, whole, altogether

But Pentheus was wounded and said 'Aunt Autonoe, help me! Think about the ghost of Actaeon!' But Autonoe did not know who Actaeon was and she ripped off Pentheus' right hand while he beseeched her; his other hand was torn apart by Ino's grip. The unlucky man did not have any

saucius ille tamen 'fer opem, matertera' dixit
'Autonoe! moveant animos Actaeonis umbrae!'
illa quis Actaeon nescit dextramque precanti
abstulit, Inoo lacerata est altera raptu.
non habet infelix quae matri bracchia tendat,

Metamorphoses 3.719–23

arms which he could reach out to his mother, but showing her his wounds, mutilated where his limbs had been seized, he said, 'Mother! Look!'. Agaue looked, howled, tossed her head and shook her hair in the air; she tore off his head, gripped it with bloodied fingers and shouted, 'Io! Comrades! This trophy shows our victory!'

trunca sed ostendens dereptis vulnera membris
'adspice, mater!' ait. visis ululavit Agaue
collaque iactavit movitque per aera crinem
avulsumque caput digitis complexa cruentis
clamat: 'io comites, opus hoc victoria nostra est!'

Metamorphoses 3.724–28

> **Actaeon** was turned into a stag and torn apart by his own hunting dogs; Ovid had retold this story a few lines earlier.

> The preference for **adjectives** in verse means that names are often used in adjectival form.

> There is a convention in verse that poets can use plural forms like **colla** even if the meaning is singular; this flexibility helps with the **rhythm**.

saucius -a -um	wounded
ops, opis, f	help
matertera, materterae, f	aunt
moveant	'may [they] move'
umbra, umbrae, f	shadow, ghost
dextra, dextrae, f	right hand
precor, precari	pray, beseech
Inous -a -um	belonging to Ino (Pentheus' aunt)
lacero, lacerare	tear apart
quae . . . tendat	'which he might reach out'
bracchium, bracchii, n	arm
truncus -a -um	mutilated
membrum, membri, n	limb
ait	'he said'
ululo, ululare, ululavi	shriek, howl
collum, colli, n	neck
iacto, iactare, iactavi	fling about
crinis, crinis, m	hair
avello, avellere, avulsi, avulsum	tear away
complector, complecti, complexus sum	embrace
cruentus -a -um	bloodied
Io	Io! (a Bacchic cry)
opus, operis, n	work, deed

DERIVATIONS

This task builds skills in deducing the meaning of one word by using a related word.

The words below derive from words in the passages above which have not been glossed.

Can you find the Latin words from which these English words derive? Can you use either the Latin or the English word to help you explain the meaning of the other?

Remember that you will need to think about the part of speech of both the Latin and English words and – if they are different – you will need to consider how to adjust the meaning to move from one part of speech to the other.

sonorous, signal, clamorous, ultimate, sylvan, pure, arboretum, campsite, insane, erratic, trepidation, violence, eloquent

Reading original Latin note 4: Poetic expression and emphasis

Verse can be harder to translate than prose partly because it is a more sophisticated and expressive medium; by using language in a highly controlled way, poets are able to convey meaning sharply, elegantly and concisely.

Poets have three important techniques at their disposal: word choice, word order and the sound of the words.

Word choice: poetry often contains lots of adjectives, adverbs and vividly nuanced words. These bring descriptive colour to the poem.

Word order: Latin poets often make use of Latin's flexible word order to create patterns in the text which echo the meaning (see, for example, how *Thisbe*, *Pyramus* are positioned next to each other at the start of *scripta* 14.4 to represent their proximity on either side of the wall).

Poets can also use word order to put words in prominent places for **emphasis**.

- **Emphasis** is achieved either by putting a word in a prominent position (such as the start or end of a sentence, clause or line) or by putting a word unusually early or late (such as promoting an adjective so that we meet it much earlier than we might expect).

- It is also possible to **emphasise** words by creating a word-order pattern which catches the reader's attention, such as an alliterated group of words, or words arranged in a chiasmus (see Chapter 10, Book 2, p129). In *scripta* 14.4, Extract 4, *indignos claro plangore lacertos* is a chiasmus because two accusatives frame two ablatives and thus a mirroring pattern is created.

Word sound: sometimes the sound of a word reinforces the meaning (for example, the *s* sounds at the end of *scripta* 14.4, Extract 3, echo the hissing sound of the water spurting out of the burst pipe). Poets can also make use of the sounds created by the poem's **rhythm**. This is explained in more detail on p85 and in Appendix 2, p215.

scripta 14.4: Pyramus and Thisbe

These extracts are taken from Ovid's Metamorphoses, *Book 4. Ovid retells the story of Pyramus and Thisbe, the Babylonian young lovers who lived in neighbouring houses but who had been forbidden by their parents to marry. Pyramus and Thisbe meet regularly in secret by speaking through a small chink in the wall which divides their gardens. One day, they plan to sneak out and meet properly in the nearby woods.*

Unfortunately, Thisbe arrives at the agreed location first; she is terrified by a lion and runs away, dropping her veil by mistake behind her. Pyramus arrives a little later, sees the veil (now mauled by the lion and covered in blood) and assumes Thisbe is dead. Horrified, Pyramus stabs himself. Thisbe returns to find her lover lying mortally wounded on the ground and – grief stricken – she kills herself.

Ovid's playful version of the tragic tale of star-crossed lovers highlights his poetic ability to create humorous melodrama and bathos. Shakespeare used the story to similar effect as a mini-comedy, set within A Midsummer Night's Dream.

Extract 1: Pyramus and Thisbe meet at the wall

Thisbe and Pyramus stand either side of the garden wall, frustrated that they are kept apart but grateful that they can at least speak to each other. Ovid creates a comical image of the two lovers pressed close to the wall, so desperate for contact that they try to catch the other's breath, but talking to the wall, rather than to each other.

Often, when Thisbe had stood on one side, and there – on the other – was Pyramus, and when in turn they had caught the breath from each other's mouth, they used to say, 'Jealous wall, we love each other – why do you stand in our way? Was it such a big thing for you to let us be together, body upon body, or – if this is too much – at least to open up so that we can kiss? We aren't ungrateful to you – we recognise that we are in your debt because at least there is a route for our words to reach our beloved's ears.'

saepe, ubi constiterant hinc Thisbe, Pyramus illinc,
inque vices fuerat captatus anhelitus oris,
"invide" dicebant "paries, quid amantibus obstas?
quantum erat ut sineres toto nos corpore iungi
aut, hoc si nimium est, vel ad oscula danda pateres?
nec sumus ingrati tibi nos debere fatemur,
quod datus est verbis ad amicas transitus aures."

Metamorphoses 4.71–77

in . . . vices	'in turn'
capto, captare, captavi, captatum	seize, catch
fuerat captatus = captatus erat	
anhelitus, anhelitus, m	breath, panting
os, oris, n	mouth
paries, parietis, m	wall
quantum erat ut sineres	'How big a thing was it to allow . . .'
aut	or
si	if
nimium	too much
vel ad oscula danda pateres	'that you open up instead so that we can give kisses'
fateor, fateri	admit, confess
transitus, transitus, m	crossing, pathway
auris, auris, f	ear

Chapter 14 Virgil and Ovid – Epic Poetry

> **Extract 2: Thisbe reaches the meeting place**
>
> *Thisbe secretly and daringly leaves the house to find the agreed meeting place. In a moment of poetic melodrama, a lion suddenly appears, her jaws smeared with the blood from a recent kill. Terrified, Thisbe flees the scene to hide in a nearby cave, leaving her veil behind by mistake.*

Thisbe cleverly opened the door, slipped out in darkness and deceived her own family. Covering her face, she reached the mound and sat under the tree as agreed. Love made her bold. But – look! – a lioness appears, her foaming jaws smeared with the fresh blood of oxen, looking to satisfy her thirst with the water of the nearby spring. By the light of the moon, Babylonian Thisbe saw the lion at a distance and fled at a terrified run into a dark cave; while she fled, her veil slipped from her back and she left it behind.

callida per tenebras versato cardine Thisbe
egreditur fallitque suos **adoperta**que **vultum**
pervenit ad tumulum dictaque sub arbore sedit.
audacem faciebat amor. venit ecce recenti
caede leaena boum spumantes oblita rictus
depositura sitim vicini fontis in unda;
quam procul ad lunae radios Babylonia Thisbe
vidit et obscurum timido pede fugit in antrum,
dumque fugit, tergo velamina lapsa reliquit.

Metamorphoses 4.93–101

In verse, the **PPP** is often paired with an accusative noun: 'covered as to her face' = 'having covered her face'.

callidus -a -um	clever, cunning
tenebrae, tenebrarum, f pl	darkness
versato cardine	'with the hinge turned', i.e. 'having opened the door'
fallo, fallere	deceive
adopertus -a -um	(having been) covered
vultus, vultus, m	face
tumulus, tumuli, m	mound
arbor, arboris, f	tree
caedes, caedis, f	slaughter
bos, bovis, m (genitive pl – **boum**)	cow, ox
spumans, spumantis	foaming
oblitus -a -um	smeared
rictus, rictus, m	open jaw
sitis, sitis, f (accusative sg – **sitim**)	thirst
vicinus -a -um	nearby
fons, fontis, m	spring, water source
procul	far off
radius, radii, m	ray
antrum, antri, n	cave
dum	while
tergum, tergi, n	back
velamen, velaminis n	veil
labor, labi, lapsus sum	fall

Chapter 14 *scripta*

> **Extract 3: Pyramus dies**
>
> *This extract starts with the moment when Pyramus decides to die. The scene is shaped as a moment of grand heroism: Pyramus presents his decision as courageous, and his emotional farewell and direct address to a prop are evocative of Greek tragedy. Ovid achieves humour, however, by combining this with bathos: Pyramus is talking to a flimsy veil (rather than, for example, the grand armour of a great warrior) and – after Pyramus has pulled his sword out again from his guts – Ovid compares the blood to the rather mundane scene of a burst water pipe.*

Pyramus lifts Thisbe's veil and takes it with him to the shadow of the tree they'd agreed on, and, as he gave his tears to the familiar garment, as he gave his kisses, he said, 'Take now also the draughts of my blood!' He plunged the sword, which he had been wearing, down into his guts – there was no delay – and, as he died, he pulled it out from the seething wound. When he lay on his back on the ground, gore shot forth, high up into the air, just like when a water pipe breaks because of a fault in its lead, and through the small, hissing crack, it spurts out much water and breaks through the air with its force.

. . . velamina **Thisbes**
tollit et ad pactae secum fert arboris umbram,
utque dedit notae lacrimas, dedit oscula vesti,
'accipe nunc' inquit 'nostri quoque sanguinis haustus!'
quoque erat accinctus, demisit in ilia ferrum,
nec mora, ferventi moriens e vulnere traxit.
ut iacuit resupinus humo, cruor emicat alte,
non aliter quam cum vitiato fistula plumbo
scinditur et tenui stridente foramine longas
eiaculatur aquas atque ictibus aera rumpit.

Metamorphoses 4.115–24

Thisbes is a Greek genitive sg.

velamen, velaminis, n	veil
pactus -a -um	agreed
arbor, arboris, f	tree
umbra, umbrae, f	shade
ut	when
osculum, osculi, n	kiss
haustus, haustus, m	drink, draught
quo	'with (the sword with) which'
accingo, accingere, accinxi, accinctum	gird on (a weapon)
ilia, ilium, n pl	guts, intestines
mora, morae, f	delay
fervens, ferventis	seething, bubbling
iaceo, iacere, iacui	lie (down)
resupinus -a -um	on his back
humo	on the ground
cruor, cruoris, m	blood, gore
emico, emicare	flash forth, burst out
cum	when
vitio, vitiare, vitiavi, vitiatum	damage, cause fault to
fistula, fistulae, f	water pipe
plumbum, plumbi, n	lead
scindo, scindere	break apart
tenuis, tenue	thin, small
foramen, foraminis, n	hole
eiaculor, eiaculari	shoot forth, hurl out
ictus, ictus, m	blow
aer, aeris, m	air (Greek accusative sg - *aera*)

Chapter 14 Virgil and Ovid – Epic Poetry

Extract 4: Thisbe weeps for Pyramus

Thisbe returns to the scene and is horrified to see her lover injured. In keeping with the melodrama of the previous scenes, Thisbe reacts with a dramatic outpouring of grief, beating her arms, tearing her hair and covering Pyramus' icy body with kisses. Pyramus opens his eyes briefly and – after one final glimpse of Thisbe – closes them for the last time.

Thisbe had been hanging back, but after she recognised her lover, she wailed loudly, she beat her undeserving arms, she tore her hair, she embraced her lover's body, she filled his wounds as she wept and mixed her tears with his blood; planting kisses on his icy face she shouted, 'Pyramus! What disaster has taken you from me? Pyramus! Answer me! It is your darling Thisbe who calls you; hear me and lift your lolling head!' At the name of Thisbe, Pyramus opened his eyes, weighed down by death and – after he had seen her – closed them again.

sed postquam remorata suos cognovit amores,
percutit indignos claro plangore lacertos
et laniata comas amplexaque corpus amatum
vulnera supplevit lacrimis fletumque cruori
miscuit et gelidis in vultibus oscula figens
'Pyrame,' clamavit, 'quis te mihi casus ademit?
Pyrame, responde! tua te carissima Thisbe
nominat; exaudi vultusque attolle iacentes!'
ad nomen **Thisbes** oculos a morte gravatos
Pyramus erexit visaque recondidit illa.

Metamorphoses 4.137–46

Thisbes is a Greek genitive sg.

remoror, remorari, remoratus sum	delay, hang back
percutio, percutere	beat hard
indignus -a -um	undeserving
plangor, plangoris, m	wailing, lamentation
lacertus, lacerti, m	arm
lanio, laniare	tear to pieces
comae, comarum, f pl	hair
amplexus -a -um	having embraced
suppleo, supplere, supplevi, suppletum	fill, add to
fletus, fletus, m	weeping, tears
cruor, cruoris, m	blood, gore
gelidus -a -um	icy
vultus, vultus, m	face
ocsculum, ocsculi, n	kiss
figo, figere	fix, fasten
casus, casus, m	fate, misfortune
adimo, adimere, ademi, ademptum	take away
iaceo, iacere	lie (down)
gravatus -a -um	weighed down
erigo, erigere, erexi	lift up
recondo, recondere, recondidi	hide, cover over

DERIVATIONS

This task builds skills in deducing the meaning of one word by using a related word.

The words below derive from words in the passages above which have not been glossed.

Can you find the Latin words from which these English words derive? Can you use either the Latin or the English word to help you explain the meaning of the other?

Remember that you will need to think about the part of speech of both the Latin and English words and – if they are different – you will need to consider how to adjust the meaning to move from one part of speech to the other.

invidious, obstacle, gratitude, deposit, lunar, obscurity, pedestrian, vestry, ferrous, claritude, nominate, audition

Reading original Latin note 5: Rhythm

As is the case for much English poetry, Latin verse is written within rhythmical patterns.

Latin's patterns are built around the **pace** of a line and are created by arrangements of long and short syllables. Lines with lots of short syllables will sound faster and more energetic in pace than lines with fewer and longer syllables.

All the extracts in this chapter are written in the hexameter metre. This means that each line has six units, known as metrical **feet**. The first four of these feet can either be made up of two long syllables (known as a **spondee**), or one long and two short syllables (known as a **dactyl**). The fifth foot is typically a dactyl and the sixth foot contains two syllables only. This metre, therefore, allows lines to be anything from 12 to 17 syllables long.

To help you hear the Latin rhythmical patterns, it can be useful to think of the sound of the English phrase *strawberry jam pot*. The word *strawberry* matches the sound of a Latin **dactyl**; the words *jam pot* matches the sound of a Latin **spondee**.

As you read the Latin lines, think about the sound of the words and their rhythm: you will hear that some lines sound fast and energetic, but others have a much smoother, calmer sound. In addition, you will notice that there are **pauses** in different places. This also helps to create rhythmic effects: an early pause in a line can be dramatic and create emphasis on the words either side. Usually, there is a pause at the end of a line too, but sometimes the sense requires you to read on without pausing (a technique known as **enjambement**). This also affects the pace and atmosphere of the text.

For more detail on what makes a syllable short or long in Latin and an overview of the rules for the hexameter metre, see Appendix 2: Latin Metre, p215.

Chapter 14 Virgil and Ovid – Epic Poetry

> ### scripta 14.5: Arachne confronts Pallas Athene
>
> In Metamorphoses, Book 6, Ovid retells the story of Arachne, a girl who was so talented at weaving that she claimed she was even better than Pallas Athena (the Greek name for the goddess Minerva). Angered by Arachne's arrogance, Pallas challenges her to a competition. Inevitably, the goddess wins and turns Arachne into a spider, condemned to spin for all time.
>
> Ovid's version of the Arachne myth focuses on the bleak limits of mortal power. During the weaving competition, Pallas weaves pictures of the gods' power while Arachne weaves scenes of mortal women powerless to escape the gods. The story is a good example of the theme of change ('metamorphosis') which ties Ovid's great epic poem together but it is also an interesting reflection on different genres of art. In his description of the weaving competition, Ovid has to imagine material art. This gives him the opportunity to demonstrate the breadth of his artistic skill, proving that he is not only skilled as a writer of words, he can also depict exceptional artworks.
>
> The extract below focuses on the first moment of direct confrontation between Arachne and Pallas. Arachne has boasted that Pallas has nothing to teach her, claiming that she would be happy to compete against her to prove her own skill. Pallas has decided to disguise herself as an old woman and appear before Arachne, giving her the chance to admit that Pallas is the superior weaver. Ovid describes the moment where Arachne contemptuously responds to the old woman's speech and Pallas then reveals her true identity.

'You have lost your mind – you come here, done in by advanced old age – it has done you harm to have lived far too long. If you have a daughter-in-law, or if you have a daughter, she can listen to your advice. I have enough good sense to think for myself; don't think that you are getting anywhere by giving me advice – you haven't changed my opinion. Why doesn't Pallas come in person? Why does she avoid this competition?' Then the goddess said, 'She's here!', discarded the old woman's disguise and showed herself to be Pallas. The nymphs and the Lydian women were in awe of the goddess; only Arachne was not terrified. Even so, she did blush, and a sudden redness marked her cheeks – although she did not want it to; then it vanished, just as the sky typically becomes red at the very beginning of dawn, and – after a short time – grows pale again at the rising of the sun.

'mentis inops longaque venis confecta senecta,
et nimium vixisse diu nocet. audiat istas,
si qua tibi nurus est, si qua est tibi filia, voces;
consilii satis est in me mihi, neve monendo
profecisse putes, eadem est sententia nobis.
cur non ipsa venit? cur haec certamina vitat?'
tum dea 'venit!' ait formamque removit anilem
Palladaque exhibuit: venerantur numina nymphae
Mygdonidesque nurus; sola est non territa virgo,
sed tamen erubuit, subitusque invita notavit
ora rubor rursusque evanuit, ut solet aer
purpureus fieri, cum primum Aurora movetur,
et breve post tempus candescere solis ab ortu.

Metamorphoses 6.37–49

> **Pallada** is a Greek accusative sg.

mentis inops (nominative sg)	'impoverished in mind' (i.e. stupid)
confectus -a -um	finished off
senecta, senectae, f	old age
nimium	too much
noceo, nocere (+ dative)	harm
audiat . . . si qua . . .	'if any . . . let them listen to'
iste, ista, istud	that

nurus, nurus, f	daughter in law, young woman
neve . . . putes	'you should not think'
monendo	'by giving advice'
proficio, proficere, profeci	make progress, be of use
sententia, sententiae, f	opinon, understanding
certamen, certaminis, n	contest
vito, vitare	avoid
ait	'she said'
anilis, anile	of an old woman
veneror, venerari	respect, worship
numen, numinis, n	divinity
Mygdonis, Mygdonidis	Lydian
erubesco, erubescere, erubui	blush, grow red
invitus -a -um	unwilling
os, oris, n	face
rubor, ruboris, m	red
rursus	again
aer, aeris, m	air
fio, fieri	become
cum primum	'when first'
Aurora, Aurorae, f	Aurora (goddess of the dawn)
candesco, candescere	grow white
ortus, ortus, m	rising

DERIVATIONS

This task builds skills in deducing the meaning of one word by using a related word.

The words below derive from words in the passages above which have not been glossed.

Can you find the Latin words from which these English words derive? Can you use either the Latin or the English word to help you explain the meaning of the other?

Remember that you will need to think about the part of speech of both the Latin and English words and – if they are different – you will need to consider how to adjust the meaning to move from one part of speech to the other.

longitude, vociferous, satisfaction, formation, exhibition, virginity, notation, vanish

Chapter 14 Virgil and Ovid – Epic Poetry

> ### scripta 14.6: Hercules dies
>
> This extract is from Ovid's Metamorphoses, Book 9. Ovid retells the gruesome story of Hercules' death. This myth gives Ovid the opportunity to rework epic poetry's most traditional material: the magical and marvellous tales of mighty heroes.
>
> Hercules was killed by a poisoned tunic, sent to him by his wife Deianira. Deianira believed that Hercules was in love with another woman and mistakenly believed that the tunic she sent him would restore their love. Unfortunately the tunic had been soaked in poison; this poison ate into Hercules' skin and caused a terrifyingly painful death.
>
> Ovid uses Hercules' death scene as a moment for Hercules – overboiling with blistering rage at what has happened to him – to retell his own story, list his great achievements and lambast the gods for not saving his life. Thus Ovid is able to create within his poem another epic poem in miniature and – at the same time – a death scene so melodramatic and implausibly prolonged as to be tinged with comedy.
>
> The extract below is from the beginning of the sensational death scene: we hear the gory details of the moment where the poison works its way into Hercules' body, its power exacerbated by the heat of the fire from the sacrifice which Hercules happened to be making on Mount Oeta.

The poison's energy grew hot, and – released by the flames – it spread, carried widely throughout Hercules' limbs. While he could, Hercules held back his groans with his usual courage, but after his resolve had been beaten by the pains, he knocked aside the altars and filled the groves of **Oeta** with his cries. There is no delay; he tries to tear off the deadly cloak but, wherever he pulls at it, the cloak pulls off his skin, and – disgusting to tell – either it sticks to his limbs (the attempt to remove it, futile) or it rips open his mangled flesh and shows his massive bones.

There is no limit: the greedy flames dissolve his heart, and dark-coloured sweat drips from all over his body.

incaluit vis illa mali, resolutaque flammis
Herculeos abiit late dilapsa per artus.
dum potuit, solita gemitum virtute repressit.
victa malis postquam est patientia, reppulit aras,
implevitque suis nemorosam vocibus **Oeten**.
nec mora, letiferam conatur scindere vestem:
qua trahitur, trahit illa cutem, foedumque relatu,
aut haeret membris frustra **temptata** revelli,
aut laceros artus et grandia detegit ossa.

nec modus est, sorbent avidae praecordia flammae,
caeruleusque fluit toto de corpore sudor.

Metamorphoses 9.161–73

Oeten is a Greek accusative sg.	incalesco, incalescere, incalui	grow hot
	vis, f (nominative sg)	force, power
	resolutus -a -um	loosened
	late	widely
	dilapsus -a -um	having slipped
	artus, artus, m	limb
	dum	while
	gemitus, gemitus, m	groan
	repello, repellere, reppuli	push away, drive back
	ara, arae, f	altar

impleo, implere, implevi	fill
nemorosus -a -um	covered in trees
mora, morae, f	delay
letiferus -a -um	death-bringing
scindo, scindere	tear away
qua	in the place where
cutis, cutis, f	skin
foedum relatu	'foul to report'
aut . . . aut	either . . or
haereo, haerere	stick to
membrum, membri, n	limb
revello, revellere	tear off
lacer, lacera, lacerum	torn, mangled
detego, detegere	uncover
os, ossis, n	bone
modus, modi, m	limit
sorbeo, sorbere	suck in
praecordia, praecordiorum, n pl	heart
caeruleus -a -um	dark-coloured
sudor, sudoris, m	sweat, moisture

DERIVATIONS

This task builds skills in deducing the meaning of one word by using a related word.

The words below derive from words in the passages above which have not been glossed.

Can you find the Latin words from which these English words derive? Can you use either the Latin or the English word to help you explain the meaning of the other?

Remember that you will need to think about the part of speech of both the Latin and English words and – if they are different – you will need to consider how to adjust the meaning to move from one part of speech to the other.

repressive, temptation, grandiose, avid, fluency, corporeal

QUESTIONS FOR DISCUSSION

1. Virgil presents the love affair between Dido and Aeneas as a tragedy: in *scripta* 14.1, which details do you think help to establish the tragic nature of Dido's love for Aeneas?

2. The *Aeneid* often focuses on moments of tension, when emotional impulse and rational thought pull a character in conflicting directions. Explore the inner conflicts at play in *scripta* 14.1 and 14.2: in which text do you think this inner turmoil is more acute and why?

3. Ovid delights in the comic potential of melodrama: discuss this claim in the context of the texts in this chapter.

4. Several of the texts in this chapter rest on an interplay with an earlier Greek text: do you think this is a powerful way to enrich the text's scope or a frustrating barrier to appreciating its meaning? What does this interplay suggest about the intended readership of these texts?

5. The description in epic poetry is often deepened by the use of similes and metaphors. Explore this technique in the context of one of the texts in this chapter.

Chapter 14: Additional Language

SECTION A14: CHAPTER 14 VOCABULARY

Exercise A14.1: Derivations

This exercise explores derivations from the vocabulary list for Chapter 14.

Give the meaning of the Latin word, an English derivation and explain the connection.

	Latin	meaning	derivation	explanation
1	sentio, sentire, sensi, sensum			
2	vulnus, vulneris, n			
3	scio, scire, scivi, scitum			
4	ago, agere, egi, actum			
5	vivo, vivere, vixi			
6	audeo, audere, ausus sum			
7	vox, vocis, f			
8	animus, animi, m			
9	labor, laboris, m			
10	pes, pedis, m			

Exercise A14.2: Parts of speech

Sort the following words from the vocabulary list for Chapter 14 into the correct categories and write the meaning next to each word.

pes   dirus   audeo   ago   ars   brevis
scio   infelix   paene   spero   gaudium   virtus

noun	verb	adjective	adverb

Chapter 14 Virgil and Ovid – Epic Poetry

Exercise A14.3: Case endings (nouns and adjectives)

Circle the stem, and identify the declension of the following nouns and adjectives from Chapter 14. Then give the case requested.

	Latin	declension	
1	pes, pedis, m		dative sg =
2	cura, curae, f		nominative pl =
3	gaudium, gaudii, n		accusative sg =
4	virtus, virtutis, f		ablative sg =
5	animus, animi, m		genitive sg =
6	vulnus, vulneris, n		nominative pl =
7	ars, artis, f		dative pl =
8	infelix, infelicis		nominative neuter sg =
9	brevis, breve		accusative masculine sg =
10	dirus, dira, dirum		accusative feminine pl =

Exercise A14.4: Verbs

The following verbs are from the vocabulary list for Chapter 14. Circle each of the stems of each verb: present, perfect and supine. Remember, not all verbs have all three stems and semi-deponent verbs only have two stems (see p232). Give the meaning of each verb and its conjugation.

	principal parts	meaning	conjugation
1	scio, scire, scivi, scitum		
2	cognosco, cognoscere, cognovi, cognitum		
3	ago, agere, egi, actum		
4	celo, celare, celavi, celatum		
5	vivo, vivere, vixi		
6	promitto, promittere, promisi, promissum		
7	sentio, sentire, sensi, sensum		
8	soleo, solere, solitus sum		
9	gaudeo, gaudere, gavisus sum		
10	audeo, audere, ausus sum		

Exercise A14.5: Cognates

In the table below are pairs of words: the first in each pair is a word from the vocabulary list for Chapter 14 and below it is a cognate word, i.e. a word which is related to it. You may not have met the cognate word before and it will not be listed in the vocabulary list at the back of this book.

Identify the part of speech of each Latin word and then give the meaning; you will have to work out the meaning of the second word by thinking about its part of speech and how it relates in meaning to the first word in each pair.

> **Note that** some of these cognates use two Latin words joined together. ***vulnificus*** involves two Latin words which you have met: *vulnus* and *facio*.

	Latin	part of speech	meaning
1	ago, agere, egi, actum		
	actor, actoris, m		
2	sentio, sentire, sensi, sensum		
	sensus, sensus, m		
3	labor, laboris, m		
	laboriosus, laboriosa, laboriosum		
4	pes, pedis, m		
	expedio, expedire, expedivi, expeditum		
5	sanguis, sanguinis, m		
	sanguineus, sanguinea, sanguineum		
6	vulnus, vulneris, n		
	vulnificus, vulnifica, vulnificum		
7	brevis, breve		
	breviloquens, breviloquentis		
8	poena, poenae f		
	poenalis, poenale		
9	nescio, nescire, nescivi		
	nescius, nescia, nescium		
10	vox, vocis, f		
	voco, vocare, vocavi, vocatum		

Chapter 14 Virgil and Ovid – Epic Poetry

SECTION B14: WORD ENDINGS

Exercise B14.1: Semi-deponent verb forms

Write out the principal parts for each of the semi-deponent verbs given below. Then identify the tense of the form given and translate into English.

		principal parts	tense	translation
1	ausi sunt			
2	gavisus est			
3	audebam			
4	solebant			
5	solita eras			

Exercise B14.2: English participle forms

In this chapter you have met more tenses of participles. The English equivalents to these may be unfamiliar. This exercise practises the meanings of these different participles, using verbs from Chapters 13 and 14. The Latin participles for each verb are given in the table below. Translate each one.

Most English verbs have a perfect active and a perfect passive participle, but remember that in Latin only one type of perfect participle exists for each verb: deponent verbs have a perfect active participle and non-deponent verbs only have a perfect passive participle. This is why one column has been blanked out for each type of verb.

	present active participle	perfect passive participle	perfect active participle	future active participle
1	celans, celantis =	celatus -a -um =		celaturus -a -um =
2	agens, agentis =	actus -a -um =		acturus -a -um =
3	promittens, promittentis =	promissus -a -um =		promissurus -a -um =
4	sciens, scientis =	scitus -a -um =		sciturus -a -um =
5	sperans, sperantis =	speratus -a -um =		speraturus -a -um =

Chapter 14 Additional Language

6	conans, conantis =		conatus -a -um =	conaturus -a -um =
7	patiens, patientis =		passus -a -um =	passurus -a -um =
8	ingrediens, ingredientis =		ingressus -a -um =	ingressurus -a -um =
9	loquens, loquentis =		locutus -a -um =	locuturus -a -um =
10	mirans, mirantis =		miratus -a -um =	miraturus -a -um =

Exercise B14.3: Participles in present, perfect and future tenses

Here is a reminder of all the tenses of participles you have met.

present active	reg**ens**, reg**entis**	ruling
perfect passive	rect**us**, rect**a**, rect**um**	having been ruled
future active	rect**urus**, rect**ura**, rect**urum**	being about to rule
perfect active (deponent verbs only)	secut**us**, secut**a**, secut**um**	having followed

This exercise uses verbs from the vocabulary lists for Chapters 13 and 14. Identify the tense of each participle given and translate.

Remember that in Latin, each verb only has one type of perfect participle: deponent verbs have a perfect active participle and non-deponent verbs have a perfect passive participle. When you meet a perfect participle, you will have to think carefully about whether the verb is deponent or not.

		tense	meaning
1	sentiens, sentientis		
2	acturus, actura, acturum		
3	speratus, sperata, speratum		
4	actus, acta, actum		
5	gaudens, gaudentis		
6	mortuus, mortua, mortuum		
7	locuturus, locutura, locuturum		
8	regrediens, regredientis		

Chapter 14 Virgil and Ovid – Epic Poetry

Exercise B14.4: Translating ablative absolutes

Each of the ablative absolute phrases below contains a noun and a participle in the ablative case and uses words from the vocabulary lists for Chapters 13 and 14. Translate the following ablative absolute phrases literally into English. Remember that deponent verbs have a perfect active participle.

1. poena cognita
2. vulneribus celatis
3. manu procedente
4. labore acto
5. arte sensa
6. animo vivente
7. gaudio sperato
8. rebus promissis
9. exercitu progresso
10. manu regresso

Exercise B14.5: Present passive infinitives and perfect active finite verbs

This exercise uses verbs from the vocabulary lists for Chapters 13 and 14. The principal parts for each verb are given in brackets. Use these to identify whether the verb form is a present passive infinitive or a perfect active finite verb. Then translate each one.

Watch out! These verb forms can be easily confused.

Deponent verbs are listed separately at the bottom of the table: remember that these take passive forms but are active in meaning.

		present passive infinitive or perfect active finite verb?	meaning
1	egi (ago, agere, egi, actum)		
2	vixi (vivo, vivere, vixi)		
3	sensi (sentio, sentire, sensi, sensum)		
4	sentiri (sentio, sentire, sensi, sensum)		
5	agi (ago, agere, egi, actum)		
6	scivi (scio, scire, scivi, scitum)		
7	sustuli (tollo, tollere, sustuli, sublatum)		
8	pati (patior, pati, passus sum)		
9	mori (morior, mori, mortuus sum)		
10	ingredi (ingredior, ingredi, ingressus sum)		

Exercise B14.6: English infinitive forms

In this chapter you have met more tenses of infinitives. The English equivalents to these may be unfamiliar. This exercise practises the meanings of these different infinitives by manipulating some of the Chapter 14 verbs in English.

Complete each row by adding in the other English infinitives.

		present passive infinitive in English	future active infinitive in English	perfect active infinitive in English	perfect passive infinitive in English
1	to hide (celare)				
2	to think (cogitare)				
3	to do (agere)				
4	to promise (promittere)				
5	to find out (cognoscere)				
6	to not know (nescire)				
7	to know (scire)				
8	to feel (sentire)				
9	to hope (spero)				

Chapter 14 Virgil and Ovid – Epic Poetry

Exercise B14.7: Infinitives in present, perfect and future tenses

Here is a reminder of all the tenses of infinitives you have met. Remember that the vowels used in the endings for the present infinitives vary across the conjugations. The infinitive endings for the future and perfect infinitives, however, are the same for all verbs.

present active infinitive – e.g. *to love*	am**a**re, terr**e**re, reg**e**re, aud**i**re
present passive infinitive – e.g. *to be loved*	am**ari**, terr**eri**, reg**i**, aud**iri**
perfect active infinitive – e.g. *to have loved*	amav**isse**
perfect passive infinitive – e.g. *to have been loved*	amat**us esse**
future active infinitive – e.g. *to be about to love*	amat**urus esse**

This exercise uses verbs from the vocabulary lists for Chapters 13 and 14. Identify the tense of each infinitive given and translate each one.

Remember, deponent verbs have present and perfect infinitives which are passive in form but active in meaning; their future infinitive is active in form and active in meaning. The infinitives of deponent verbs are at the bottom of the table.

		tense	meaning
1	celatus esse		
2	agi		
3	promissurus esse		
4	vixisse		
5	cognosci		
6	egredi		
7	profectus esse		
8	secuturus esse		
9	mori		
10	locutus esse		

SECTION C14: ENGLISH TO LATIN SENTENCES

Exercise C14.1: Ablative absolute

The sentences below contain subordinate clauses in bold, each of which could be translated into Latin as an ablative absolute.

Recast each of these as a participle phrase in English introduced by the word *with*. Then translate into Latin as an ablative absolute.

1. **When the army had been defeated**, the soldiers returned to their homes.
2. **While the leader was dying**, the citizens wept.
3. **After the matter had been announced**, the people rejoiced.
4. **Although the town had been burned**, the citizens still did not despair.
5. **When their voices had been heard**, the people wondered at the skill of the poets.
6. **After their toils had been done**, the women felt much joy.
7. **After the children had been punished**, the father set off from the house.
8. **While the messenger was speaking** in the forum, no voice could be heard.
9. **Because gold had been promised to the gods**, the people offered them many gifts.
10. **After many soldiers had been wounded**, the others did not want to die.

Exercise C14.2: Indirect statement

Each sentence below contains an indirect statement. Underline all the words which make up the indirect statement and identify the tense of the infinitive which would be needed to translate its verb into Latin. You should also identify whether the infinitive needed would be active or passive.

1. The woman hoped that her husband would not suffer.
2. The leader of the army noticed that many soldiers were being captured.
3. The woman reported that the same senator was still alive.
4. He announces in the forum that the leader is setting out with a huge army.
5. They say that there will be much blood and many wounds.
6. I promised that he would suffer.
7. We do not know that the army will destroy the enemy.
8. I knew that good things had been done.
9. The inhabitants thought that there was no hope.
10. The father found out that the children had dared to go out.

Exercise C14.3: Sentences to translate into Latin

1. With his feet hidden by much blood, the soldier knew that he had been badly wounded.
2. The defeated leader dared to hope that he would return home.
3. On the third day, the ships, which were carrying many troops, were destroyed by the wind.
4. The boy whose father had been killed promised to weep for a long time.
5. It was very difficult to see the messenger who was speaking in the forum.
6. All the children thought that their parents did not understand about new things.
7. The sailors were accustomed to set out by ship, but soldiers always advanced on foot.
8. They say that one mother is suffering but the other has died.
9. He reports that the inhabitants want to return but the enemy are trying to advance.
10. They seemed to be returning to their homes, having suffered many wounds.

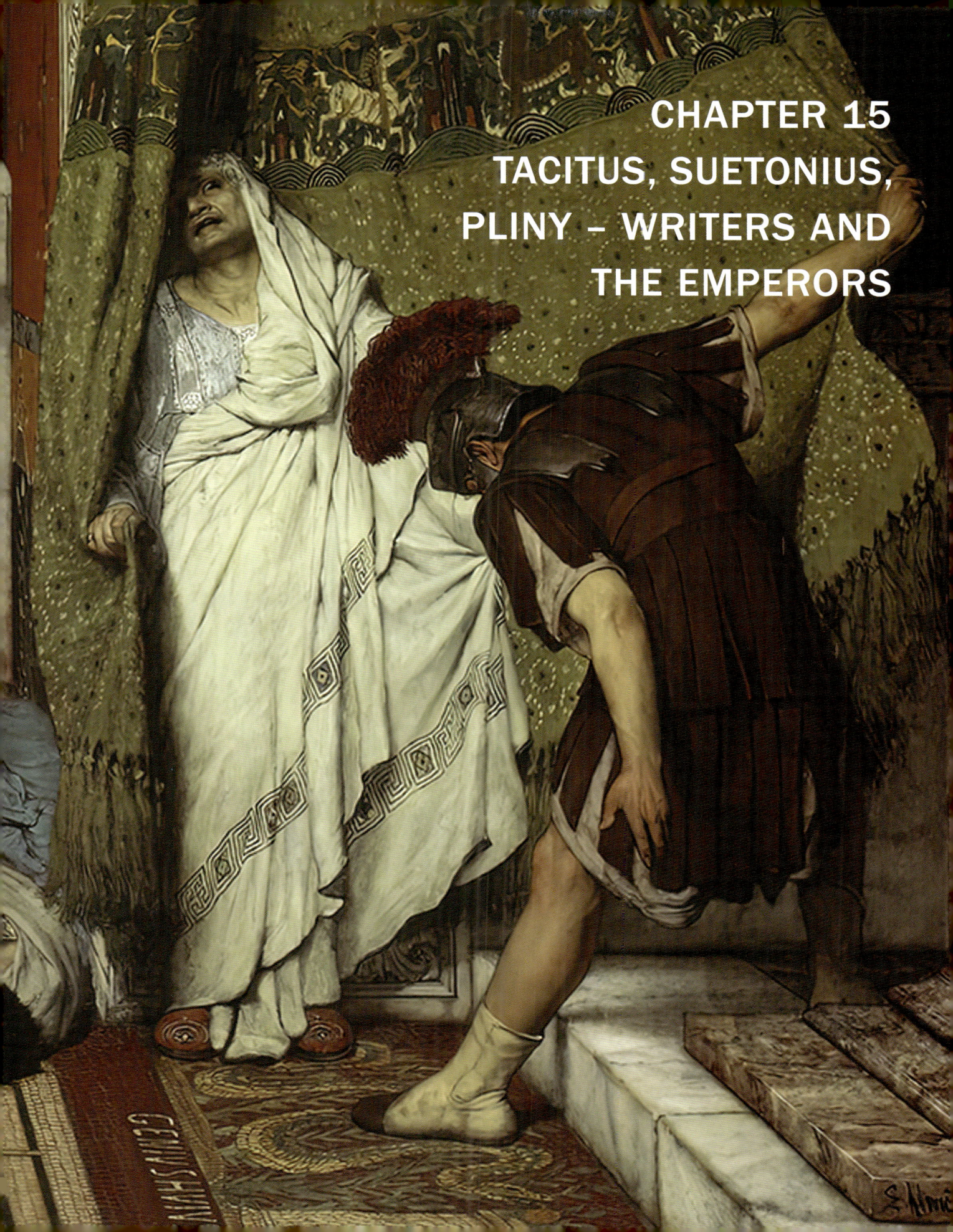

CHAPTER 15
TACITUS, SUETONIUS, PLINY – WRITERS AND THE EMPERORS

Chapter 15: Introduction

Writing under the emperors

> The Latin adjective *principalis* means *first, most important*. Explain the meaning of *principles*.

As you read in Chapters 9–13, Romans such as Julius Caesar, Pompey, Mark Antony and Octavian greatly changed the power structures in Rome. By the time of Augustus' death, the power-sharing principles of the Republic were altered and Rome had returned to one-man rule. Augustus, a master of propaganda, avoided the toxic label of *rex*. Instead, he was called **princeps** or **imperator**. From the 1st century AD, the term **Roman Empire** is used not just to refer to the land Rome governed, but the political structure where one man, an **emperor**, held ultimate power.

FIGURE 15.1: Temple of the Divine Caesar

In this picture you can see under the canopy the remains of the Temple of Divine Caesar. This temple was completed by Octavian – later known as Augustus – in 29 BC as part of his triumphal celebrations for his victories in Illyricum, Egypt and the Battle of Actium. Octavian used his divine ancestry (via Julius Caesar) as a way to highlight his personal authority. Connection with the divine was one of the ways in which the Roman emperors cemented their exceptional power. In *scripta* **15.3** you can read more about this.

Rule-by-emperor impacted writers. Chapter 8 focused on oratory, and a core part of this within the Republic was open criticism, such as the vociferous attacks by Cicero against Catiline and Mark Antony. Under the emperors, political **criticism brought greater risk** and many Romans lost their lives as punishment for crimes against the *maiestas* (the status or reputation) of the emperor. In *scripta* **15.1** you can read Tacitus' analysis of the **challenges of writing contemporary history** within this climate.

Roman history, however, had always **blended fact with imagination**. Much of the material you read in Books 1 and 2 came from authors writing about the distant past, interweaving traditional tales with their own imaginative representation of speech, thought and feeling. It is important to remember that historical texts served to entertain as well as to educate. In the *scripta* for this chapter you will see that this approach continued within the work of the two most famous imperial historians, **Tacitus** and **Suetonius**, both of whom delight in vivid anecdotes about the scandal and intrigue which took place within the imperial household.

> The Latin noun *vox* means *voice* and the Latin verb *fero* means *carry*. Explain the meaning of *vociferous*.

An heir for Augustus

As discussed in Chapter 11, during the 20s BC Augustus engineered a new power structure, disguising the scale of his power and wrapping up his multiple offices with the title of *princeps*. There remained, however, the question of what would happen after his death. In 23 BC, Augustus became gravely ill; he recovered, but his illness had been serious enough to cause him to fear a power vacuum and civil unrest without a **clear successor**.

Though he had no sons, Augustus had one daughter, Julia, and a nephew, Marcellus. He also had a step-son, Tiberius. Unfortunately, Marcellus died while still a young man. Augustus arranged for his daughter Julia to marry his long-time friend and ally, Agrippa. The couple produced five children. Augustus adopted two of these children as his own sons but they both died young and Augustus had to look again for a successor.

His choices were now limited to **Agrippa Postumus** (Julia and Agrippa's third son) or his step-son, **Tiberius**. Augustus adopted them both but neither had the full support of the senate or the people. Many considered Tiberius to be arrogant and immoral, while Agrippa Postumus was thought to be short-tempered, mean-spirited and lacking experience. The historian Tacitus, writing roughly a century later, described discussions among the senators at the time, debating the qualities of both Tiberius and Agrippa Postumus. Tacitus' account reflects the sense of **uncertainty surrounding the succession**; you can read an extract of this in *scripta* **15.2**.

> The Latin verb *succedo* means *come next, follow*. Explain the meaning of *succession*.

In AD 6, Agrippa Postumus was exiled from Rome. The reasons for his banishment are uncertain but he was accused of *ferocia*, a wildness of character. His exile removed him as a possible heir to Augustus, leaving **Tiberius** as the only remaining candidate. When Augustus died, Tiberius inherited not just Augustus' wealth, but – at the senate's request – his role and titles too, establishing him as **Rome's second emperor**.

The imperial family

To some extent, political power in Rome had always partly rested on inheritance since wealth, family connections and the *auctoritas* that came with these had always been needed

Chapter 15 Tacitus, Suetonius, Pliny – Writers and the Emperors

FIGURE 15.2 **Bust of Tiberius**

After a number of possible successors died young, Augustus' step-son Tiberius became his heir. This bust shows Tiberius as a young man; it was sculpted between AD 14 and 23. Though Tiberius was in power at this point, he is shown here without any insignia of rank or symbols of military victory. The bust is currently in the Musée Saint-Raymond in France.

for prestige. However, it was a major departure from Republican norms that another *princeps* would be chosen by the previous *princeps* and from within his own family. In effect, the senate had confirmed a new *status quo* where ultimate, hereditary power rested within the **imperial family**.

The imperial family, therefore, achieved an importance above and beyond any other Roman. In addition, the link to Julius Caesar (Augustus' adopted father) provided a **semi-divine status**. Julius Caesar had been deified after his death; this honour was given to Augustus too. **scripta 15.3** provides an example of how **Roman emperors were treated like gods**.

Emperors in the 1st and 2nd century AD: the Julio-Claudian dynasty

The transfer of power from Augustus to Tiberius established what is now known as the **Julio-Claudian dynasty**, a series of emperors who were all from the same family. Initially, **Tiberius** ruled well: following Augustus' advice, Tiberius did not seek foreign conquests and rejected many honours offered by the senate. After the death of his son, however, Tiberius withdrew from Rome and retreated to the island of Capri in the Bay of Naples. He delegated much of his authority to Sejanus, the commander of the only troops stationed in Rome – the Praetorian Guard. Historians such as Tacitus, however, describe Sejanus as cruel and he is a sinister figure in Roman history. Tiberius never returned to Rome but remained on Capri, where he reportedly took part in perverse sexual activities all while suffering from a debilitating illness. He died in AD 37.

> The Latin adjective *debilis* means *weak*. Explain the meaning of *debilitating*.

Tiberius' only son had died and Tiberius had named his great-nephew, **Caligula**, and his grandson, Gemellus, as co-heirs. Within the first year of their joint rule, Caligula became seriously ill after which his behaviour became erratic. He executed Gemellus, the only other

FIGURE 15.3 Claudius becomes emperor

The 19th-century Dutch painter Lawrence Alma-Tadema frequently chose classical subjects for his paintings. In this piece, painted in 1871, we can see the moment when Claudius, hiding behind a curtain after Caligula was murdered, was found by the Praetorian Guard and acclaimed emperor. You can read Suetonius' description of this moment in *scripta* 15.4.

contender for power. He himself was killed by the Praetorian Guard in AD 41, after ruling for less than four years.

After the assassination of Caligula, the Praetorian Guard announced his uncle **Claudius** as emperor. You can read about this in *scripta* 15.4. Claudius was an excellent administrator and, as you read in Chapter 12, expanded the Roman empire to include Britain. **Claudius' second wife, Agrippina**, wanted **Nero**, her son from a previous marriage, to be the next emperor. Suetonius tells us that in order to achieve this, Agrippina murdered Claudius in AD 54.

FIGURE 15.4 Coin of Nero

After the death of Claudius, his step-son Nero became emperor. This aureus was made early in Nero's rule. On one side, elephants are pulling a chariot containing statues of the divine Augustus and Claudius as part of Claudius' funeral. On the other side, the profiles of Nero and his mother, Agrippina, appear. The similar size of their faces indicates Agrippina's significant power. Over time, Nero came to resent his mother's influence.

Nero was less than twenty years old when he became emperor. At first, his mother greatly influenced his rule. As time went on, Nero asserted his own power. Tacitus and Suetonius both record that Nero was considered a cruel and egotistical emperor. In AD 59, resentful of Agrippina's control, Nero is believed to have arranged for **his mother to be murdered**; you can read about this in *scripta* 15.5. Nero is perhaps equally infamous for the **great fire of Rome** in AD 64, although historians are uncertain what responsibility, if any, he bore; you can read about this in *scripta* 15.6. In *scripta* 15.7 you can read Tacitus' suggestion that Nero tried to shift blame for the fire onto the **Christians**. Over time, public opposition to him grew until he was declared a public enemy by the senate. Abandoned by the Praetorian Guard, Nero fled Rome and committed suicide in AD 68. The Julio-Claudian dynasty was over.

The Latin adjective *clarus* means *clear*. Explain the meaning of *declared*.

The Flavian dynasty, Trajan and Hadrian

The following year, AD 69, is sometimes referred to as the **year of the four emperors**: Galba, Otho, Vitellius and Vespasian. The last of these, Titus Flavius Vespasian, established the next family of emperors: the **Flavian dynasty**. **Vespasian** ruled until his death in AD 79. His son Titus completed the **Colosseum** which Vespasian had begun. After his death, his brother, **Domitian**, took over in AD 81. Domitian was more tyrannical; his heavy-handed

Chapter 15 Tacitus, Suetonius, Pliny – Writers and the Emperors

treatment of Roman nobles made him unpopular with the senate and he was assassinated in AD 96. He left no sons and the Flavian dynasty ended with his death.

Next, Nerva ruled from AD 96 to 98. Nerva had no children, so he adopted **Trajan** as his heir. Trajan was a skilled administrator and under his leadership the Roman empire reached its greatest size. *scripta* **15.8** offers an example of the way Trajan communicated with his **governors in the Roman provinces** and his careful attention to detail. On his deathbed, Trajan supposedly named his cousin, **Hadrian**, as his successor. Hadrian ruled from AD 117 to 138, and, as discussed in Chapter 12, completed Hadrian's Wall, stretching from the east to the west coast of northern England. When Hadrian died in AD 138, emperors had been ruling for nearly 125 years. Rule by Roman emperors would continue to dominate the Mediterranean until the 5th century AD.

> The Latin verb *administro* means *help, manage*. Explain the meaning of *administrator*.

What difference did rule-by-emperors make?

The shift to rule-by-emperor had a major impact on Roman society. As you read in Chapter 8, within the Republic the *cursus honorum* provided a route to power for ambitious nobles. Under the emperors, however, power became concentrated in one man whose time in office was not limited. In addition, the emperor's power was likely to pass to a member of his family. This meant that the **traditional routes to power were reduced**. It is no surprise that high-ranking senators such as Tacitus found this frustrating. In his *Annals*, Tacitus offers a biting analysis of imperial rule, highlighting the **absence of frank debate and open decision making**.

The concentration of power in the hands of the imperial household also impacted who could influence the emperor. Wary of rivals and the risk of assassination, some emperors, such as Claudius, gave significant political power to their own **freedmen**, believing that the loyalty between ex-slave and master would protect the emperor. In addition, the low social status of freedmen prevented the risk of genuine rivalry.

> The Latin adverb *frustra* means *in vain*. Explain the meaning of *frustrating*.

The centrality of the imperial family also meant that **women had unprecedented influence. Livia**, Augustus' wife and Tiberius' mother, whom you read about in Chapter 11, is portrayed as an ambitious manipulator. Tacitus suggests Livia murdered Augustus to transfer power to her son, Tiberius. According to Suetonius, Claudius' third wife **Messalina** is suspected of killing members of the Julio-Claudian family and was executed as a result. The relationship between the emperor Nero and his mother, **Agrippina**, is a notorious part of Roman history. *scripta* **15.6** focuses on their dark and possibly incestuous relationship; in this text you can read Suetonius' description of **Agrippina's murder**.

The importance of the military also changed because of the system of imperial succession. As you read in Chapter 9, by the end of the Republic powerful Romans were using military support for their own purposes. With the system of inherited power, however, the most influential soldiers were not in the legions but in the **Praetorian Guard**. Created in 27 BC by the emperor Augustus, these nine cohorts were stationed near Rome. As the only armed force within marching distance of the city these soldiers became an important part of securing and maintaining power. As noted above, Tiberius gave increased political power to Sejanus, the commander of the Praetorian Guard and – as you can read in *scripta* **15.4** – the **Praetorian Guard was involved in making Claudius the new emperor**, establishing a significant precedent.

CHAPTER 15: READ THE *SCRIPTA* IN ENGLISH

The texts for each scripta *are printed in this book in Latin and English. These texts can be read in English, Latin or a combination of the two. The* scripta *texts for this chapter start on p122. They follow the Core Language section because their Latin versions contain new grammar and vocabulary from this chapter.*

The questions below can be answered by reading the scripta *in English. Available on the Companion Website are copies of the English version of each* scripta *along with the questions for each text.*

scripta 15.1 in English (p124): Tacitus discusses the challenges of writing history

1 According to Tacitus, what engages the interest of readers?
2 What does Tacitus say he will be writing about instead?
3 Explain why Tacitus thinks that writing about recent events is unlikely to please his audience. Why do you think he chose this content despite these challenges?

scripta 15.2 in English (p126): Tacitus describes the political uncertainty at the prospect of Augustus' death

1 According to Tacitus, how did people respond to the prospect of Augustus' death? Do you find this surprising in the context of Augustus' success?
2 Why do you think some people desired civil war?
3 Tacitus says that Tiberius was preferred to Agrippa; from what you can read in this extract, who do you think sounds like the better choice for the next princeps?
4 One of Tacitus' central criticisms about life under the emperors is that Romans had less political freedom as a result. Find as many different details as you can in this passage which suggest that the Romans felt limited in what they could say or do.

Chapter 15 Tacitus, Suetonius, Pliny – Writers and the Emperors

scripta 15.3 in English (p128): Tacitus comments on the emperor as a god

1. Tacitus writes that Romans are seeking protection by holding onto a statue of the emperor. Explain how he suggests that this has become a problem.
2. What does Gaius Cestius say to try to stop the practice that anyone could be protected from punishment if they held onto a statue of the emperor?
3. Explain in your own words what Annia Rufilla had done and why Cestius thinks this is so shocking.
4. What impression do you get from this text of political life in Rome at this time?

scripta 15.4 in English (p130): Suetonius describes how Claudius became emperor

1. What does Claudius do when he hears that Caligula is dead? How does Suetonius create an image of Claudius as unimpressive here?
2. Suetonius tells us that Claudius was worried about the prospect that the Roman consuls might declare liberty for all. What do you think this means and what risk might it pose to Claudius as a member of the imperial family?
3. Suetonius suggests that the Romans were not really committed to restoring liberty for all: which details from the passage show this?
4. How does Suetonius highlight the Praetorian Guard's power? Give as many details from the text as you can to support your answer.

scripta 15.5 in English (p133): Suetonius describes Agrippina's murder

1. At the start of this extract, what evidence is there that Nero's relationship with his mother had deteriorated?
2. Nero tries to kill his mother in a variety of ways: explain in your own words what these were.
3. Suetonius seems to relish the horror of this murder: which moments do you find most horrific and why?
4. Using this extract as your evidence, write character descriptions of Nero and Agrippina.

Chapter 15: Read the *scripta* in English

scripta 15.6 in English (p136): Tacitus describes the great fire in Rome

1. Tacitus tells us that he does not know for sure why the fire happened but he offers two possible causes. What were these?
2. List as many details as you can from this passage which emphasise the severity of the fire.
3. How does Tacitus create a sense of chaos during the fire?
4. How does Tacitus use this episode to criticise Nero?

scripta 15.7 in English (p138): Tacitus describes Nero's treatment of the Christians

1. What rumour was Nero trying to stop and how did he try to do this initially?
2. Why did Nero choose the Christians as targets for blame?
3. Explain in your own words how the Christians were killed.
4. What does this passage imply about the relationship between Nero and the Roman people?

scripta 15.8 in English (p140): Pliny writes to the emperor Trajan

1. According to Pliny, why did the fire spread so widely?
2. Why is Pliny cautious about creating a society of firemen?
3. Trajan tells Pliny not to set up a society of firemen: what reasons does he give for this?
4. From these two letters, what impression do you get of Pliny as a governor and of Trajan's priorities as emperor?

Chapter 15: Core Language Vocabulary List

faveo	favere, favi, fautum (+ dative)	favour; support
iaceo	iacere, iacui	lie (down)
accido	accidere, accidi	happen
opprimo	opprimere, oppressi, oppressum	crush; overwhelm
pello	pellere, pepuli, pulsum	drive
resisto	resistere, restiti (+ dative)	resist
victoria	victoriae, f	victory
captivus	captivi, m	captive; prisoner
castra	castrorum, n pl	(military) camp
imperium	imperii, n	empire; power; command
praemium	praemii, n	prize; reward; profit
imperator	imperatoris, m	emperor; general; leader
legio	legionis, f	legion
princeps	principis, m	chief; emperor
scelus	sceleris, n	crime
lentus	lenta, lentum	slow
scelestus	scelesta, scelestum	wicked
diligens	diligentis	careful
vehementer		violently; loudly
simul		at the same time
antea		before
interea		meanwhile
libenter		willingly; gladly
postridie		on the next day
umquam		ever
dum		while, until
nisi		if . . . not; unless; except
si		if
simulac, simulatque		as soon as
ut		as; when

castra is a plural noun in Latin but *military camp* is a singular noun in English.

Sentence structure: subordinate clauses and phrases

Every sentence must have a **finite verb**; this is a verb with a **person** and a **tense**. Because Latin finite verbs reveal tense and person via their stem and ending, it is possible for a Latin sentence to be only one word long.

lacrimavi.   I wept.

Sentences often contain more than one finite verb and this means that they contain more than one **clause**. A **clause** is made up of all the words which are grammatically centred around a finite verb.

The sentence below has **two clauses** because it has **two finite verbs**.

puer lacrimavit sed puella risit.   The boy wept but the girl laughed.

A word which connects a clause to another clause is known as a **conjunction**. In the sentence above, **sed** is the conjunction.

Some sentences contain **subordinate clauses**. A subordinate clause is a clause which is connected to another clause by a **subordinating conjunction**. A **main clause** is a clause which is **not** introduced by a subordinating conjunction and which could stand on its own as a complete sentence.

postquam dux interfectus est, milites fugerunt.   After the leader was killed, the soldiers fled.
  subordinate clause   main clause

postquam, ubi, qui etc. are all examples of **subordinating conjunctions**.

Sentences often contain subordinate information which does not form a separate clause; a group of words which are working together and which do not contain a finite verb is called a **phrase**.

currentes per vias, liberi matrem conspexerunt.   **Running through the streets**, the children caught sight of their mother.

currentes per vias is a **phrase** because it does not contain a finite verb.

Chapter 15 Tacitus, Suetonius, Pliny – Writers and the Emperors

> **Why it is important to distinguish between clauses and phrases**
>
> It is important to distinguish between **clauses** and **phrases** because the grammatical rules are different.
>
> The most important of these rules is that when there is a **new finite verb** the **case structure resets**.
>
> | conspexi **pueros qui** per vias currebant. | I saw the boys who were running through the streets. |
>
> **pueros** and **qui** are in different cases because they are working with **different finite verbs**.
>
> A sentence which conveyed the same information via a **phrase**, however, would not reset the case structure:
>
> | conspexi **pueros** per vias **currentes**. | I saw the boys running through the streets. |
>
> **pueros** and **currentes** are both in the accusative case because they are both working as the object of the **same finite verb**.

Consolidation: subordinate clauses

Here are all the Latin **subordinating conjunctions** which you have met so far:

quod	because
antequam	before
postquam	after; when
quamquam	although
ubi	when; where
qui, quae, quod	who; which

Each of these introduces a **subordinate clause**. This clause must have its own **finite verb**. Its case structure will **reset** and the cases in it will depend upon the relationship with the **finite verb**.

EXERCISE 15.1

1. quamquam captivi **vulnerati sunt**, etiam nunc **vivunt**.
2. cives principi **favebant** quod victoriam magnam **rettulerat**.
3. imperator huius legionis praemia **dedit** militibus qui fortiter et libenter **pugnaverunt**.
4. dux, ubi in castra **ingressus est**, suos dormientes **invenit**.
5. cives, antequam de scelere senatoris **audiverunt**, non **credebant** eum scelestum esse.
6. miles diligens, postquam legionem fugientem **vidit**, hostibus resistere **volebat**.
7. **cognovisti**ne de rebus quae prope castra **acciderunt**?
8. Romani, quod multas gentes **vicerunt**, imperium maximum **habebant**.
9. postridie **adveni** ad castra ubi captivi **custodiebantur**.
10. hic exercitus, contra quem hostes vehementer **procedebant**, nunc **oppressus est**.

> The finite verbs are in bold. Which are in **main clauses** and which are in **subordinate clauses**? You will need to use the **subordinating conjunctions** to help you work this out.

scripta in Latin you could now look at the Latin version of *scripta* 15.1

New subordinating conjunctions

Here are the new **subordinating conjunctions** for this chapter; each is used to introduce a subordinate clause. Each subordinate clause must contain a finite verb. The case structure within this subordinate clause will be centred around the clause's finite verb.

dum	while; until
si	if
nisi	if . . . not; unless; except
ut	as; when
simulac, simulatque	as soon as

Chapter 15 Tacitus, Suetonius, Pliny – Writers and the Emperors

Labelling subordinate clauses

Subordinate clauses connect in meaning to the main clause in different ways. For example, sometimes they give information which **relates** to a noun in the main clause, sometimes they give information about the **time** of the main clause, sometimes they explain the **cause** of the main clause, sometimes they state the **condition** on which the main clause action took place, sometimes they **concede** that although something happened, the main clause action took place all the same.

These different types of clauses are given different names to explain **how** they connect to the main clause. Here are the different types of subordinate clause you have met so far.

name	connection	Latin conjunction
relative clause	information which **relates** to a noun in the main clause	qui, quae, quod
temporal clause	sets the **time frame** of the main clause	antequam, postquam, ubi, simulac, simulatque, dum, ut
causal clause	gives the **cause** of the main clause	quod
concessive clause	**concedes** that although something else happens, the main clause action still took place	quamquam
conditional clause	states the **condition** on which the main clause action takes place	si, nisi

Tenses in subordinate clauses

English and Latin have slightly different **idioms** for the **tense** of the finite verb in the subordinate clause.

For a **past-time action** in a subordinate clause, Latin typically uses the **perfect tense** but English often uses the **pluperfect tense**.

> ubi milites **fugerunt**, incolae ridebant.   When the soldiers **had fled**, the inhabitants began to laugh.

For a **future-time action** in a subordinate clause, Latin typically uses a **future tense**, but English often uses the **present tense**.

> si diligenter **laborabitis**, laetus ero.   If **you work** carefully, I shall be happy.

EXERCISE 15.2

1. 'si fortissime,' **inquit** imperator, '**pugnabitis**, victorias maximas clarissimasque **habebitis**.'
2. quod legiones omnes **aberant**, castra ab hostibus **incensa sunt**.
3. nisi prope urbem **manebitis**, **nescietis** de sceleribus senatorum.
4. simulatque nuntius in oppidum **ingressus est**, cives in forum **cucurrerunt** quod omnia audire **volebant**.
5. princeps, ubi exercitus **deletus est**, magnopere et vehementer **lacrimabat**.
6. interea, dum liberi **gaudebant**, pater materque lentissime domum **regrediebantur**.
7. nisi victoriam **sperabitis**, numquam **vincetis**.
8. ancilla, simulac sanguinem **vidit**, pedes vulneratos esse **sciebat**.
9. si aurum in agro diligenter **celatum est**, tutum **est**.
10. nisi servi cibum **emerunt**, cenam diram **habebimus**.

> All the **finite verbs** are in bold. Who is the **subject** of each finite verb?

scripta in Latin you could now look at the Latin version of *scripta* 15.2 and 15.3

Consolidation: subordinate phrases (indirect statement, ablative absolute)

In Latin, the **indirect statement** and the **ablative absolute** are examples of **subordinate phrases**. In Latin, neither uses a finite verb and – because they are phrases, not clauses – neither starts with a subordinating conjunction.

The **infinitive** and **participle** operate differently from finite verbs: the **time** indicated by their tense is **relative to the main verb**.

- **perfect** tense infinitive or participle = action which took place **before** the main verb
- **present** tense infinitive or participle = action **at the same time as** the main verb
- **future** tense infinitive or participle = action **at some point later** than the main verb.

Latin's indirect statement and ablative absolute can be difficult to translate into English because it is more idiomatic in English to use a **subordinate clause**; this means that you have to:

- add a subordinating conjunction
- convert the infinitive / participle to a finite verb; this means that its tense may change.

    e.g. **sciebat cives principi favere.**
        He knew the citizens to support their emperor.
    → He knew **that** the citizens **supported** their emperor.

militibus resistentibus, oppidum non oppressum est.
        With the soldiers resisting, the town was not overwhelmed.
    → **Because** the soldiers **were resisting**, the town was not overwhelmed.

EXERCISE 15.3

1. princeps novus timebat quod sciebat **nonnullos sibi non favere**.
2. captivi sentiunt **se hodie morituros esse**.
3. **praemiis datis**, milites maxime gaudebant.
4. **voce poetae audita**, liberi gaudium magnum sentiebant.
5. ancillae, quae cognoverunt **servos laborem non coepisse**, iratissimae erant.
6. dux promisit **se postridie exercitum Romam reducturum esse**.
7. **corpore mortuo conspecto**, omnes sciebant de scelere filiorum scelestorum.
8. senator quidam, **templo novo aedificato**, artem mirabatur.
9. nonne putas **principem ipsum de victoria locuturum esse**?
10. **equis vulneratis**, nunc malumus ambulare.

> Look at the **phrases** in bold. Which are **indirect statements**? Which are **ablative absolutes**?

---

scripta in Latin — you could now look at the Latin version of *scripta* 15.4 and 15.5

GRAMMAR HUNT

Can you find in Exercise 15.3 an example of the following:

1. a perfect active verb (3rd person pl)
2. an imperfect active verb (3rd person sg)
3. a future active infinitive with a plural subject
4. a genitive pl noun
5. a superlative adverb
6. an irregular verb in the present tense
7. a perfect active infinitive
8. an imperfect deponent verb (3rd person sg)
9. a nominative pl noun
10. a present active infinitive

Chapter 15 Tacitus, Suetonius, Pliny – Writers and the Emperors

> *Agenda* comes from the Latin for *[things] needing to be done.*

Gerundives

Latin has another type of non-finite verb: the **gerundive**.

This is a part of a verb which behaves like an **adjective**: it often describes a noun as 'needing-to-be-something-ed'. It uses the **present stem** and so its endings vary by conjugation.

1st conjugation	am**andus**, am**anda**, am**andum**	needing to be loved
2nd conjugation	terr**endus**, terr**enda**, terr**endum**	needing to be terrified
3rd conjugation	reg**endus**, reg**enda**, reg**endum**	needing to be ruled
4th conjugation	aud**iendus**, aud**ienda**, aud**iendum**	needing to be heard

The gerundive form for the mixed conjugation is given in the Reference Grammar on p246.

Deponent verbs form their gerundives in exactly the same way as the non-deponent verbs in their conjugation, e.g. *sequendus – needing to be followed*. Note that in this form deponent verbs are passive in form and passive in meaning.

Like the other non-finite forms of the verb, the gerundive's tense operates **relative** to the **main verb**.

cives audiendi sunt.   The citizens **are needing to be heard**.
→ The citizens **must be heard**.

praemia danda erunt.   The prizes **will be needing to be given**.
→ The prizes **will have to be given**.

captivi opprimendi erant.   The prisoners **were needing to be crushed**.
→ The prisoners **had to be crushed**.

A **dative noun** can be used to show the person by whom the action is to be done.

captivus **militi** interficiendus est.   The prisoner must be killed **by the soldier**.

EXERCISE 15.4

> The **gerundives** are in bold. Translate each one literally.

1. haec castra militibus nostris **incendenda** sunt.
2. hodie praemia **offerenda** sunt; cras iterum pugnabimus.
3. interea illi servi et illae ancillae **interficiendi** sunt.
4. omnes sciebant scelus **puniendum** esse.
5. cur mater **necanda** erat? ei qui hoc fecerunt scelestissimi sunt.
6. hoc templum **mirandum** est, nam maximum est et plus auri habet quam illum.
7. nunc – si spem pacis habere volumus – res nobis libenter **agenda** est.
8. hostes ab urbe nostra **pellendi** sunt.
9. quamquam hostes nostri sunt, cibus captivis **offerendus** est.
10. in hoc bello magnopere passi sumus; nunc consilium novum **capiendum** erit.

> **Note that** deponent verbs have gerundives which are passive in meaning, just like non-deponent verbs.

scripta in Latin   you could now look at the Latin version of *scripta* 15.6

ad + gerundive

It is very common to meet *ad* + noun + gerundive. In this use, the gerundive simply means 'being something-ed'.

The *ad* + noun + gerundive phrase is often best translated idiomatically as a simple **phrase of purpose**.

imperator in forum advenit ad captivos spectandos.	The emperor arrived in the forum **for the purpose of** the captives **being looked at.**
	→ The emperor arrived in the forum **to look at** the captives.

119

Chapter 15 Tacitus, Suetonius, Pliny – Writers and the Emperors

EXERCISE 15.5

Translate each of the **ad** + **gerundive phrases** in bold.

1. agricola ad oppidum festinabat **ad equum novum emendum**.
2. ancillae fideles diligenter laborabant **ad cenam parandam**.
3. imperator ad castra progressus est **ad milites videndos**.
4. nautae nonnulli e nave egressi sunt **ad amorem quaerendum**.
5. milites in castris manebunt **ad praemia accipienda**.
6. interea in foro adsumus **ad principem audiendum**.
7. dux breviter locutus est **ad virtutem militum laudandam**.
8. in bello homines scelera dira faciunt **ad pecuniam rapiendam**.
9. omnes ad portas cucurrerunt **ad nuntium conspiciendum**.
10. simul milites et dux pugnare coeperunt **ad hostes opprimendos**.

scripta in Latin   you could now look at the Latin version of *scripta* 15.7

Consolidation: expressions of time

Latin has lots of different ways to express time.

Temporal clauses: these are introduced by *ubi*, *postquam*, *antequam*, *ut*, *dum*, *simulac / simulatque* and contain a finite verb.

   ubi de scelere cognovit, princeps   When he found out about the crime,
     iratissimus erat.   the emperor was very angry.

Adverbs of time such as *interea*, *antea*, *umquam*, *simul*, *postridie*, *mox*, *cras*, *heri* are used at the start or within a clause to set the time-frame for the main verb's action.

Prepositions of time must be followed by a noun, e.g. *post bellum* – *after the battle*.

Noun phrases in a particular case can create a **time phrase** of the following types:

- the **accusative case** to denote **how long** something lasted
  tres horas hostibus resistebamus.   **For three hours** we were resisting the enemy.

- the **ablative case** to show **when** an action took place
  quarto die princeps mortuus est.   **On the fourth day** the emperor died.

EXERCISE 15.6

Translate each of the **time words and phrases** in bold.

1. cur haec **umquam** promisisti? scelesta sunt nec spem ullam pacis offerunt.
2. **tres horas** milites fortiter pugnabant; **nunc** paene omnes mortui sunt.
3. **postquam** nuntius in urbem advenit, cives de victoria desperabant.
4. castra **antea** paranda erant; nunc milites non tuti sunt.
5. **ante lucem** primam naves ad insulam navigabant.
6. **die secundo**, senator Romam rediit; **postridie** interfectus est.
7. **post mortem patris** diu gaudium nullum sentiebam.
8. **dum** senex lentus progrediebatur, liberi scelesti, celeriter currentes, ridebant.
9. **interea** nuntius forum ingressus est; **mox** loquetur de rebus quas copiae passae sunt.
10. alter frater **iam** domum regressus est; alter prope mare sedet et **mox** regredietur.

---

scripta in Latin — you could now look at the Latin version of *scripta* 15.8

DERIVATION HUNT

Can you find in Exercise 15.6 the Latin words from which the following English words derive? Can you use the Latin word to help you explain the meaning of the English word?

1. impugn
2. mortuary
3. regressive
4. secondary
5. advent
6. horological
7. ingredients
8. alternative
9. domestic
10. passion

Chapter 15: *scripta*

For guidance on how to make use of these Latin texts and their English translations, see pp.viii–ix.

On the Companion Website you will find resources to accompany these texts:

- in the **scripta in English** section you will find copies of each text in English only, with questions on each one
- in the **scripta in Latin** section you will find notes for each of the Latin texts: these contain glosses for all words not yet met in a Core Language vocabulary list, explanations to help you understand the Latin and material designed to help you build your appreciation of literary style.

Meet the *scriptores*: Tacitus, Suetonius, Pliny

Publius Cornelius Tacitus (AD 56–120) rose up the *cursus honorum* but his greatest accomplishments were his works of history. Born in the reign of Nero, he lived under several emperors, including the tyranny of Domitian. No doubt his personal experience contributed to his acerbic criticism of the principate as a political structure.

Tacitus is highly critical of imperial rule, highlighting the lack of meaningful debate, the fear and the abuse of power within this system. Tacitus' most famous text – the *Annals* – is written in concise and analytical prose; Tacitus explores the interplay of appearance versus reality of government, often focusing on the gap between private opinion and what could be said more publicly in the senate. He acknowledges that Augustus had brought peace and stability but laments that successive emperors reduced political freedom.

Unlike Tacitus, **Gaius Suetonius Tranquillus** (AD 69–c. 122) did not pursue the *cursus honorum*, though he did serve in a secretarial capacity under Trajan and Hadrian. **Suetonius** is famous for his **biographies**; the most well-known of these are commonly referred to as *The Lives of the Twelve Caesars*. Suetonius shows comparatively little interest in military or legal administration of the empire. Instead, he focuses on the private lives, relationships and personalities of the emperors. Whereas Tacitus seemed to find the lack of morality and political freedom distressing, Suetonius appears to find delight in recounting scandalous or sensational anecdotes.

Gaius Plinius Caecilius Secundus ('**Pliny the Younger**') (AD 61–113) gives us another view of life under the emperors. Unlike Tacitus' fiercely critical chronological history or Suetonius' sensational series of biographies, Pliny's contributions to history take the form of **personal letters** which cover events ranging from the eruption of Mount Vesuvius in AD 79 to first-person accounts of social, legal and personal events.

FIGURE 15.5 Statue of Trajan

The emperor Trajan is shown here in military regalia in the *adlocutio* pose to indicate he is addressing his troops. Correspondence between Trajan and Pliny the Younger offers us a unique insight into the governance of the Roman empire at this time. In *scripta* 15.8 you can read one of Pliny's letters and Trajan's reply.

Through his letters, **Pliny** paints a less harsh picture of life under the emperors. Pliny had a long career, serving as a judge, senator, tribune, priest and, eventually, governor of Bithynia and Pontus (modern-day northern Turkey). Pliny's letters offer a much more personal approach to writing; this approach, seen in the writing of others, will be explored in more depth in the poetry included in Chapter 16.

> ## Reading original Latin note 6: Latin's concision and sentence length
>
> The passages in this chapter are more idiomatic and have been adapted more lightly than those you met in Chapter 13. As a result, you will find that the differences between a literal and idiomatic translation are even greater.
>
> Latin is a very concise language. This is because:
>
> - **grammatical role** is typically shown in Latin by the ending of a word but English often needs several words instead, e.g. *regebam – I was ruling*
>
> - **emphasis** can be created in Latin by unusual word order or by promoting important words to the start or end of a sentence, whereas English often adds words to create emphasis, e.g. *I really am happy*, *this is the book I like*
>
> - **variety** can be achieved in Latin by different word order but English tends to achieve the same vitality of style by varying the vocabulary and constructions used instead.
>
> In addition, Latin sentences can be very long. Elegant English, however, tries to mitigate its natural wordiness by keeping sentence length short. As a result, one Latin sentence is often best translated by several English sentences, and this means that the clause structure often has to change. In particular, bits of a sentence which have been subordinated as a clause or phrase in Latin may work best as a main clause in a shorter English sentence.
>
> As you explore the idiomatic English translations, think about where and why they are different from the most literal translation of the Latin. It will be helpful to think about what the English is trying to achieve in tone and emphasis, and how this was achieved in a different way in Latin.
>
> Remember, you may end up disagreeing with the English translation and thinking that it would have been better to translate the Latin in a different way: discussing translations critically in this way is a really constructive part of understanding both English and Latin better.

Chapter 15 Tacitus, Suetonius, Pliny – Writers and the Emperors

> ### *scripta* 15.1: Tacitus discusses the challenges of writing history
>
> *This text is taken from Tacitus, Annals 4.33. Tacitus reflects on the challenges facing a writer of contemporary history: the historians who wrote about events from long ago were able to focus on delighting their reader and they were at liberty to colour their history without fearing the personal bias of their readers.*
>
> *In contrast, as a writer of contemporary history, Tacitus thinks that he has to deal with content which is unremitting in its bleakness and with a readership who are too close to the reality of what he describes not to be personally impacted by his choice of what to praise or to criticise.*

It's the geographical location of tribes, battles of different types and the famous deaths of generals which capture the attention and keep the minds of the readers engaged. In contrast I am knitting together savage edicts, never-ending accusations, friendships which could not be trusted, the destruction of men who did not deserve it and always the same reasons for their death. Then there is the fact that it's rare to find anyone who objects to the ancient writers, and it does not matter much to anyone whether you present the Carthaginian or Roman battle lines in a more sparkling fashion. But the descendants are still alive today of many of the men who were punished or humiliated when Tiberius held power; even when the actual families have now died out, you will still find men who, because they have similar characteristics, think that the bad actions of others are held out as criticisms directed at themselves. Even glory and praise make readers hostile, since it creates too clear a contrast with the opposite actions.

nam situs gentium, varietates proeliorum, clari ducum exitus retinent ac redintegrant legentium animum: **nos** saeva iussa, continuas accusationes, fallaces amicitias, perniciem innocentium et easdem exitii causas coniungimus. tum quod antiquis scriptoribus est rarus obtrectator, neque refert cuiusquam Punicas Romanasne acies laetius extuleris: at multorum qui Tiberio regente poenam vel infamias subierunt, posteri manent utque familiae ipsae iam extinctae sunt, invenies eos qui propter similitudinem morum aliena malefacta sibi obiectari putant. etiam gloria ac virtus infensos habet, ut nimis diversa arguens.

Note that plurals can be used in Latin for emphasis.

situs, situs, m	location
redintegro, redintegrare	restore
fallax, fallacis	untrustworthy
pernicies, perniciei, f	ruin
exitium, exitii, n	death
obtrectator, obtrectoris, m	someone who criticises, a detractor
refert (+ genitive) . . . extuleris	'does it make a difference (to x) . . . whether you present'
quisquam, quaequam, quicquam	anyone, anything
acies, aciei, f	battle line
vel	or
infamia, infamiae, f	disgrace
posteri, posterorum, m pl	descendants
mos, moris, m	custom, habit
infensus – a -um	hostile
nimis	too much
diversus – a -um	opposite
arguo, arguere	make clear

DERIVATIONS

This task builds skills in deducing the meaning of one word by using a related word.

The words below derive from words in the passages above which have not been glossed.

Can you find the Latin words from which these English words derive? Can you use either the Latin or the English word to help you explain the meaning of the other?

Remember that you will need to think about the part of speech of both the Latin and English words and – if they are different – you will need to consider how to adjust the meaning to move from one part of speech to the other.

variety, continual, innocence, causation, conjunction, antiquated, rarely, extinction, similar, objection

Reading original Latin note 7: The importance of indirect speech

As you read in Chapter 8, oratory was a central part of Roman education, and skill in public speaking was an important ingredient in winning power and prestige. As a result, Roman history often reports what people said or thought. Reported speech aids characterisation, it often conveys an analysis of the reasons for an action or situation, and it allows the author to display their own oratorical skill in constructing a plausible version of a famous speech.

This means that as a reader of historical Latin prose, you need to be ready to meet indirect statements very frequently. Because Latin leans towards concision, the words which introduce the indirect statement are often left out because the **accusative + infinitive** construction makes the move to indirect speech very obvious.

Notice how often the accusative + infinitive construction appears in the text below and how **English has to keep adding** *they said* or similar, even though these words are not there in Latin.

Chapter 15 Tacitus, Suetonius, Pliny – Writers and the Emperors

> ### scripta 15.2: Tacitus describes the political uncertainty at the prospect of Augustus' death
>
> This text is taken from Tacitus, Annals 1.4, and describes the fraught political uncertainty at the time of Augustus' death.
>
> As discussed in Chapter 11, Augustus' propaganda focused on the claim that he had restored the Republic. The potential power vacuum at his death brought with it the opportunity for a more meaningful return to Republican structures and the liberty that these promoted. It also, however, brought the risk of civil war if ambitious Romans decided to fight it out in order to move themselves to the top spot. In AD 14 Tiberius, Augustus' adopted son, was declared the next princeps; this created the precedent for what became in effect a hereditary monarchy, cementing the end of the Roman Republic.
>
> In this section, Tacitus acerbically re-creates the private discussions which might have taken place at the time, and focuses on the Romans' thoughts about the possible contenders for Augustus' position. A contrast is drawn between the young and hot-headed Agrippa and the more seasoned Tiberius. The passage focuses on the Romans' fear about the sort of ruler Tiberius would prove to be, the sexual perversions which had dominated his time when he retreated from public life to the island of Rhodes, and the overbearing influence of his mother, Livia.
>
> The passage is an excellent example of Tacitus' interest in rumour and private opinion as a way to provide a contrast with what could be said openly. Tacitus' approach to writing history demonstrates that, for the Romans, history was as much a work of creative imagination and interpretation as it was a matter of unbiased facts.

Augustus had now reached advanced old age and he was weakened by ill-health. The end of his life was near and this led to fresh hope: a few men began to talk again about liberty; a greater number feared civil war while others craved it. The greatest number by far began to discuss their likely masters privately in various ways. Some believed Agrippa to be psychopathic and already enraged by his humiliation, and they did not think that he had the age or experience to make him ready for so great a role. In contrast, they thought that Tiberius Nero was seasoned by life-experience, tried and tested in war, but that he had the age-old and ingrained arrogance of the Claudian family. What's more, they thought that many indications of his savage nature were to the fore. They said that he was a man who had been brought up from infancy in a house laced with a royal mindset; consulships and military triumphs had been heaped upon him from an early age and – when he had withdrawn from public life to the island of Rhodes under the pretence of a retreat – he had done nothing other than indulge his aggression, deception and his secret lusts. They said that his mother was taking the stage with her unrestrained female power and that they would end up enslaved to a woman.

postquam provecta iam senectus aegro corpore fatigabatur aderatque finis et spes novae, pauci de libertate loquebantur, plures bellum pavescebant, alii cupiebant. pars multo maxima inminentes dominos variis rumoribus differebant: **trucem Agrippam** et ignominia incensum, non aetate neque rerum experientia tantae moli parem; Tiberium Neronem maturum annis, spectatum bello, sed vetere atque insita Claudiae familiae superbia, multaque indicia saevitiae erumpere. hunc et prima ab infantia eductum in domo regnatrice; congestos esse iuveni consulatus, triumphos; ne iis quidem annis, quibus Rhodi specie secessus exul egerit, aliud quam iram et simulationem et secretas libidines meditatum esse. accedere matrem muliebri inpotentia: **serviendum** esse feminae.

> The accusative **trucem** marks the beginning of the indirect speech; supply *esse*.

> **serviendum** is a form of the verb used to express obligation. This is explained on p118.

provectus -a -um	advanced
aeger, aegra, aegrum	sick
fatigo, fatigare	wear out, tire
pavesco, pavescere	grow frightened
differo, differre	distinguish between
trux, trucis	savage, fierce
ignominia, ignominiae, f	disgrace, insult
aetas, aetatis, f	age
tantus -a -um	so big, so great
moles, molis, f	burden, undertaking
par, paris	equal
spectatus -a -um	tried, tested
vetus, veteris	old
insitus -a -um	innate
superbia -ae, f	arrogance
erumpo, erumpere	break out
congero, congerere, congessi, congestum	pile up
ne . . . quidem	not even
species, speciei, f	appearance
secessus, secessus, m	retreat
exul egerit	'he had lived as an exile'
libido, libidinis, f	sexual pleasure, lust
meditor, meditari	consider, think over
accedo, accedere	step forward

DERIVATIONS

This task builds skills in deducing the meaning of one word by using a related word.

The words below derive from words in the passages above which have not been glossed.

Can you find the Latin words from which these English words derive? Can you use either the Latin or the English word to help you explain the meaning of the other?

Remember that you will need to think about the part of speech of both the Latin and English words and – if they are different – you will need to consider how to adjust the meaning to move from one part of speech to the other.

finish, liberty, imminent, various, incendiary, experience, mature, indicator, infancy, simulator, servitude

Chapter 15 Tacitus, Suetonius, Pliny – Writers and the Emperors

> ### scripta 15.3: Tacitus comments on the emperor as a god
>
> *This text is taken from Tacitus, Annals 3.36. Tacitus highlights how the position of emperor had started to blur the boundaries between human and divine and thus cement the idea that the imperial family brought with it a power which was beyond the reach of other Roman citizens. It had long been established in Roman custom that individuals could seek refuge in temples and appeal to the power of the gods to protect them from human aggression. This passage highlights that Roman citizens had taken to clinging to statues of the imperial family in a similar way in order to escape punishment.*
>
> *The passage describes events that took place in AD 21. At the start of this year, the emperor Tiberius had decided to leave Rome for a temporary retreat in Campania. In his absence, his son Drusus held power in Rome.*

The basest individuals had taken on the lawlessness of stirring up – with impunity – complaints against their betters by holding onto a statue of **Caesar**. This extended even to freedmen and slaves who, while attacking their patron or master verbally or physically, began to strike fear into others. Therefore Gaius Cestius, a senator, said that although the imperial family were indeed equal to the gods, everyone should remember that prayers were not heard by the gods if they were not lawful, and that it was not a good thing that bad men, wanting divine support for their shameful actions, were taking refuge in the Capitol or in the other temples of the city. He spoke about the example of Annia Rufilla who, in the forum, on the steps of the senate-house, even though she had been found guilty of fraud, directed threats at Cestius himself because she had positioned herself right in front of a statue of the emperor. Other senators started to shout out about examples not dissimilar to this and indeed even worse; they kept begging Drusus to set an example of punishment until he ordered that Annia Rufilla be held under public guard.

incedebat enim pessimis hominibus licentia impune invidiam in bonos excitandi arrepta imagine **Caesaris**: libertique etiam ac servi, patrono vel domino dum voces, dum manus intentabant, alios terrebant. igitur C. Cestius senator dixit principes quidem instar deorum esse, sed preces a deis nisi iustas non audiri neque bonum esse malos, volentes auxilium deorum ad flagitia, perfugere in Capitolium aut in alia urbis templa. locutus est de Annia Rufilla quae in foro, in limine curiae, quamquam fraudis damnata est, minas C. Cestio ipsi intendit quod ob effigiem imperatoris opposita est. haud dissimilia alii senatores et atrociora circumstrepebant precabanturque Drusum daret ultionis exemplum, donec Anniam Rufillam attineri publica custodia iussit.

Caesar was passed down as a name for the emperors; this probably refers to the current emperor, Tiberius.

incedo, incedere	advance upon
licentia, licentiae, f	freedom, lawlessness
invidia, invidiae, f	ill-will
excitandi	'of stirring up'
vel	or
intento, intentare	stretch towards (threateningly)
quidem	indeed
instar (+ genitive)	equal to
preces, precum, f pl	prayers
flagitium, flagitii, n	disgraceful action
aut	or
limen, liminis, n	threshold
curia, curiae, f	senate-house
damno, damnare	condemn
minae, minarum, f pl	threats
ob (+ accusative)	in front of
haud	not
circumstrepo, circumstrepere	make a loud noise all around
precabantur . . . daret	'they kept praying that [Drusus] should give'
ultio, ultionis, f	revenge
donec	until
attineo, attinere	hold

DERIVATIONS

This task builds skills in deducing the meaning of one word by using a related word.

The words below derive from words in the passages above which have not been glossed.

Can you find the Latin words from which these English words derive? Can you use either the Latin or the English word to help you explain the meaning of the other?

Remember that you will need to think about the part of speech of both the Latin and English words and – if they are different – you will need to consider how to adjust the meaning to move from one part of speech to the other.

impunity, patronage, justice, fraudulent, opposition, dissimulation, atrocity, custody

Chapter 15 Tacitus, Suetonius, Pliny – Writers and the Emperors

scripta 15.4: Suetonius describes how Claudius became emperor

This text is taken from Suetonius' biography of Claudius, Section 10. As discussed in Chapter 12, Claudius was an unlikely emperor who had been kept away from the public eye and shamed for his physical disabilities. When Caligula was assassinated, Claudius was terrified, no doubt because he realised that, as a blood relative of the previous emperor, he was a potential threat to whomever took power next.

Suetonius reports that when Claudius heard the news of Caligula's assassination, he hid behind a set of curtains. In a surprising turn of events, Claudius was found by a member of the Praetorian Guard, brought under their protection and then hailed as emperor by the soldiers. Suetonius comments that the money Claudius gave to these soldiers established the precedent that future emperors could (and would) buy the support of Rome's soldiers in order to shore up their power in Rome.

Claudius came to power in his fiftieth year, in a rather surprising way. He had been shut out along with the others by Gaius Caligula's assassins and he had retreated into a separate room, which was known as the Hermaeum. Not long afterwards, terrified by the news of the murder, he had crawled into the nearest window alcove and hidden himself within the curtains. A soldier, running past by chance, caught sight of his feet, realised he was hiding there and dragged him out. Claudius – in fear – fell at the knees of the soldier, but the soldier greeted him as emperor.

quinquagesimo anno imperium cepit quantumvis mirabili casu. exclusus inter ceteros ab insidiatoribus **Gai**, in diaetam, cui nomen est Hermaeum, recesserat; neque multo postea rumore caedis exterritus prorepsit ad solarium proximum interque vela se celavit. latentem discurrens forte miles, conspectis pedibus, agnovit extractumque et propter timorem ad genua sibi accidentem imperatorem salutavit.

Gai is the genitive sg form of Gaius, the first name of the emperor Caligula.

quinquagesimus -a -um	fiftieth
quantumvis	'as much as you like' (i.e. 'really rather')
casus, casus, m	event
insidiator, insidiatoris, m	a man in ambush
diaeta, diaetae, f	living room
caedes, caedis, f	murder
prorepo, prorepere, prorepsi	creep, crawl forward
solarium, solarii, n	a balcony, sunny area
velum, veli, n	curtain
lateo, latere	hide
agnosco, agnoscere, agnovi	recognise
genu, genus, n	knee

After this, the soldier led him to the rest of his division. These men put Claudius in a litter and carried him, wretched and fearful, to their camp. Those who passed him on his way pitied him, thinking that he was an innocent man who was being hauled off for punishment. Claudius was taken inside the camp's defences and spent the night amongst the military guard, slightly more confident than he had been, but with very little optimism even so because the consuls, along with the senate and the urban cohorts had taken up position in the forum and on the **Capitoline Hill**, ready to declare liberty for all. But, on the next day, the senate had become rather less purposeful through their own weariness and in-fighting and the mob, who were gathered all around, kept demanding that one man take the lead, calling for Claudius by name. Because of this, Claudius let the armed guard swear loyalty to his name and promised them 15,000 sesterces each. He was the first of the Caesars to gain surety about the loyalty of the soldiers by means of a reward given in advance.

hinc ad alios commilitones perduxit; ab his lecticae impositus et in castra delatus est tristis ac trepidus, miserante obvia turba quasi ad poenam raperetur insons. receptus intra vallum inter excubias militum pernoctavit, aliquanto minore spe quam fiducia. nam consules cum senatu et cohortibus urbanis forum **Capitolium**que occupaverant asserturi communem libertatem: sed postero die et senatu segniore per taedium ac dissensionem et multitudine, quae circumstabat, unum rectorem iam et nominatim exposcente, armatos iurare in nomen suum passus est promisitque singulis quina dena sestertia, primus Caesarum fidem militis etiam praemio pigneratus.

> The **Capitoline Hill** was an important area politically and contained some of Rome's most sacred temples.

lectica, lecticae, f	litter (for carrying someone)
obvius -a -um (+ dative)	in the way, meeting
quasi . . . raperetur	'as if he were being seized'
insons, insontis	innocent
vallum, valli, n	fortification
excubiae, excubiarum, f pl	watchmen
aliquanto	to some extent
fiducia, fiduciae, f	trust, confidence
assero, asserere, adseri, adsertum	claim, assert
segnis, segne	slow
taedium, taedii, n	weariness
exposco, exposcere	demand
iuro, iurare	swear an oath
quina dena	150 each
pigneror, pignerari, pigneratus sum	take as a pledge

Chapter 15 Tacitus, Suetonius, Pliny – Writers and the Emperors

DERIVATIONS

This task builds skills in deducing the meaning of one word by using a related word.

The words below derive from words in the passages above which have not been glossed.

Can you find the Latin words from which these English words derive? Can you use either the Latin or the English word to help you explain the meaning of the other?

Remember that you will need to think about the part of speech of both the Latin and English words and – if they are different – you will need to consider how to adjust the meaning to move from one part of speech to the other.

exclusion, recess, extract, accidental, communal, posterity, dissent, singular

Reading original Latin note 8: Vividness

As discussed in the Introduction to this chapter, literary historical texts were closer to a modern-day historical novel than to a history textbook. Writers such as Livy, Tacitus and Suetonius were judged partly on their vividness, i.e. how well they brought the past to life. As a reader of Latin historical prose, you will get more from the Latin text if you are alert to this vividness and use your imagination to create a living, breathing scene in your mind.

Vivid writing often involves the following:

- **vivid tenses** such as the imperfect and present tense. These tenses are vivid because they encourage us to think about the action while it is still happening. In a technique known as the **historic present**, Roman writers often used the present tense to make a past action more vivid.

- **speech**: Roman writers often tell us what people said, thought or felt. This helps the reader to understand and **empathise** with how events affected the people involved.

- **descriptive detail**: the 17th-century French playwright Racine described Tacitus as 'the finest painter of antiquity' and many have admired Tacitus' skill in creating a vibrant scene. It is useful to pause and consider the descriptive detail which shows us what we would have **seen** if we had been there, what we would have **heard** and what we would have **felt**.

- **metaphors and similes**: metaphors and similes deepen a description by interweaving something else into it. English is rich in metaphor too and, as a result, sometimes we take metaphors for granted; it is useful to ask yourself how often something is described in a way which is not literally true, and then consider what the impact of this is.

- **nouns rather than verbs**: it sometimes has greater impact to use a noun rather than a verb, because a noun places the focus on the action that took place rather than the people who did it (e.g. *there was a* **fight** *v.* **they fought**). Notice how often nouns are used in the passage below for information which could have been presented via a verb instead. In particular, Latin sometimes uses an infinitive instead of a main verb. This is known as the **historic infinitive**. An infinitive refers to the action itself and so an historic infinitive allows a writer to express an action in a way which is closer to a noun than a verb.

scripta 15.5: Suetonius describes Agrippina's murder

This text is made up of extracts from Suetonius' biography of Nero, section 34. Nero's relationship with his mother Agrippina is a central part of Suetonius' account: ruthless and ambitious, Agrippina had pushed Nero into power, but he soon tired of her overbearing dominance and decided to kill her. Suetonius lingers (at much greater length than the extracts given below) on the dramatic, deceitful and perverted details of this matricide.

In the passages below, Suetonius describes Nero's decision to murder his mother and his crazed guilt afterwards. Suetonius reminds the reader of the incestuous relationship between mother and son, and the final details focus on Nero's sexual fascination with her body. As you read in Chapter 14, Latin texts often echoed literary predecessors, either within the same genre or beyond it. In Suetonius' text, Nero's decision to kill his mother is reminiscent of the dysfunctional family relationships often present in Greek tragedy: the reference to the Furies shows the influence of this genre. In Greek tragedy, the Furies were terrifying divine beings who came to haunt people who had committed brutal crimes against their families.

His mother kept asking him more pointedly about what he was doing and saying and she kept on taking him to task. Nero found this increasingly heavy going and so he repeatedly exposed her to public resentment, acting as if he was about to step back from his power and go away to Rhodes. Then he stripped her of all her status and power, took away the body guard of Roman and German soldiers and drove her out from his private quarters and his palace on the **Palatine Hill**.

matrem facta dictaque sua quaerentem <u>acerbius</u> et <u>corrigentem gravabatur</u>; itaque <u>invidia</u> identidem <u>oneravit quasi cessurus</u> erat imperio Rhodumque abiturus erat, mox et honore omni et potestate <u>privavit</u> abductaque militum et Germanorum statione, <u>contubernio</u> ac **Palatio** expulit.

> The **Palatine Hill** was the location for Nero's grand palace.

acerbius	more bitterly, more keenly
corrigo, corrigere	put straight, chastise
gravor, gravari	be annoyed at, wearied by
invidia, invidiae, f	ill-will
onero, onerare	weigh down, make worse
quasi	as if
cedo, cedere, cessi, cessum	go away
privo, privare	strip, deprive
contubernium, contubernii, n	private dwelling

Chapter 15 Tacitus, Suetonius, Pliny – Writers and the Emperors

At last, terrified by her threats and her violent nature, he decided to kill her. He tried to do this three times with poison, but realised that she had defended herself by taking antidotes in advance. Then he prepared ceiling panels which would fall down on top of her as she slept. This plan, however, was not concealed well enough by those who knew about it and so he obtained a collapsible boat and – after faking a reconciliation – in a most charming letter he invited Agrippina to **Baiae** to join in with his celebrations of the festival of Minerva. He dragged out the party and when she wanted to return to Bauli, he offered her this boat, accompanying her to it cheerfully and even kissing her breasts at the moment of departure.

tandem minis eius ac violentia territus perdere constituit; et ubi ter veneno temptavit et sentiebat eam antidotis praemunitam esse, lacunaria, quae noctu super dormientem decisura erant, paravit. hoc consilio per conscios parum celato solutilem navem commentus est atque ita reconciliatione simulata iucundissimis litteris **Baias** evocavit ad sollemnia Quinquatruum simul celebranda; protraxit convivium repetentique Baulos machinosum illud obtulit, hilare prosecutus atque in digressu papillas etiam exosculatus.

> **Baiae** was a popular sea-side town, famous for its lavish parties.

minae, minarum, f pl	threats
perdo, perdere	destroy
ter	three times
venenum, veneni, n	poison
praemunio, praemunire, praemunivi, praemunitum	fortify / make safe in advance
lacunar, lacunaris, n	ceiling panel
decido, decidere, decidi, decisum	fall down
parum	too little
solutilis, solutile	collapsible
comminiscor, comminisci, commentus sum	contrive, invent
iucundus -a -um	agreeable, delightful
sollemnia Quinquatruum (accusative)	festival of Minerva
convivium, convivii, n	banquet, party
machinosum, machinosi, n	adapted (boat)
hilare	cheerfully
papillae, papillarum, f pl	breasts
exosculor, exosculari	kiss

He stayed awake for the intervening time – greatly on edge – waiting for the end of what he had begun. But when he found out that she had escaped by swimming, at a loss for his next move, he ordered that his mother be killed. Trustworthy sources report actions even worse than these: they say that Nero hurried to inspect the corpse, that he fondled her limbs, that he criticised some parts of her body and praised others. Afterwards, however, although he was fortified by congratulations from the soldiers, senate and Roman people, he was not able to bear his memory of the crime and confessed that he was tormented by his mother's ghost and by the **Furies**' lashes and their burning torches.

reliquum temporis cum magna trepidatione vigilavit opperiens coeptorum exitum. sed ut eam nando effugisse cognovit, inops consilii, iussit matrem occidi. adduntur his atrociora nec incertis auctoribus: Neronem ad cadaver visendum accurrisse, contrectavisse membra, alia vituperavisse, alia laudavisse. postea tamen, quamquam et militum et senatus populique gratulationibus confirmabatur, conscientiam sceleris ferre non potuit, saepe confessus se exagitari materna specie verberibusque **Furiarum** ac taedis ardentibus.

> The **Furies** were the ancient Greek spirits of revenge.

opperior, opperiri	wait for
nando	'by swimming'
inops, inopis (+ genitive)	lacking
cadaver, cadaveris, n	corpse
contrecto, contrectare	touch, handle
membrum, membri, n	limb
vitupero, vituperare	criticise
confirmo, confirmare	strengthen, reassure
confiteor, confiteri, confessus sum	confess, admit
exagito, exagitare	chase, harass
species, speciei, f	ghost
verber, verberis, n	whip
taeda, taedae, f	torch

DERIVATIONS

This task builds skills in deducing the meaning of one word by using a related word.

The words below derive from words in the passages above which have not been glossed.

Can you find the Latin words from which these English words derive? Can you use either the Latin or the English word to help you explain the meaning of the other?

Remember that you will need to think about the part of speech of both the Latin and English words and – if they are different – you will need to consider how to adjust the meaning to move from one part of speech to the other.

enquiry, identical, honour, station, expulsion, attempt, sentient, antidote, reconciliation, evocative, protracted, trepidatious, vigil, congratulations, conscience, ardent

Chapter 15 Tacitus, Suetonius, Pliny – Writers and the Emperors

scripta 15.6: Tacitus describes the great fire in Rome

This text is made up of sections from Tacitus, Annals 15.38. Tacitus vilifies the emperor Nero, presenting his reign as a time of extreme cruelty, perversion and self-indulgence. One of Nero's defining characteristics was his love of performing on the stage, something which was seen as culturally low-grade and unsuitable therefore for a Roman as exalted as the emperor.

In this famous passage, a terrible fire gripped Rome but Nero – who was away from the city at the time – is reported to have reacted by taking to the stage and performing a song about the destruction of Troy. Tacitus' account gives a vivid account of the human despair caused by this disaster and the contrast between this and those who were keen to make use of it for their own benefit. The passage starts and ends with the suggestion that Nero may have caused the blaze, perhaps with the intention of clearing space in the city for an overwhelmingly lavish new imperial palace.

Tacitus' account is much longer than the sections given below. Taken in full, it is an excellent example of his skill in picture-painting and his empathetic account of past events.

Disaster followed. It is unclear whether it came about by chance or because of some devious plan of the Princeps, but it was more serious and more devastating than anything which had happened to this city previously during violent outbreaks of fire. The flames surging through the city made their attack first on the low-lying areas, then rose up to the higher ground and, in the speed of its damage, outran the preventative measures.

sequitur clades, forte an dolo principis incertum est, sed omnibus, quae huic urbi per violentiam ignium acciderunt, gravior atque atrocior. impetu pervagatum incendium plana primum, deinde in edita adsurgens anteiit remedia velocitate mali.

clades, cladis, f	disaster
an	whether . . . or . . .
dolus, doli, m	deceit, trick
impetus, impetus, m	attack
pervagatus -a -um	widespread
planus -a -um	flat (ground)
editus -a -um	high (ground)
adsurgo, adsurgere	rise up against

In the face of this, there were the wails of terrified women; there were people who were thinking about themselves and people who were thinking about others; some were dragging the weak with them, some were waiting for them, in some places there was hesitation, in others a mad dash, and all of this made it harder to get out. Many found that while they were pausing to look behind them, they then became surrounded by the fire to the front and the sides. Finally, people filled the streets or just lay down in the fields, some in despair because they had lost all their possessions, others in grief for their relatives whom they had not been able to save, even though an escape route lay open. No one dared to defend themselves because of the repeated threats of the many men who were forbidding anyone to extinguish the fire; others were openly throwing fire-brands about, either because they wanted to loot more freely or because they had been ordered to do this.

ad hoc lamenta paventium feminarum, quique sibi quique aliis consulebant, dum trahunt invalidos aut opperiuntur, pars mora, pars festinans, cuncta impediebant. et saepe, dum in tergum respectant, lateribus aut fronte circumveniebantur. postremo, **complere** vias, **sterni** per agros; quidam amissis omnibus fortunis, alii caritate suorum, quos eripere nequiverant, quamquam effugium patebat. nec quisquam defendere audebat, crebris multorum minis restinguere prohibentium, et quod alii palam faces iaciebant, sive ut raptus licentius exercerent seu iussu.

> *complere* and *sterni* are examples of **historic infinitives** (see p132).

paveo, pavere	quake with fear
consulo, consulere (+ dative)	take thought for
aut	or
opperior, opperiri	wait for
mora, morae, f	delay
cunctus -a -um	all
tergum, tergi, n	the back, rear
latus, lateris, n	side
compleo, complere	fill up
sterno, sternere	lay flat, strike down
caritas, caritatis, f	love
nequeo, nequere, nequivi	be unable
pateo -ere	lie open
quisquam, quaequam, quicquam	anyone, anything
creber, crebra, crebrum	frequent, numerous
minae, minarum, f pl	threats
palam	openly
fax, facis, f	torch, fire-brand
sive . . . seu	whether . . . or
ut . . . exercerent	'so that they might carry out'
licentius	more freely

Chapter 15 Tacitus, Suetonius, Pliny – Writers and the Emperors

At that time, Nero did not return to the city before the fire had reached his own home. The rumour spread that at the very moment when the city burned, Nero had stepped up upon his private stage and had sung of the destruction of Troy, likening the present ills to the ancient disaster.

eo in tempore Nero non in urbem regressus est, antequam domui eius ignis appropinquavit. pervaserat rumor ipso tempore flagrantis urbis eum inisse domesticam scaenam et cecinisse Troianum excidium, praesentia mala vetustis cladibus adsimulantem.

pervado, pervadere, pervasi	go through, spread
flagro, flagrare	burn, blaze
scaena, scaenae, f	stage
cano, canere, cecini	sing, sing of
excidium, excidii, n	overthrow, destruction
vetustus -a -um	ancient

DERIVATIONS

This task builds skills in deducing the meaning of one word by using a related word.

The words below derive from words in the passages above which have not been glossed.

Can you find the Latin words from which these English words derive? Can you use either the Latin or the English word to help you explain the meaning of the other?

Remember that you will need to think about the part of speech of both the Latin and English words and – if they are different – you will need to consider how to adjust the meaning to move from one part of speech to the other.

sequence, violence, ignite, remedial, velocity, lamentation, impediment, circumvent, extinguish, prohibition, regression, domesticate, presently

scripta 15.7: Tacitus describes Nero's treatment of the Christians

This text is taken from Tacitus, Annals *15.44. In the aftermath of the fire, Nero was keen to distract attention away from the rumour that he was responsible. When Nero's attempts to win back popular support by cash handouts did not work, Tacitus writes that Nero decided to try to redirect the public anger onto the new religious movement – the Christians – instead.*

In this extract, Tacitus describes how the Christians were publicly and hideously executed.

Human resources and the emperor's bribery did not work – and neither did the appeasements offered to the gods: the rumour did not go away and large numbers believed that the fire had been ordered by Nero. And so, because he wanted to get rid of this rumour, Nero used the Christians as scapegoats and inflicted on them the most novel punishments.

sed non ope humana, non largitionibus principis aut deorum placamentis discedebat infamia et plurimi credebant iussum esse incendium. itaque, quod abolere rumorem volebat, Nero subdidit reos eos quos per flagitia invisos vulgus Christianos appellabat et novissimis poenis adfecit.

The common people already hated these men because of their shameful practices. Jesus Christ, the source of their name, had been killed at the hands of the procurator, Pontius Pilate, while Tiberius held power. Their deadly cult had been suppressed temporarily, but was beginning to spread again, not only throughout Judaea – the origin of this blight – but even through the city of Rome. Therefore, at first men were arrested who confessed, then – by their evidence – a huge number were convicted not so much for the crime of arson but because they were hateful to the human race. Wrapped in animal skins they were mauled by dogs and died, or they were tied to crosses and, when the daylight failed, they were burned to provide night-time light. Nero had offered his own gardens for this spectacle and he put on a public show in the Circus. As a result, pity started to grow on the basis that these men were being destroyed not really for the public benefit but to satisfy the savagery of one man.

auctor nominis eius, Christus, Tiberio imperitante per procuratorem Pontium Pilatum interfectus est; repressaque in praesens exitiablilis superstitio iterum erumpebat, non modo per Iudaeam, originem eius mali, sed per urbem etiam. igitur primum correpti sunt ei qui fatebantur, deinde indicio eorum multitudo ingens haud proinde in crimine incendii quam odio humani generis convicti sunt. ferarum tergis contecti laniatu canum perierunt aut crucibus adfixi, ubi defecit dies, in usum nocturni luminis urebantur. hortos suos ei spectaculo Nero obtulerat, et circense ludicrum edebat. itaque miseratio oriebatur, tamquam non utilitate publica, sed in saevitiam unius absumebantur.

ops, opis, f	power, means
largitio, largitionis, f	bribery
aut	or
placamentum, placamenti, n	appeasement
infamia, infamiae, f	disgrace
subdo, subdere, subdidi	substitute
reus, rei, m	a person accused of a crime
flagitium, flagitii, m	disgraceful action
invisus -a -um	hateful
vulgus, vulgi, n	crowd, mob
exitiabilis, exitiabile	deadly
modo	only
corripio, corripere, corripui, correptum	seize
fateor, fateri	confess
indicium, indicii, n	evidence
haud proinde . . . quam	'not so much . . . as . . .'
tergum, tergi, n	hide, skin
contego, contegere, contexi, contectum	cover
laniatus, laniatus, m	mangling, tearing
deficio, deficere, defeci	fail, run out
uro, urere	burn
ludicrum, ludicri, n	theatrical performance, show
orior, oriri	rise
absumo, absumere	waste, destroy

DERIVATIONS

This task builds skills in deducing the meaning of one word by using a related word.

The words below derive from words in the passages above which have not been glossed.

Can you find the Latin words from which these English words derive? Can you use either the Latin or the English word to help you explain the meaning of the other?

Remember that you will need to think about the part of speech of both the Latin and English words and – if they are different – you will need to consider how to adjust the meaning to move from one part of speech to the other.

humane, abolition, appellation, novel, superstition, original, multitude, criminal, conviction, feral, crucify, useful, horticulture, commiserate

scripta 15.8: Pliny writes to the emperor Trajan

This text is taken from Pliny's collection of letters. The majority of these provide a window into day-to-day life for Rome's ruling elite in the 1st to 2nd centuries AD, but the tenth book of letters is made up of correspondence between Pliny and the emperor Trajan.

Pliny had been sent to Bithynia as governor of the province in AD 110, and his correspondence highlights the process of imperial government. The letters offer a much calmer view of Roman history than the sensationalist biographies of Suetonius or the sharply critical analysis written by Tacitus. The letters below (10.33 and 10.34), however, highlight that in running the provinces, Trajan's first priority was to maintain Roman control.

Pliny to Trajan: When I was touring a different part of the province, an enormous fire destroyed many private homes in **Nicomedia** and two public buildings. The fire spread more widely, first because of the force of the wind, and second because of the idleness of the men: it is generally agreed that the people watching that disaster stood by inactive and motionless; what's more there is no fire hose anywhere, no fire-buckets, in short no equipment at all for fighting fires. These things, as I have already instructed, will now be obtained. But you, **master**, do you think that a society of firemen should be set up, numbering roughly 150 men? I shall watch out that no one joins it unless they are a fireman and that they do not use the rights they have been granted for any other purpose. It will not be difficult to keep an eye on so few men.

C Plinius Traiano Imperatori: ubi diversam partem provinciae circumibam, **Nicomediae** vastissimum incendium multas privatorum domos et duo publica opera, absumpsit. sparsum est autem latius, primum violentia venti, deinde inertia hominum: satis constat otiosos et immobiles tanti mali spectatores perstitisse; et alioqui nullus usquam in publico sipho, nulla hama, nullum denique instrumentum ad incendia compescenda. et haec quidem, ut iam praecepi, parabuntur; tu, **domine**, putasne collegium fabrorum instituendum esse, dumtaxat hominum CL? ego attendam ne quis nisi faber recipiatur neve iure concesso in aliud utantur; nec erit difficile custodire tam paucos.

> **Nicomedia** was the most important city in the province of Bithynia.

> Pliny calls Trajan **domine** as a mark of respect.

opus, operis, n	building
absumo, absumere, absumpsi	destroy
spargo, spargere, sparsi, sparsum	scatter, spread
latius	more widely
satis constat	'it is generally agreed'
otiosus -a -um	idle
tantus -a -um	so great
persto, perstare, perstiti	stand firm
alioqui	otherwise, in general
usquam	anywhere
sipho, siphonis, m	fire hose
hama, hamae, f	bucket
denique	in short, finally
compesco, compescere	hold in, restrain
quidem	indeed
praecipio, praecipere, praecepi	instruct
faber, fabri, m	workman
dumtaxat	not more than
ne quis . . . recipiatur	'so that no one is admitted'
neve . . . utantur (+ ablative)	'and that they should not use'
ius, iuris, n	right, entitlement
tam	so

Chapter 15 Tacitus, Suetonius, Pliny – Writers and the Emperors

Trajan to Pliny: Indeed, following the examples of many, it has come into your mind that a society of firemen could be set up among the Nicomedians. But you ought to remember that this province and especially these cities have been troubled by factions of this type. Whatever the name, whatever the reason we give to the men who have been brought together for a shared purpose, they will soon become a secret society. It is more than enough, therefore, to obtain the equipment which is helpful for controlling fires and to tell the masters of the estates to put the fires out themselves. Tell them that, if the situation requires it, they should summon others quickly and make use of their help.

Traianus Plinio: tibi quidem secundum exempla complurium in mentem venit posse collegium fabrorum apud Nicomedenses constitui. sed debes meminisse provinciam istam et praecipue eas civitates eius modi factionibus esse vexatas. quodcumque nomen ex quacumque causa damus iis, qui in idem contracti sunt, hetaeriae brevi tempore fient. satius itaque est comparare ea, quae ad coercendos ignes auxilio sunt, iubereque dominos praediorum ipsos inhibere ac, si res poposcerit, accursu populi ad hoc uti.

secundum (+ accusative)	following
complures, complurium	several
apud (+ accusative)	among
constituo, constituere, constitui	establish
meminisse	'to remember'
praecipue	especially
modus, modi, m	type
vexo, vexare	trouble, harass
quicumque, quaecumque, quodcumque	whoever, whatever
hetaeria, hetaeriae, f	secret society
fio, fieri, factus sum	become
auxilio sunt	'are a help'
praedium, praedii, n	large estate
si . . . poposcerit	'if [the situation] requires'
utor, uti (+ ablative)	make use of

DERIVATIONS

This task builds skills in deducing the meaning of one word by using another, related word.

The words below derive from words in the passages above which have not been glossed.

Can you find the Latin words from which these English words derive? Can you use either the Latin or the English word to help you explain the meaning of the other?

Remember that you will need to think about the part of speech of both the Latin and English words and – if they are different – you will need to consider how to adjust the meaning to move from one part of speech to the other.

diverse, inert, instrument, collegiate, institute, concession, faction, contract, coercive, inhibition

QUESTIONS FOR DISCUSSION

1. Tacitus is famous for his criticisms of Roman politics under the emperors: what criticisms does he make in the texts in this chapter? Do you think his criticisms are justified?

2. Suetonius seems to delight in scandal and sensational stories: do you think that entertainment is a good enough justification for his imaginative recreation of the past or do you think that his writing is impaired by details which seem too extreme at times to be believable?

3. What picture of power do you get from the texts in this chapter? Who had power and why? Does power shape a person's personality and actions? If so, how and why?

4. Both Tacitus and Suetonius are famous for their vivid descriptions and ability to create dramatic scenes. Explore the techniques used to create a striking scene in *scripta* 15.4, 15.5, 15.6 or 15.7.

5. Speech, rumour and private opinion offered Roman historians a chance to be imaginative and to colour their accounts with potentially controversial views. Explore the use of speech in these extracts and consider what this adds to the texts.

Chapter 15 Tacitus, Suetonius, Pliny – Writers and the Emperors

Chapter 15: Additional Language

SECTION A15: CHAPTER 15 VOCABULARY

Exercise A15.1: Derivations

This exercise explores derivations from the vocabulary list for Chapter 15.

Each of the words below derives from a Latin word. Find this Latin word and use it to help you explain the meaning of the English word. You may not know some of these words; think about what part of speech they might be and see if you can work out their meaning based on the Latin.

	derivation	Latin word and translation	meaning of the English derivation
1	vehement		
2	diligent		
3	imperious		
4	principal		
5	impulse		
6	captivate		
7	adjacent		
8	accidental		
9	simultaneous		
10	premium		

Exercise A15.2: Parts of speech

Sort the following words from the vocabulary list for Chapter 15 into the correct categories and write the meaning next to each word.

simul   praemium   antea   nisi   diligens   faveo
pello   umquam   iaceo   ut   dum   legio

noun	verb	adjective	adverb	conjunction

Exercise A15.3: Case endings (nouns and adjectives)

Circle the stem, and identify the declension of the following nouns and adjectives from Chapter 15. Then give the case requested.

	Latin	declension	
1	imperium, imperii, n		dative sg =
2	scelus, sceleris, n		nominative pl =
3	castra, castrorum, n pl		ablative pl =
4	legio, legionis, f		accusative pl =
5	victoria, victoriae, f		ablative sg =
6	captivus, captivi, m		dative pl =
7	princeps, principis, m		accusative sg =
8	lentus, lenta, lentum		ablative feminine pl =
9	scelestus, scelesta, scelestum		accusative masculine pl =
10	diligens, diligentis		accusative neuter pl =

Exercise A15.4: Verbs

The following verbs are from the vocabulary list for Chapter 15. Circle each of the stems of each verb: present, perfect and supine. Remember, not all verbs have all three stems. Then give the meaning of each verb and its conjugation.

Remember: some verbs don't have a supine.

	principal parts	meaning	conjugation
1	faveo, favere, favi, fautum (+ dative)		
2	iaceo, iacere, iacui		
3	accido, accidere, accidi		
4	resisto, resistere, restiti (+ dative)		
5	opprimo, opprimere, oppressi, oppressum		
6	pello, pellere, pepuli, pulsum		

Chapter 15 Tacitus, Suetonius, Pliny – Writers and the Emperors

Exercise A15.5: Cognates

In the table below are pairs of words: the first in each pair is a word from the vocabulary list for Chapter 15 and below it is a cognate word, i.e. a word which is related to it. You may not have met the cognate word before and it will not be listed in the vocabulary list at the back of this book.

Identify the part of speech of each Latin word and then give the meaning; you will have to work out the meaning of the second word by thinking about its part of speech and how it relates in meaning to the first word in each pair.

	Latin	part of speech	meaning
1	scelus, sceleris, n		
	scelestus, scelesta, scelestum		
2	victoria, victoriae, f		
	victor, victoris, m		
3	pello, pellere, pepuli, pulsum		
	pulsus, pulsus, m		
4	imperium, imperii, n		
	impero, imperare, imperavi, imperatum		
5	libenter		
	liber, libera, liberum		
6	captivus, captivi, m		
	captivitas, captivitatis, f		
7	legio, legionis, f		
	legionarius, legionaria, legionarium		
8	castra, castrorum, n pl		
	castrensis, castrense		
9	faveo, favere, favi, fautum (+ dative)		
	favor, favoris, m		
10	opprimo, opprimere, oppressi, oppressum		
	oppressio, oppressionis, f		

SECTION B15: WORD ENDINGS

Exercise B15.1: English finite verbs, participles and infinitives

This exercise uses verbs from the vocabulary lists for Chapters 13–15.

Sort the following English verbs into the table below according to whether they are finite verbs, participles or infinitives; identify the tense of each one and whether it is active or passive.

to have been overwhelmed speaking we were dying it was done
to resist I lie down having been driven they began
to have spoken to be hidden being about to offer we had begun
having spoken it was being felt to be about to rejoice

finite verb	participle	infinitive

Exercise B15.2: Labelling clauses and identifying conjunctions

Each of the English sentences below contains a main clause and a subordinate clause.

Underline the subordinate clause in each sentence, name what type of subordinate clause it is and select the correct Latin subordinating conjunction for it from the list below.

It may be useful to refer to the table on p114 to help you remember the names of the different types of subordinate clause.

quod   postquam   ubi   nisi   quam
    dum   quod   quamquam   si   qui

1. If you ever do wicked things, you will pay the penalty.
2. Because our feet were now tired, we were not rejoicing.
3. Unless we resist, all the captives will die.
4. The soldier was hiding his wound which was dreadful and large.
5. Although we were accustomed to rejoice, after the battle we did not feel joy.
6. She alone suffered while she supported the wicked emperor.
7. When they returned home, they were amazed at the courage of the children.
8. The unlucky captives, who did not know about the punishments, willingly entered the camp.
9. The whole legion, which the general had praised, suddenly overwhelmed the camp.
10. The faithful legions, after they had received a great victory, were greeted by the emperor.

Exercise B15.3: Turning phrases into clauses: indirect statement

This exercise uses vocabulary from Chapters 13–15.

Each of the sentences below contains an indirect statement. Practise translating these indirect statements by converting them into a subordinate clause in English, introduced by the conjunction *that*.

Each pair of sentences starts with a sentence with a present tense main verb and is then followed by a sentence with a past tense main verb: notice how the tense of the verb in the English subordinate clause changes when the main verb becomes a past tense.

1. exercitus sperat imperatorem praemia sibi oblaturum esse.
   exercitus sperabat imperatorem praemia sibi oblaturum esse.

2. scimus principem ipsum lentissime mortuum esse.
   sciebamus principem ipsum lentissime mortuum esse.

3. imperator sentit captivos libenter loqui.
   imperator sentiebat captivos libenter loqui.

4. captivi promittunt se voces non sublaturos esse.
   captivi promiserunt se voces non sublaturos esse.

5. imperator refert exercitum poenas dedisse.
   imperator rettulit exercitum poenas dedisse.

Exercise B15.4: Turning phrases into clauses: ablative absolute

Each of the sentences below contains an ablative absolute. For each sentence, translate the ablative absolute literally first, and then convert it into a subordinate clause in English, introduced by *when / while / after / since / because / although*.

Each pair of sentences starts with a present tense main verb and is then followed by a sentence with a past tense main verb: notice how the tense of the verb in the English subordinate clause changes when the main verb becomes a past tense.

1. femina resistente, filius non aufertur.
   femina resistente, filius non ablatus est.

2. hostibus vulneratis, milites arma colligunt.
   hostibus vulneratis, milites arma collegerunt.

3. militibus fugientibus, dux lacrimat.
   militibus fugientibus, dux lacrimabat.

4. castris oppressis, captivi effugiunt.
   castris oppressis, captivi effugerunt.

5. legionibus ad mare pulsis, princeps desperat.
   legionibus ad mare pulsis, princeps desperabat.

6. praemiis promissis, exercitus fortiter pugnat.
   praemiis promissis, exercitus fortiter pugnabat.

7. exercitu vehementer oppresso, pauci vivunt.
   exercitu vehementer oppresso, pauci vivebant.

8. victoria accepta, princeps scelestus imperium maximum habet.
   victoria accepta, princeps scelestus imperium maximum habebat.

Exercise B15.5: Gerundives

This exercise practises gerundives from the verbs in the vocabulary lists for Chapters 13–15.

Give a literal translation of each of the gerundives in the table below.

Remember: deponent verbs' gerundives have the same meaning as non-deponent verbs: e.g. *sequendus* – *needing to be followed*.

	gerundive	translation
1	celandus, celanda, celandum	
2	agendus, agenda, agendum	
3	patiendus, patienda, patiendum	
4	cognoscendus, cognoscenda, cognoscendum	
5	pellendus, pellenda, pellendum	
6	referendus, referenda, referendum	
7	tollendus, tollenda, tollendum	
8	sentiendus, sentienda, sentiendum	
9	cogitandus, cogitanda, cogitandum	
10	opprimendus, opprimenda, opprimendum	

Chapter 15 Tacitus, Suetonius, Pliny – Writers and the Emperors

Exercise B15.6: Forming gerundives

The following exercise uses verbs from the vocabulary lists for Chapters 13–15.

For each of the verbs given below, circle the present tense stem, identify the conjugation, and then give and translate its gerundive.

Remember that deponent verbs form their gerundive in exactly the same way as the non-deponent verbs in their conjugation.

	principal parts	conjugation	gerundive (in Latin and English)
1	sequor, sequi, secutus sum		
2	conor, conari, conatus sum		
3	scio, scire, scivi, scitum		
4	spero, sperare, speravi, speratum		
5	audeo, audere, ausus sum		
6	loquor, loqui, locutus sum		
7	ago, agere, egi, actum		
8	opprimo, opprimere, oppressi, oppressum		
9	miror, mirari, miratus sum		
10	cogito, cogitare, cogitavi, cogitatum		

Exercise B15.7: Expressions of time

The following Latin words are all used to express time. Translate each word and label as an adverb, preposition or subordinating conjunction.

		meaning	part of speech
1	postquam		
2	postea		
3	post (+ accusative)		
4	ante (+ accusative)		
5	antea		
6	antequam		
7	simulac		
8	simul		
9	ubi		
10	nunc		

SECTION C15: ENGLISH TO LATIN SENTENCES

Exercise C15.1: Cases and clauses

This exercise practises identifying cases within clauses. Remember that every finite verb creates its own clause and the case of a noun / pronoun will depend upon its role in that clause.

Identify the case of each of the nouns / pronouns in bold in the sentences below by thinking about its relationship to the finite verb in its clause. Then translate each noun / pronoun into Latin.

1. While several **legions** were advancing, the **emperor** preferred to write a letter.
2. After the **camp** was overwhelmed, the **army** captured the **enemy** fleeing towards the sea.
3. As soon as the **voice** of the **emperor** was heard, the **crowd** was silent.
4. I began to steal the **gold, which** was in the temple, because I did not fear **the punishment**.
5. If we did good **things**, **we** will be praised by our friends.
6. Your **toils**, unless **you yourself** work quickly, will be long and difficult.
7. Although the **general** spoke violently before the battle, now we see **him** rejoicing.
8. These **crimes**, **which** I shall show to **you**, are dreadful and wicked.
9. We noticed the **camp**, **which** had been burned by your army.
10. When the **voice** of the bold leader was heard, all the **captives** sensed danger.

Exercise C15.2: Expressions of time

The English sentences below contain different expressions of time. Match the Latin phrases below to the words in bold in the English sentences.

multos dies   cras   postea   tertio die
     antequam   interea   diu   paucas horas
postquam   totam diem   post   dum

1. **After** the army arrived, the chief began to speak.
2. Light arrives **after** a long night.
3. The battle was long and difficult. **Afterwards**, we all wept greatly.
4. The town was quickly overwhelmed. **For many days** the captives suffered.
5. **On the third day**, the prisoner was killed.
6. Rejoice! **Tomorrow**, you will be set free.
7. **While** you were walking in the forum, the senator was speaking many words.
8. **Before** the enemy entered the city, there was peace **for a long time**.
9. I was alone **for the whole day**. I read my books **for a few hours**.
10. The women were captured by the soldiers. **Meanwhile** the daring children escaped.

Chapter 15 Tacitus, Suetonius, Pliny – Writers and the Emperors

Exercise C15.3: Sentences to translate into Latin

1. With several people speaking, many voices from the crowd were heard.
2. When my dreadful crime had been found out, I knew that I would pay the penalty.
3. After the cruel punishments had been given, the commander promised that he would soon set out.
4. With his hands raised to the sky, the emperor spoke boldly to the legion.
5. If today there is hope of victory, tomorrow we shall rejoice.
6. The emperor, whom the legions favoured, gave many rewards to his faithful army.
7. A certain captive resisted, but the rest put down their weapons.
8. Because the legion, having set out before first light, had advanced for five days, the emperor was able to win.
9. We live without many cares and we often rejoice in our souls, because at home our toils are brief.
10. While the army was advancing towards the camp, the soldiers were hoping that the generals would not capture them.

CHAPTER 16
CATULLUS, HORACE,
TIBULLUS, MARTIAL –
SHORTER POEMS

Chapter 16: Introduction

> The Latin verb *erudio* means *teach, refine*. Explain the meaning of *erudite*.

Shorter poems: the influence of the Alexandrian poets

In the 1st century BC a group of Roman poets began to take their inspiration from the **Alexandrian poets** of the 3rd century BC rather than from epic poetry. The Alexandrian writers had developed an approach to poetry which was wide-reaching in its content and self-consciously erudite in its reference to myth, other texts and in the way words were used in an overtly clever way.

The Alexandrian writers produced material which included mini-epics, religious hymns, pastoral poetry celebrating the countryside, didactic poems and very short epigrams. The Roman poets made use of the Alexandrian variety of content and metrical forms but injected into it a personal approach and **depth of feeling** which was their own. These poets are sometimes referred to as the **neoterics** ('new poets') and their work marked the beginning of several new genres of Latin poetry.

Genre and metre

Because of the tight relationship between Latin literature and its Greek precedents, different metrical forms brought with them different expectations. This means that the concept of genre within Roman literature is as much connected with metre as it is with content. Chapter 14 explored epic poetry, a genre characterised by the hexameter metre. Much of the poetry in this chapter, however, is written in a lighter metre known as **elegiac couplets** (you can read more about this in *Appendix 2: Latin Metre*, p215). Since these poems often focused on love affairs, the term '**Latin elegy**' gradually became associated with **love poetry** of this period, but elegiac poems were not restricted solely to this.

FIGURE 16.1 Mosaic of Erato, the muse of love poetry

This is a section from a much larger mosaic from *c.* AD 240. The mosaic depicts the 9 muses, the goddesses who inspired artistic endeavour. In this section we can see Erato, the muse of love poetry. Epic poets traditionally opened their poems with a call to the muses for inspiration but in *scripta* 16.1 you can find Tibullus taking a different approach: rejected by his beloved he begs the divine muse to leave him alone. The mosaic is now in Luxembourg in the MNAHA Collections.

Shorter poems in a Roman context

In this chapter you will meet a broad range of content taken from the poems of **Catullus, Horace, Tibullus** and **Martial**. Their work spans the time period from the late Republic through to the Augustan age and into the reigns of the emperors Domitian, Nerva and Trajan.

Rome's shorter poems can feel intensely personal and it can seem like they reveal the true feelings of the writer. Literary expectations, however, required writers to prove their worth by their ability to **imitate or create a wide range of content and styles**: sometimes a poem which seems very personal is largely a reworking of a Greek precedent. Each poem offers us the chance to step into a set of feelings or a scenario which feels real and immediate, but it is important not to be surprised if one poem seems to contradict the values or the viewpoint of another poem written by the same poet.

> The Latin verb *praecedo* means *go before*. Explain the meaning of *precedent*.

In *scripta* 16.1, you can read thoughts about the **power and purpose of poetry** from three different poets. You might find surprising the degree to which poetry seems to be self-serving and viewed as a way to impress or win favour with others. In a society as competitive as Rome, the need to impress others never seems to be far away. The intensity of the emotions expressed in many of the poems often seems like the most important aspect of the poem, but it will be useful to keep thinking about the way each poem is also a vehicle for the poet to display their own poetic skill, inventiveness or ability to re-work a Greek model within a Roman context.

Culture and customs

The poets in this chapter are part of a **cultural elite**, writing for a highly educated audience. It would be inappropriate to take their work as representative of Roman society on a broader scale, but the personal nature of their poetry still offers a window into some forms of daily life in Rome and some of the values at that time.

Religious observance remained an important aspect within Roman society, and praise for the gods is a common theme within Roman poetry. In *scripta* 16.2, you can read a **Latin hymn**, a religious poetic song, by Catullus in praise of the goddess Diana. This hymn reflects the importance of the goddess to the Romans but it also acts as a vehicle for demonstrating Catullus' **poetic skill**. As you read the poem you may find it interesting to think about how Catullus manages to combine breath of content with concision and how he creates elegance through his use of sound and word order, balancing repetition against variation.

Not all poetry, however, focused on such solemn and serious content. Shorter poetry often discussed simple, **every-day matters** and interpersonal relationships, often in a bitingly critical way. *scripta* 16.3 offers us insight into Roman attitudes to **patronage**, **marriage**, **friendship**, **justice** and **slavery**. Running through several of the *scripta* 16.3 poems is the importance of **money** and its power. Catullus writes a poem in praise of his patron; this poem acts as a reminder of the give-and-take nature of the **patron–client** relationship. As you read in Chapter 11, a wealthier Roman could act as a patron and offer financial support to his less wealthy clients; in return they could be relied upon to demonstrate their patron's status through flattery and personal support. Other poems within the *scripta* 16.3 selection indicate that money could be a reason for marriage or that bribery could be a convenient

FIGURE 16.2 Statue of Diana

This statue of Diana is a Roman copy of a lost Greek statue. The original Greek version was made from bronze. Diana was worshipped as the patron goddess of hunters, the moon and young girls; this statue represents her mastery over the untamed wilderness. The statue is currently in the Louvre in Paris.

Chapter 16 Catullus, Horace, Tibullus, Martial – Shorter Poems

> The Latin noun *exemplum* means *example*. Explain the meaning of *exemplified*.

way to secure a particular outcome in the law courts. The power of shorter poems to deliver cutting **criticism** is also exemplified in this selection and you might think it interesting to think about what gets criticised and why.

Grief, love, hatred and laughter

Within Roman society, there were a number of *virtutes* – moral traits – which the Romans believed to be important. Three of the most important of these were *pietas* (dutifulness), *prudentia* (discretion or self-restraint) and *severitas* (self-control). Each of these conceptualises the belief that it is necessary to some degree to have control or restraint over strong emotions or impulses and to be ready to act as society requires even if these actions are painful or difficult.

The more personal nature of much of Rome's shorter poetry provided the opportunity to explore this concept. The **emotional intensity** of many of the poems in this chapter reveals moments where self-control or restraint breaks down and the poem provides an outlet for grief, love or hatred. In *scripta* **16.4**, grief is to the fore: the poet exemplifies *pietas* in his commitment to performing **funeral rites for his brother**, but *severitas* breaks down when Catullus weeps and hands over tear-soaked offerings. In the same section, Horace offers a different view on *pietas*: he describes his decision to **worship the gods** again but this is a decision which has arisen because of the extent of his fear of their power.

The poems in the *scripta* **16.5** selection focus on the feelings caused by **falling in love**. Catullus' poems convey how love affairs often bring with them a mixture of joy, hatred, jealousy and pain; the extract from a much longer poem by Tibullus conveys the powerlessness of someone experiencing uncontrollable feelings. The poets' readiness to describe the intensity of these emotions challenges the traditional Roman *virtutes* of self-restraint; in addition, their decision to characterise themselves as lovers deepens this challenge. Writers such as Catullus and Tibullus highlighted the personal choice available to Roman men: rather than seeking military glory or political power, the love poets chose to fight for or to be enslaved to love. Love poetry also brings the experience of women to the fore; the love poets often explore the dynamics of power and control, highlighting the contrast between the restrictions married women faced and their power over their potential lovers.

Despite the Roman interest in self-restraint, there seemed to be very little need for Romans to be restrained in the criticisms they made of other Romans. In Chapter 8, Source 8.3, you met an example of how oratory could be used to create savage attacks on personal or political enemies. The final selection of poems – *scripta* **16.6** – provides examples of the ways in which poetry could also be used for **personal attacks**. The poems by Catullus and Martial aim to entertain by encouraging the reader to laugh at or look down on someone else.

FIGURE 16.3 Lesbia and her sparrow

Many of Catullus' love poems describe his love affair and fascination with a woman called Lesbia. This relationship has provided inspiration for other artists for centuries. The 19th-century English painter, Edward Poynter, painted this image of Lesbia, inspired by Catullus 2 and 3. In Catullus 2, the author describes the affectionate relationship between Lesbia and her pet sparrow, even expressing envy for the way the sparrow lifts Lesbia's mood. Catullus laments the death of the sparrow in poem 3 and the great sorrow felt by Lesbia. You can read more about Lesbia in *scripta* **16.5**.

Roman poetry: then and now

As you read the *scripta* for this chapter, you will find much that still rings true but you will also find content which allows you to reflect on how different attitudes and cultural values are today. At times you may find the content of the poetry in this chapter **shocking or unattractive**, but the selection of texts printed serve to remind us of poetry's ability to **distil, engage and provoke** even at a distance of thousands of years.

> The Latin participle *tentus* means *held, contained*. Explain the meaning of *content*.

FIGURE 16.4 Tibullus in the company of his lover, Delia

This painting by the 19th-century artist Lawrence Alma-Tadema, depicts a party with Delia, Tibullus' lover and the focus of much of his poetry. In ***scripta* 16.5** you can read an extract from one of his poems about Delia, highlighting the turbulent nature of their relationship.

Chapter 16 Catullus, Horace, Tibullus, Martial – Shorter Poems

CHAPTER 16: READ THE *SCRIPTA* IN ENGLISH

The texts for each scripta *are printed in this book in Latin and English. These texts can be read in English, Latin or a combination of the two. The* scripta *texts for this chapter start on p. 176. They follow the Core Language section because their Latin versions contain new grammar and vocabulary from this chapter.*

The questions below can be answered by reading the scripta *in English. Available on the Companion Website are copies of the English version of each* scripta *along with the questions for each text.*

scripta 16.1 in English (p178): Reflections on the role of poetry

1. What benefit does Martial say he gets from his poetry?
2. What role has poetry played in Catullus' feelings for Licinius? Why are these feelings a mixture of joy and pain?
3. The extracts from Tibullus' poem suggest that he feels powerless: explain why this is, supporting your answer with as many details as possible from the poem.
4. Martial, Catullus and Tibullus all suggest that writing poetry can bring some sort of personal benefit. Are you surprised by this? What do you think the purpose of poetry is?

scripta 16.2 in English (p182): Religious poetry

1. Diana is worshipped in this hymn by virgin boys and girls: what does this symbolise about her power?
2. Like many other Roman gods, Diana was believed to have power that reached over a wide range of contexts. List as many different domains for her power as you can find in this poem.
3. Which details in this poem focus on Diana's identity as a female deity?
4. Religious hymns were designed to flatter a god and thus win their approval: how does Catullus praise Diana in this poem?

scripta 16.3 in English (p184): Roman customs and daily life

1. In each poem what does the poet (or central character) seem to care about most?
2. Think about the tone of Martial's poetry: can you find examples of sarcasm, humour and scorn?
3. Martial and Catullus are both famous for their concision. Which poem do you think manages to convey the most information relative to its length?
4. Which poem do you think shows the most unappealing aspect of Roman society, and why?

scripta 16.4 in English (p188): Death, grief and fear

1 Catullus has travelled a long way in order to perform funeral rites for his brother; he seems to have mixed feelings about the value of these rites. What are these feelings and which are the details in the poem which convey them?
2 How does Catullus convey his grief at his brother's death?
3 Horace uses a sailing metaphor to describe his changed relationship with the gods. What is this change and why has Horace altered the way he worships the gods?
4 Horace describes Jupiter in a way which emphasises his power. What are the details in his description which convey this?
5 What image is used to convey Fortune's frightening power to change someone's circumstances? What is terrifying about this image?

scripta 16.5 in English (p191): Love poetry

1 Read the first two poems by Catullus (48 and 85). These poems give a different impression of how it feels to be in love. Describe in your own words how the poet is feeling in each poem.
2 Read the three poems about Lesbia (Catullus 58, 83 and 87).
  a Who is angry in these poems and why?
  b How do you interpret the tone of poem 87: do you think Catullus is angry or does this poem convey a different emotion? Explain your answer.
3 How does the extract from Tibullus' poem convey feelings of powerlessness and pain? You might like to discuss the imagery used as well as other details from the poem.
4 Think about these poems in the context of modern-day love poems or songs: how do they compare? Do you think attitudes to writing about love have changed over time or not?

scripta 16.6 in English (p194): Insults

1 Summarise the insults in each of the poems.
2 Which poem do you find the most interesting and why?
3 These poems are all written by men but each poem contains at least one female character. What impression do you get of male attitudes towards women and female attitudes towards men at this time?

Chapter 16: Core Language Vocabulary List

hortor	hortari, hortatus sum	encourage; urge
impero	imperare, imperavi, imperatum (+ dative)	order; command
oro	orare, oravi, oratum	beg
cogo	cogere, coegi, coactum	force; compel
reddo	reddere, reddidi, redditum	give back; restore
surgo	surgere, surrexi	get up; stand up; rise
verto	vertere, verti, versum	turn
conficio	conficere, confeci, confectum	finish; wear out
ianua	ianuae, f	door
vita	vitae, f	life
inimicus	inimici, m	(personal) enemy
modus	modi, m	manner; way; kind
consul	consulis, m	consul
custos	custodis, m/f	guard
tempestas	tempestatis, f	storm
summus	summa, summum	highest; greatest; top (of)
proximus	proxima, proximum	nearest; next to
quantus?	quanta? quantum?	how big? how much?
qualis?	quale?	what sort of?
quomodo?		how?
quot?		how many?
talis	tale	such; of such a kind
tantus	tanta, tantum	so great; such a great
adeo		so much; so greatly; to such an extent
ita		in this way; to such an extent; so
tam		so
tot		so many

cum	+ subjunctive	when; since; although
ne	+ subjunctive	that . . . not; so that . . . not; that; lest
ut	+ subjunctive	that; so that; in order that
num		whether

Further notes on tense: aspect

So far, you have learned how **tense** denotes **time**. Chapter 15 focused on how the time denoted by a verb's tense operates differently for finite and non-finite forms of the verb:

- the tense of the **finite verbs** you have met so far shows whether an action belongs to **past**, **present** or **future time**

- the tense of the **non-finite verbs** shows whether an action was **before**, **at the same time** or **yet to happen** at the time of the main verb.

There is another important dimension, however, to the tenses of verbs. This dimension is called **aspect** and denotes **how the action is viewed**.

One and the same action can be viewed in different ways: different aspects are possible for actions which took place at the same time. Consider the following English sentences:

Yesterday, **I ran** for 5 minutes at 3pm.   past time, completed aspect
Yesterday, **I was running** for 5 minutes at 3pm. past time, continuous aspect

PRACTISE YOUR VERBS

Think about each of the following verbs: is the action viewed as finished / completed or continuous / not-yet finished?

1. **They were fighting** against the enemy.
2. **They conquered** the enemy.
3. **I saw** the ship.
4. **I am running**.
5. **You will hear** the poet.
6. **She had learned** the words.

Chapter 16 Catullus, Horace, Tibullus, Martial – Shorter Poems

> The label **perfect** derives from the Latin verb *perficio, perficere, perfeci, perfectum* – *finish, complete*.

The aspects of the Latin verb

There are two different **aspects** for Latin's finite verbs.

- Tenses that use the **present stem** have a **continuous aspect**, i.e. the action is viewed as something on-going or not-yet finished.

- Tenses that use the **perfect stem** or **PPP** have a **completed aspect**, i.e. the action is viewed as something finished or complete.

The table below shows how Latin's finite verb tenses operate in time and in aspect. The stem of each verb is in **bold** to highlight that forms that **share the same stem, share the same aspect**.

aspect = viewed as continuous / not-yet finished	
past time	imperfect active – **reg**ebam – I was ruling
	imperfect passive – **reg**ebar – I was being ruled
present time	present active – **reg**o – I rule / I am ruling
	present active – **reg**or – I am ruled / I am being ruled
future time	future active – **reg**am – I shall rule
	future passive – **reg**ar – I shall be ruled

aspect = viewed as finished	
past time	perfect active – **rex**i – I ruled
	pluperfect active – **rex**eram – I had ruled
	perfect passive – **rectus** sum – I was ruled
	pluperfect passive – **rectus** eram – I had been ruled
present time	
future time	future perfect – **rex**ero – I shall have ruled
	future perfect passive – **rectus** ero – I shall have been ruled

There is no verb tense which denotes viewed-as-finished aspect in present time: this is because if an action is taking place right now, it is necessarily viewed as not-yet finished.

> You have not met the **future perfect** before. It is explained in full in Appendix 1, p209.

EXERCISE 16.1

English verb forms can be very complex and there are more variations of finite verb forms than in Latin. Consider the verbs in **bold** below and decide which Latin tense would be used to translate them. To do this, you will need to think about **time** and **aspect** and work out which Latin tense is the best fit for the English.

1. Every day **we used to resist** the enemy.

    past time, not-yet finished aspect → imperfect tense

2. Tomorrow, **I am going to be lying** in the garden.
3. Today, **I do beg** you, but yesterday **I was silent**.
4. Every day during the last war the soldiers **would fight** bravely.
5. Yesterday **we kept on resisting** the troops, but today **we are being overwhelmed**.
6. **Did you stand up**?
7. Tomorrow, **will you have finished** the work?
8. Tomorrow, **will you be commanding** the soldiers?
9. Yesterday, **you resisted** the inhabitants for many hours.
10. Today **I am returning** to the city and **I rejoice**.

Chapter 16 Catullus, Horace, Tibullus, Martial – Shorter Poems

> **Subjunctive** derives from the Latin *subiungo* – join to; subordinate

The subjunctive

The finite verb tenses you have met so far are all known as **indicatives**. This is because they **indicate** an action in past, present or future time.

Latin has another type of finite verb, known as the **subjunctive**. It is used primarily in **subordinate** clauses.

The two most common tenses of the Latin subjunctive are the **imperfect** and **pluperfect**. These names can be confusing because the imperfect and pluperfect subjunctives are often different in meaning from the imperfect and pluperfect indicatives. Furthermore, they do not have a fixed English translation: instead, their translation depends on the type of subordinate clause they are in.

For the subjunctive, tense reveals **aspect**, not time:

- **imperfect subjunctive**: actions which are viewed as continuous / not-yet finished;
- **pluperfect subjunctive**: actions which are viewed as finished.

The imperfect and pluperfect subjunctive are shown in the table below; note that the **stem used** matches the **aspect** of the verb.

No translation is given in the table since the Latin subjunctive is **translated differently** in **different clauses**.

	imperfect subjunctive – continuous / not-yet finished aspect	pluperfect subjunctive – finished aspect
active	reg**erem** reg**eres** reg**eret** reg**eremus** reg**eretis** reg**erent**	rex**issem** rex**isses** rex**isset** rex**issemus** rex**issetis** rex**issent**
passive	reg**erer** reg**ereris** reg**eretur** reg**eremur** reg**eremini** reg**erentur**	rect**us** essem rect**us** esses rect**us** esset rect**i** essemus rect**i** essetis rect**i** essent

> **Note that** the ending for the PPP has to **agree** with its subject; a feminine subject will require feminine endings and so forth.

Because the imperfect subjunctive uses the **present stem**, the vowels used depend on the **conjugation**; the forms for all conjugations are listed in full in the Reference Grammar on p241.

Fear clauses

Originally, the Latin subjunctive was used for actions which were in some way in the mind of the subject of the sentence's main clause. Fear clauses are a good example of this.

The consul feared that the citizens would not support the new emperor.
— main clause — — fear clause —

The action in the fear clause is something which the sentence's subject – the consul – is thinking about; it may, or may not, actually happen.

Latin uses the subordinating conjunction **ne** to introduce a fear clause. The verb in the fear clause will be a subjunctive and its tense will depend upon the **aspect** of the action feared.

A fear that something **would happen** / **was already happening**	aspect = viewed as ongoing / not-yet finished	**ne** + imperfect subjunctive
A fear that something **had happened**	aspect = viewed as finished	**ne** + pluperfect subjunctive

Adverbs can be used to help make the time of the action clear:

consul timebat ne cives principi non faverent.
  The consul feared that the citizens would not support the new emperor.

consul timebat ne cives principi non iam faverent.
  The consul feared that the citizens did not support the emperor now.

EXERCISE 16.2

1. consul timebat ne tempestas naves **delevisset**.
2. custos timebat ne captivi **morerentur**.
3. inimici mei timebant ne ad urbem **regrederer**.
4. imperator timebat ne hostes iam **progrederentur**.
5. legio timebat ne imperator praemia sibi non **offerret**.
6. civis timebat ne princeps scelus **cognosceret**.
7. timebatis ne nullam spem vitae **haberemus**.
8. magister timebat ne labor a liberis non **confectus esset**.
9. incolae timebant ne Romani se **opprimerent**.
10. mulier, simulac domum regressa est, timebat ne ancillae **fugissent**.

The **subjunctive** verbs are in bold. Identify the **tense** for each one and whether the subjunctive is **active** or **deponent**.

Chapter 16 Catullus, Horace, Tibullus, Martial – Shorter Poems

> **Further notes on verbs of fearing**
>
> Note that verbs of fearing are not always followed by a clause. Sometimes, an **object** or **action** is feared, rather than an **event**.
>
> | fearing an **object** | fear-verb + **accusative noun** |
> |---|---|
> | | bellum timebam.   I feared the battle. |
> | fearing an **action** | fear-verb + **infinitive** |
> | | pugnare timebam.   I was afraid to fight. |
> | fearing an **event** | fear-verb + **ne** + **subjunctive** |
> | | timebam ne hostes urbem oppugnarent.   I was afraid that the enemy would attack the city. |

EXERCISE 16.3

Look at the words in bold. Identify each as either an **accusative** noun / pronoun, **infinitive** or **subjunctive**.

1. omnes cives **mortem** principis timebant.
2. in magna tempestate nautae **navigare** timent.
3. senator timebat ne cives sibi non **faverent**.
4. 'in ludis,' inquiunt liberi, 'leones **nos** terrebant. volebamus domum redire.'
5. cur, o milites, timebatis ad castra **procedere**?
6. quod oppidum incensum est, nunc de vita maxime timemus.
7. 'numquam,' inquit miles fortissimus, '**periculum** timere solebam.'
8. poeta, quod putabat cives se non audituros esse, in foro **loqui** timebat.
9. consules vehementer timebant pecuniam **reddere** et scelus **ostendere**.
10. milites huius legionis timebant ne castra **deleta essent**.

Purpose clauses and indirect commands

A **purpose clause** states an action which is the intended **purpose** of the main clause:

> The slave got up | so that she might hurry to the temple.
> main clause | purpose clause

An **indirect command** reports what someone **commanded / told / asked** someone else to do.

> The consul urged the citizens | that they should crush their enemies.
> main clause | indirect command

It is easy to confuse these types of expression because it is much more natural in English to express them in the same way with an **infinitive phrase** instead of a clause:

> The slave got up **to hurry to the temple**.
> The consul urged the citizens **to crush their enemies**.

Latin, however, typically uses a **clause**: the same construction is used for both **purpose clauses** and **indirect commands**

intending **to do something** / telling someone **to do something**	**ut** + imperfect subjunctive
intending **not to do something** / telling someone **not to do something**	**ne** + imperfect subjunctive

The subjunctive is used because these actions are in the mind of the sentence's subject; they may not actually happen. The **imperfect subjunctive** is used in these clauses because an intended / commanded action is necessarily something which is **viewed as not-yet finished**.

> **Note that** some Latin verbs match the English infinitive construction, for example *iubeo* + infinitive.

Chapter 16 Catullus, Horace, Tibullus, Martial – Shorter Poems

> Look at the **subjunctives** in bold. Is each one **active**, **passive** or **deponent**?

EXERCISE 16.4

1. dux militibus imperavit ut fortissime **pugnarent**.
2. in foro cives surrexerunt ut principem novum **salutarent**.
3. consul a civibus iratis coactus est ut Roma **fugeret**.
4. mater paterque liberos hortati sunt ut diligenter **laborarent**.
5. ego custodem orabam ne me **occideret**.
6. cur imperator milites non hortatus est ut celerrime **progrederentur**?
7. poeta amicos oravit ut hos libros **legerent**.
8. ad mare processimus ne prope domum **inveniremur**.
9. libenter turba consules hortabatur ut pacem incolis **offerrent**.
10. haec dona ad templa portavisti ut dei laeti **essent**.

| *scripta* in Latin | you could now look at the Latin version of *scripta* 16.1 |

Demonstrative adjectives and adverbs

In Chapter 7 you met two **demonstrative pronouns**.

| hic, haec, hoc | this, these |
| ille, illa, illud | that, those |

> *Demonstrative* derives from the Latin verb ***demonstro*** – show

Demonstrative words point something out. They are used to draw attention to something or to emphasise it.

Latin also has **demonstrative adjectives** and **adverbs**.

tantus	tanta, tantum	so great; such a great
talis	tale	such; of such a kind
tot		so many
ita		in this way; to such an extent; so
tam		so
adeo		so much; so greatly; to such an extent

Although **tot** is used to describe a noun, it never changes its form.

ita is an adverb which emphasises the **extent to which** or **how** an action took place; *tam* is an adverb which emphasises the **degree** to which an adjective or adverb applies.

Romani **ita** pugnaverunt.   The Romans fought **in this way**.
mater **tam** laeta est.   My mother is **so** happy.
Romani **tam** fortiter pugnaverunt. The Romans fought **so** bravely.

EXERCISE 16.5

1. quod **tot** amicos habemus, laeti sumus!
2. poeta **tam** diligenter laboravit quod librum optimum scribere volebat.
3. agricola **tales** equos conspexit et statim illos emere volebat.
4. quod multas horas **ita** pugnabant, milites confecti sunt.
5. Romani, quod **tantum** imperium habebant, clarissimi erant.
6. 'miserrimus sum!' inquit nauta, 'nam tempestas **tanta tot** naves delevit!'
7. quod **tot** inimicos habebat, consul **ita** desperabat.
8. 'malo **ita** vivere,' inquit civis. '**illa** vita dira est.'
9. **hoc** oppidum est proximum; **tot** incolae ibi habitant.
10. liberi **tam** vehementer lacrimabant quod vulnerati sunt.

Translate each of the **demonstrative** words in bold.

| *scripta* in Latin | you could now look at the Latin version of *scripta* 16.2 |

Chapter 16 Catullus, Horace, Tibullus, Martial – Shorter Poems

> ### Result clauses
>
> Although the subjunctive was originally used in subordinate clauses where the action was in some way in the mind of the main clause's subject, over time its use spread into other types of subordinate clauses, such as **result clauses**.
>
> A **result clause** states an action which happened, or was likely to happen, **as a result of** the main clause.
>
> The Romans fought bravely with the result that they won.
>   main clause   result clause
>
> In Latin, **ut** + **subjunctive** is used.
>
> It is very common for the main clause to contain a **demonstrative** word to **emphasise** why the result took place.
>
> cives **tam** fortiter pugnaverunt **ut** dux non iam **timeret**.
>   The citizens fought so bravely that their leader was no longer afraid.
>
> Notice that because the action expressed by the subjunctive is **not** 'in the mind' (see p165), its translation **is the same as** the equivalent tense of the **indicative**.

EXERCISE 16.6

> Look at each of the **subjunctive** verbs in bold: is it **active**, **passive** or **deponent**?

1. consul novus tot amicos habebat ut multi cives ei **faverent**.
2. hic hortus tam pulcher erat ut ab omnibus **laudaretur**.
3. captivi adeo vulnerati erant ut dormire non **possent**.
4. milites cum hostibus tot horas pugnabant ut tandem fugere **vellent**.
5. dux tales copias habebat ut hostes vehementer **terrerentur**.
6. hic exercitus tanta castra posuit ut incolae, qui prope castra habitabant, **mirarentur**.
7. cives tantam spem pacis habebant ut contra principem novum non **pugnarent**.
8. hoc templum tanta arte aedificatum est ut dei laetissimi **essent**.
9. poenas ita dedimus ut postea nullum amorem sceleris **haberemus**.
10. custos tam scelestus erat ut omnes captivos interfecturus **esset**.

scripta in Latin   you could now look at the Latin version of *scripta* 16.3

Subordinate clauses introduced by *cum*

As explained in Chapter 15, in Latin **temporal clauses** introduced by *ubi, postquam, antequam, dum, simulac / simulatque* usually use the **indicative**.

cum (*when, since, although*), however, is typically followed by a subjunctive. Like result clauses, because the action in this type of subordinate clause is **not** in the mind, the translation of the subjunctive **is the same as** the equivalent tense of the **indicative**.

> cum hostes **fugerent**, Romani castra ceperunt.
> Since the enemy **were fleeing**, the Romans captured their camp.
>
> cum hostes **fugissent**, dux praemia militibus dedit.
> When the enemy **had fled**, the general gave rewards to his soldiers.

Note that this is a different word from the preposition *cum* – *with*.

EXERCISE 16.7

1. frater sororque, cum domum redire **vellent**, quam celerrime per silvas festinaverunt.
2. cum castra ab hostibus **incensa essent**, milites magnopere desperabant.
3. cum **vulnerata esses**, o domina, sanguinem plurimum conspexisti.
4. cum tanta praemia militibus **oblata essent**, dux sperabat se victoriam clarissimam habiturum esse.
5. cum parentes **mortui essent**, filia tristissima curas magnas habebat.
6. cum epistulam diram a principe missam **accepissem**, tamen maxime gaudebam.
7. cum pedes vestri fessi **essent**, ambulare non poteratis.
8. amici poetae, cum eum laetum esse **vellent**, verba laudaverunt.
9. cum ad flumen **progrederemur**, ancillam lacrimantem prope domum vidimus.
10. cum senatores irati **essent**, consul de imperio suo timebat.

Look at each of the **subjunctives** in bold: is it **imperfect** or **pluperfect** tense?

When **cum** means *although*, **tamen** is often used at the start of the main clause.

| *scripta* in Latin | you could now look at the Latin version of *scripta* 16.4 |

Chapter 16 Catullus, Horace, Tibullus, Martial – Shorter Poems

Question words

You have now met the following **question words**:

quis	quis, quid	who? what? which?
quantus	quanta, quantum	how big? how great?
qualis	quale	what sort of?
quo		to where?
ubi		where?
quot		how many?
quomodo		how?
cur		why?

> Although **quot** is used to describe a noun, it never changes its form.

quis, quis, quid is a pronoun; its forms are listed in full in the Reference Grammar on p226. Like all pronouns, it will take the gender and number of the noun it represents and its case will depend upon its role in its clause.

quantus, quanta, quantum is a 2-1-2 adjective; **qualis, quale** is a 3rd declension adjective. Their endings follow the usual patterns, as listed in the Reference Grammar on p221–2. Like all adjectives, *quantus* and *qualis* must agree with the noun they describe in case, gender and number.

In addition, you have also met the following words at the start of a *yes / no* question.

-ne	indicates that the answer to the question is *yes* or *no*
num	indicates that the question invites the answer *no*
nonne	indicates that the question invites the answer *yes*

EXERCISE 16.8

> Translate each of the **question words** in bold.

1. ubi me loquentem audivisti, **cur** caput non vertisti?
2. '**quot** equos emisiti?' filia patrem rogavit. 'sunt**ne** pulcherrimi celerrimique?'
3. **qualem** villam aedificare volebatis?
4. **ubi** liberos lacrimantes vidistis? obtulistis**ne** eis auxilium?
5. **cur** civis notissimus in foro non ambulabat? nolebat**ne** amicos salutare?
6. **quis** pecuniam meam abstulit? quamquam pecuniam in loco tuto celavi, nunc eam invenire non possum.
7. **quomodo** tot hostes occidisti? fortior es quam ceteri milites.
8. '**quanta** erat victoria?' cives nuntium rogaverunt. 'omnia audire volumus!'
9. **quo** servi fugerunt? quod dominum interfecerant, timebant ne punirentur.
10. in hoc domo nemo adest: mater, pater, filii, filiaeque absunt. **quem** primum quaeremus?

scripta in Latin — you could now look at the Latin version of *scripta* 16.5

LABELING VERBS

The verbs below are all from Exercise 16.8. Is each verb a finite verb or not?

If it is a finite verb, which person is it? If it is not a finite verb, is it a participle or an infinitive?

1. aedificare
2. loquentem
3. ambulabat
4. punirentur
5. salutare
6. lacrimantes
7. celavi
8. audivisti
9. interfecerant
10. quaeremus

Chapter 16 Catullus, Horace, Tibullus, Martial – Shorter Poems

Indirect questions

An **indirect question** is a subordinate clause **introduced by a question word**.

He asked the sailors **what sort of** storm had destroyed the boats.

    main clause   indirect question

Notice that an indirect question does not have to seem particularly question-like. For example, the subordinate clause in the sentence below is still an indirect question because it is introduced by a question word.

He knew **why** the boats had been destroyed.

In Latin, **indirect questions** use the **subjunctive**. The translation of the subjunctive **is the same as** the equivalent tense of the **indicative**.

rogavit cur custos dormiret.	He asked why the guard was sleeping.
sciebat quomodo inimicus interfectus esset.	He knew how his enemy had been killed.

Notice that it is fairly common to meet a **future participle** + the **imperfect subjunctive** of the verb *to be* in an indirect question as a way of asking about something which was going to happen later.

quaesivi quot epistulas scripturus esses.	I asked how many letters you were going to write.

All the question words you have met so far can be used to introduce an indirect question, with the following exceptions:

- *-ne* – this is never used at the start of an indirect question;
- *nonne* – this is never used at the start of an indirect question;
- *num* – this is used at the start of an indirect question but with a different meaning: for **indirect questions**, *num* means **whether**.

EXERCISE 16.9

1. custos iratissimus rogavit cur tot captivi **advenissent**.
2. ad proximum oppidum progrediebamur: nesciebamus enim ubi illa nocte dormituri **essemus**.
3. cur me non rogavisti quantam pecuniam **haberem**?
4. heri magister iuvenibus ostendit quot libros legere **deberent**.
5. mater filiam rogavit num maritum petere **vellet**.
6. dixistine qualis dux his militibus imperaturus **esset**?
7. omnes cives cognoverunt quis consulem interficere **conatus esset**.
8. nonnulli rogare coeperunt quot nautae in tempestate **mortui essent**.
9. ad summum montem ascendebamus quod videre volebamus ubi hostes castra **posuissent**.
10. liberi nesciebant quis per ianuam domum **ingrederetur**.

> Look at each of the **subjunctives** in bold; is it **imperfect** or **pluperfect** tense? Is the verb **active**, **passive** or **deponent**?

| *scripta* in Latin | you could now look at the Latin version of *scripta* 16.6 |

Chapter 16: *scripta*

For guidance on how to make use of these Latin texts and their English translations, see pp.viii–ix.

On the Companion Website you will find resources to accompany these texts:

- *in the **scripta in English** section you will find copies of each text in English only, with questions on each one*
- *in the **scripta in Latin** section you will find notes for each of the Latin texts: these contain glosses for all words not yet met in a Core Language vocabulary list, explanations to help you understand the Latin and material designed to help you build your appreciation of literary style.*

Meet the *scriptores*: Catullus, Horace, Tibullus, Martial

Gaius Valerius Catullus was the first known Roman poet to imitate the Alexandrians. **Catullus** lived from *c.* 84–54 BC and he was a contemporary of Julius Caesar and Cicero. There is little known about his life but it is likely that he was born into a wealthy equestrian family and came from Verona to Rome as a young man. Rather than pursue the *cursus honorum*, Catullus devoted his life to writing poetry and he is famous for poems which are dazzling in their literary skill, bold in their innovation and often shocking or scandalous in their content.

> The Latin adjective *novus* means new. Explain the meaning of *innovation*.

Much of Catullus' work concerns his tumultuous relationship with a woman he calls Lesbia. Many scholars believe Lesbia was a pseudonym for the patrician aristocrat Clodia, a woman notorious for several high-profile extra-marital affairs. Catullus' poetry describes the stages of their relationship: the euphoria of meeting and the early passion of a new love affair, followed by equally passionate jealousy, anger and pain. Catullus is best known for his love poetry, but his poetry covers a broad canvas of emotions and styles, including grief, flattery, religious devotion, playful teasing and sharp criticism.

Changeability of fortune and circumstance is a key theme in the poetry of **Quintus Horatius Flaccus** (65–8 BC). The poems in this chapter exemplify his personal poetry but **Horace** is also famous for the insight he provides into Roman political history. In Chapter 10, one of Horace's poems was used as Source 10.4 to explore the characterisation of Cleopatra from a Roman viewpoint. Horace is often referred to as an Augustan poet, partly because his poetry contributed to public perceptions of Augustan politics. His interest in political commentary also led him to develop the Roman genre of satire into a more finessed form.

> The Latin adjective *arduus* means *steep, difficult*. Explain the meaning of *arduous*.

Like Virgil and Horace, **Albius Tibullus** lived from *c.* 55–19 BC and seems to have lost much of his family land in the political turbulence of the time. His poems are characterised by a deep love for the countryside and an interest in the immediacy of feelings which arise from love-affairs. In his poetry, **Tibullus** often sets up a contrast between a life of political ambition, ensnared in dangerous and arduous military and political manoeuvres, and the simple pleasures of a life focused on the here and now, given over to delight in the countryside and the pleasure and pains of love. Tibullus' style is more meandering than Catullus' and Horace's; the length of his poems means that extracts only are included in this chapter. These extracts highlight Tibullus' ability to convey feelings and to reflect on the role that poetry can play in navigating affairs of the heart.

Probably the pithiest and the most controversial poet in this chapter is **Marcus Valerius Martialis** (*c.* AD 40–*c.* 103). **Martial** was born in what is now Spain and moved to Rome as a young man. A true observer of human nature, Martial is known for his epigrams; short, often scathing, poems which satirise both people and circumstances. Martial conveys the minutiae and the broader socio-political currents of life in Imperial Rome; his epigrams create a picture of the sounds, sights and smells of Rome – sometimes in sordid detail – and they create a vehicle for criticisms of the perceived moral hypocrisy of the those in power. Through his witty observations, Martial's epigrams remain some of the most immediately enjoyable and accessible examples of Latin literature.

FIGURE 16.5 **Twentieth-century bust of Martial**

This bronze bust of the poet Martial was sculpted by the Spanish artist Juan Cruz Melero (1910–86). The artist chose to depict Martial looking serious and calm without a hint of the wicked humour for which Martial is best known. This work is evidence of the enduring interest in the works of Martial.

Reading original Latin note 9: Displays of literary skill

As discussed in Chapter 8, skill with words was a central part of winning prestige in Rome and Roman poets often seem to write with this in view. The quality of a Latin poem, therefore, rests partly in the skill with which it has been written. Literary skill is often demonstrated by:

- **connection with Greek language, poems and other famous literary texts**. Chapter 14 focused on the relationship between Roman epic and Greek epic. Many of the poems below are closely related to Greek texts or make use of Greek grammatical forms (e.g. *epigrammaton* in Martial 1.1 below).

- **patterns**: the flexibility of Latin word order is used to great effect in Latin poetry and writers often position words into elegant patterns (notice, for example, the adjective, adjective, preposition, noun, noun pattern in line 2 of Martial 1.1 below, or how often a framing pattern is used such as the participle, noun, participle structure in line 5).

- **clever word-play**, such as repeating words or using variants. For example, see how the three diminutive forms used by Catullus (*tabellis, versiculos, ocellos*) in Catullus 50 give a playful tone to the poem.

- **density**: by use of allusions, imagery and a careful choice of descriptive detail, a skilful Roman poet was able to weave a wide range of emotions and flavours into a very short space: notice, for example, the movement from energetic and companionable laughter to restless torment and isolated desire in Catullus 50 below, or how Tibullus makes use of slave and fire metaphors to highlight the powerlessness of his pain.

Chapter 16 Catullus, Horace, Tibullus, Martial – Shorter Poems

> **scripta 16.1: Reflections on the role of poetry**
>
> *Roman poets often wrote poetry in a self-conscious way, discussing both the process of writing poetry and its likely after-effects. In the extracts below, three different views are presented about the value of poetry to the writer.*
>
> *Martial focuses on the fame and glory which accompanies his clever wit. Catullus creates a portrait of the playful fun which came with writing poetry, and the way in which someone could impress via their skill with words. Tibullus speaks with the voice of a disempowered lover, craving some return from his beloved: in despair that his poetry has not yet won her round, Tibulllus tells the divine Muse to leave him alone. If poetry cannot win him his girl, there is no point in writing it.*

Here he is! The poet you are reading, the poet you are looking for! Martial, famous throughout the whole world with his incisive little books of epigrams. Attentive reader, you have given glory to him while he is alive and alert to it; few poets have such glory after death.

hic est quem legis ille, quem requiris,
toto notus in orbe Martialis
argutis **epigrammaton** libellis:
cui, lector studiose, quod dedisti
viventi decus atque sentienti,
rari post cineres habent poetae.

Martial 1.1

> **epigrammaton**
> is a transliterated Latin version of a Greek genitive pl noun.

argutus -a -um	expressive, incisive, acute
epigrammaton (genitive pl)	epigrams
decus, decoris, n	glory, distinction
cinis, cineris, m	ashes

Yesterday, Licinius – a day off – we had great fun at my writing tablets, since it had suited us to take it easy: each of us writing our poems played about now in this metre, now in that, exchanging shared jokes in the midst of fun and wine. I went away from there fired up by your charm, Licinius and your wit, and the result was that food did me no good, nor did sleep close my eyes peacefully, but, wild with emotion, I tossed and turned all over my bed, desperate to see daylight so that I could speak with you, and so that I could be with you. But after my limbs, exhausted from exertion, were spread corpse-like across my bed, I wrote this poem for you – you mean so much to me – so that you might understand my pain.

hesterno, Licini, die otiosi
multum lusimus in meis tabellis,
ut convenerat esse delicatos:
scribens versiculos uterque nostrum
ludebat numero modo hoc modo illoc,
reddens mutua per iocum atque vinum.
atque illinc abii tuo lepore
incensus, Licini, facetiisque,
ut nec me miserum cibus iuvaret
nec somnus tegeret quiete ocellos,
sed toto indomitus furore lecto
versarer, cupiens videre lucem,
ut tecum loquerer, simulque ut essem.
at defessa labore membra postquam
semimortua lectulo iacebant,
hoc, iucunde, tibi **poema** feci,
ex quo perspiceres meum dolorem.

Catullus 50 (lines 1–17)

poema is a Greek accusative sg noun.	hesternus -a -um	yesterday's
	otiosus -a -um	at leisure
	tabella, tabellae, f	small writing tablet
	convenerat	'it had suited us'
	delicatus -a -um	luxurious, at ease, soft
	uterque, utraque, utrumque	each
	numerus, numeri, m	metre
	modo . . . modo . . .	'at one time . . . at another time . . .'
	illoc = illo	
	iocus, oci, m	joke
	lepor, leporis, m	charm, wit
	facetia, facetiae, f	humour, wit
	ut (+ subjunctive)	'with the result that . . .'
	iuvo, iuvare	help, benefit
	tego, tegere	cover, close
	ocellus, ocelli, m	(little) eye
	indomitus -a -um	untamed, wild
	furor, furoris, m	passion
	lectus, lecti, m	bed
	verso, versare	turn about
	at	but
	membrum, membri, n	limb
	ex quo (+ subjunctive)	'from which [you might . . .]'
	dolor, doloris, m	pain

Chapter 16 Catullus, Horace, Tibullus, Martial – Shorter Poems

Here I see slavery for me and a ready mistress: now I say goodbye to my own ancestral freedom. Instead, a grim servitude is before me and I am held in chains; Love never releases me – wretched – from its bonds. Whether I have deserved it in any way or whether I have done nothing wrong, it burns me. I am burned – oh! – cruel girl, take away the fire-brands.

. . .

Elegiac poems are no benefit to me and neither is Apollo, the inspiration for poetry. That woman keeps on demanding payment with an empty hand: Muses, go elsewhere if you do no good for a lover. I do not worship you in order to have to write epic poetry, nor do I write about the paths of the sun and what shape the Moon is when she completes her orbit, wheels around her horses and returns. I am looking for an easy way in to my mistress through my poems. Muses, if these poems have no power, then go elsewhere.

hic mihi servitium video dominamque paratam:
   iam mihi, libertas illa paterna, vale.
servitium sed triste datur, teneorque catenis,
   et numquam misero vincla remittit Amor,
et seu quid merui seu nil peccavimus, urit.
   uror, io, remove, saeva puella, faces.

. . .

nec prosunt elegi nec carminis auctor Apollo:
   illa cava pretium flagitat usque manu.
ite procul, Musae, si non prodestis amanti:
   non ego vos, ut sint bella canenda, colo,
nec refero Solisque vias et qualis, ubi orbem
   complevit, versis Luna recurrit equis.
ad dominam faciles aditus per carmina quaero:
   ite procul, Musae, si nihil ista valent.

Tibullus 2.4 (lines 1–6, 13–20)

vale	'farewell'
catena, catenae, f	chain
vinclum, vincli, n	chain, fetter
seu . . . seu . . .	whether . . . whether . . .
quid	'anything, in any way'
mereo, merere, merui	deserve
pecco, peccare, peccavi	do wrong, sin
uro, urere	burn
fax, facis, f	torch, fire-brand
prosum, prodesse (+ dative)	benefit
carmen, carminis, n	poem, song
auctor, auctoris, m	creator, author
cavus -a -um	hollow, empty
pretium, pretii, n	reward, price
flagito, flagitare	demand repeatedly
usque	continuously
procul	far away
ut sint . . . canenda	'so that [. . .] have to be sung'
colo, colere	worship, cultivate
compleo, complere, complevi	fill up, finish
iste, ista, istud	that
valeo, valere	be strong

DERIVATIONS

This task builds skills in deducing the meaning of one word by using a related word.

The words below derive from words in the passages above which have not been glossed.

Can you find the Latin words from which these English words derive? Can you use either the Latin or the English word to help you explain the meaning of the other?

Remember that you will need to think about the part of speech of both the Latin and English words and – if they are different – you will need to consider how to adjust the meaning to move from one part of speech to the other.

requisition, studious, rarify, versify, semi-detached, jocund, perspective, dominate, orbit, recurrent

Reading original Latin note 10: Patterns in word order and sound

Latin's natural concision is used to great effect in Roman poetry. The sparseness of Latin phrasing and the flexibility of its word order allows words to be positioned in elegant or emphatic positions. Much of the beauty in *scripta* 16.2 comes from the careful refinement of its word order. Notice how often a word is positioned in a way that creates a pattern.

For example:

- the chiastic structure of *puellae . . . pueri . . . pueri . . . puellae* in lines 1–4
- the patterning of *Dianae, Dianam* at the start of the lines and *integri, integri* at the end of the lines in lines 1–3;
- the juxtaposition of *maximi / magna* in lines 5–6
- the patterning of *Deliam . . . olivam*, both at the end of their lines in lines 7–8
- the genitive plurals at the start of each of the lines in lines 9–12 and the interweaving of 3rd and 2nd declension genitive plurals at the ends of lines 10–12
- the alliterative juxtaposition of *menstruo / metiens* in lines 17–18 or the *s*- alliteration running through lines 21–24.

Set against this delight in patterns is the need for a poet to avoid monotony or predictability in composition. This is particularly important within the **sound** patterns in a poem. Because many Latin words share the same endings, Roman poetry aims to **avoid rhyme**, preferring to interweave sound repetition at the start or in the middle of a word instead. Poets also take care to avoid a jangle of repeated endings: notice how carefully the genitive plural words in lines 10–12 have been arranged to avoid two-syllable rhyme within any adjacent pair.

Chapter 16 Catullus, Horace, Tibullus, Martial – Shorter Poems

> ### scripta 16.2: Religious poetry
>
> *Latin poetry was typically modelled on Greek prototypes, and one of the oldest forms of Greek poetic song was a hymn to a god or goddess. Here, Catullus offers a hymn to Diana, goddess of chastity and hunting. As is typical of this type of poetry, he lists the names by which she is known and celebrates the wide reach of her powers.*

We are loyal to Diana, we are untouched girls and boys; as untouched boys and girls let us sing to Diana.

O daughter of Leto, you are the great offspring of greatest Jupiter, the goddess whom her mother set down near to the Delian olive grove

so that you might be the mistress of the mountains and the green woods and the hidden groves, and the resounding rivers.

You are named Juno Lucina for mothers in the pains of childbirth, you are the powerful **Trivia** and you are named Luna in the reflected light of the moon.

You, goddess, with your monthly route measuring out your yearly journey, you fill the rustic houses of the farmer with good crops.

May you be honoured with whatever name pleases you, and, as has been your custom of old, may you look after the race of Romulus with your bountiful help.

Dianae sumus in fide
puellae et pueri integri:
Dianam pueri integri
puellaeque canamus.

o Latonia, maximi
magna progenies Iovis,
quam mater prope Deliam
deposuit olivam,

montium domina ut fores
silvarumque virentium
saltuumque reconditorum
amniumque sonantum:

tu Lucina dolentibus
Iuno dicta puerperis,
tu potens **Trivia** et notho es
dicta lumine Luna.

tu cursu, dea, menstruo
metiens iter annuum,
rustica agricolae bonis
tecta frugibus exples.

sis quocumque tibi placet
sancta nomine, Romulique,
antique ut solita es, bona
sospites ope gentem.

Catullus 34

Trivia was the Roman name for Hecate, the goddess of witchcraft, ghosts and crossroads.

integer, integra, integrum	complete, unspoilt, pure
canamus	'let us sing'
ut fores	'so that you might be'
virens, virentis	green, healthy
saltus, saltus, m	grove, glade
reconditus -a -um	concealed, mysterious
amnis, amnis, m	river, stream
sonans, sonantis	resounding
doleo, dolere	suffer pain
puerpera, puerperae, f	a woman in childbirth
nothus -a -um	hybrid, false, borrowed
metior, metiri	measure
tectum, tecti, n	building, house
fruges, frugum, f pl	crops
expleo, explere	fill
sis	'may you be'
quocumque (ablative)	'with whatever'
placeo, placere (+ dative)	be pleasing to
sanctus -a -um	holy, sacred
sospites	'may you keep safe'
ops, opis, f	help, wealth

DERIVATIONS

This task builds skills in deducing the meaning of one word by using a related word.

The words below derive from words in the passages above which have not been glossed.

Can you find the Latin words from which these English words derive? Can you use either the Latin or the English word to help you explain the meaning of the other?

Remember that you will need to think about the part of speech of both the Latin and English words and – if they are different – you will need to consider how to adjust the meaning to move from one part of speech to the other.

fidelity, progeny, luminary, menstrual, rustic, antiquarian

Chapter 16 Catullus, Horace, Tibullus, Martial – Shorter Poems

Reading original Latin note 11: Implication, inference and wit

The creative potential offered by Latin's concision reaches its peak in its shortest poems. The brevity necessary for these poems means that **much of the message lies beyond what is actually said**; for example, Martial implies in 1.10 that a quick route to wealthy inheritance is what is firing up a particular suitor and he does this via a single word: *tussit*. The reader needs to infer or understand that the cough is life-threatening, that the woman is wealthy, and that this is why the suitor is in such a rush.

This gap between words and meaning brings with it the potential for the poets to enjoy the friction between what the poem might imply and what a reader might understand for themselves. In Catullus 49 below, Catullus implies that he is in awe of Cicero's oratorical skill, but the reader can infer from the overtly rhetorical patterning in the poem that Catullus is in no doubt about his own skill with words too. This allows for the poem to be playfully double-edged.

Martial is famous for the wit he displays in navigating the art of implication, often encouraging the reader to imagine scandalous content to fill in the gaps in what he writes. In Martial 2.82 the reader is left wondering what is the secret that needs to be hushed up; in 2.13 we wonder how much money changed hands in bribes and why.

As you read through these poems, remember that the small number of words in the poem is only the first step to its interpretation: enjoy letting your imagination bring colour to the skeletal narrative and especially so when there is room for more than one route through its meaning.

scripta 16.3: Roman customs and daily life

The genre of epic poetry required its poets to write about things which were grand and important, but the expectations of shorter poetry were much looser. Significant numbers of poems were written about day-to-day contemporary Roman life, and the collection below gives an interesting snap-shot of the power-dynamics, concerns and priorities of elite Roman life.

Catullus writes a poem with overblown praise for his patron; Martial's epigrams offer biting criticism of self-interested Romans. Epigram 1.10 suggests that a suitor is interested only in the prospect of inheritance if he marries a wealthy but sick woman, 1.23 suggests that a dinner-party host only invites men he finds sexually attractive, 21.3 suggests that someone has only escaped justice because he has bribed the judge and because his patron has intervened on his behalf, and 2.82 highlights the gruesome and pointless cruelty of a man who is keen to stop the gossip about whatever shameful events have taken place at his home.

Chapter 16 scripta

Marcus Tullius, most eloquent of the descendants of Romulus, as many as there are today and as many as there ever have been, and as many as there ever will be in the years to come; Catullus, the lowliest of all the poets, gives the greatest thanks to you. Just as Catullus is the lowliest of all the poets, you are the best of all the patrons.

disertissime Romuli nepotum,
quot sunt quotque fuere, **Marce Tulli**,
quotque post aliis erunt in annis,
gratias tibi maximas Catullus
agit pessimus omnium poeta,
tanto pessimus omnium poeta,
quanto tu optimus omnium patronus.

Catullus 49

> **Marcus Tullius** refers to Cicero, the great orator and Catullus' patron.

disertus -a -um	eloquent
nepos, nepotis, m	descendant
quot	'as many as'
fuere = fuerunt	
post = postea	
tanto . . . quanto	'to the same extent . . . as . . .'

Gemellus seeks marriage with Maronilla: he's desperate for it! He pushes it along, prays for it and gives her presents. Is she really so beautiful? Not at all – nothing is uglier. So, what is he after in her case and why is she attractive to him? She has a cough.

petit Gemellus nuptas Maronillae
et cupit et instat et precatur et donat.
adeone pulchra est? immo foedius nil est.
quid ergo in illa petitur et placet? Tussit.

Martial 1.10

nuptiae, nuptiarum, f pl	marriage
insto, instare	pursue eagerly
precor, precari	pray
immo	indeed no!
foedus -a -um	ugly, foul
ergo	therefore
placeo, placere	be pleasing to
tussio -ire	have a cough

Chapter 16 Catullus, Horace, Tibullus, Martial – Shorter Poems

Cotta, you don't invite anyone to dinner if you do not go to the public baths with them. Indeed the baths alone provide party companions for you. I was amazed, Cotta, as to why you had never invited me: now I know that when I was naked, I did not please you.

invitas nullum nisi <u>cum quo</u>, Cotta, <u>lavaris</u>
　et dant <u>conviviam</u> <u>balnea</u> sola tibi.
mirabar <u>quare</u> numquam me, Cotta, **vocasses**:
　iam scio me nudum <u>displicuisse</u> tibi.

Martial 1.23

Note that long perfect-stem verb forms are difficult to fit into a poem's rhythm and sometimes get shortened. **vocasses** = *vocavisses*.

cum quo . . . lavaris	'someone you go to the baths with'
conviva, convivae, m	dinner-guest
balnea, balneorum, n pl	baths
quare . . . vocasses	'why you had called'
displiceo, displicere, displicui	displease

Both the judge and your patron ask for their money. Sextus, I recommend that you pay back your creditor.

et iudex petit et petit patronus:
　<u>solvas censeo</u>, Sexte, creditori.

Martial 2.13

solvas censeo	'I recommend that you pay back.'

Ponticus, why do you crucify your slave with his tongue cut out? Don't you know that the general public voices what he keeps silent?

<u>abscisa</u> servum quid <u>figis</u>, Pontice, lingua?
　nescis tu populum, quod tacet ille, loqui?

Martial 2.82

abscindo, abscindere, abscidi, abscisum	cut off
figo, figere	fix (here, 'crucify')

DERIVATIONS

The words below derive from words in the passages above which have not been glossed.

Can you find in the passages above the Latin words from which these English words derive? Can you use either the Latin or the English word to help you explain the meaning of the other?

Remember that you will need to think about the part of speech of both the Latin and English words and – if they are different – you will need to consider how to adjust the meaning to move from one part of speech to the other.

gratitude, pessimistic, patronise, donate, invitation, judicial, creditor, language

Reading original Latin note 12: Extended imagery

As discussed in Chapter 15, vivid description often involves interweaving other material to enrich the scene. Sometimes this is done with a **simile**. English tends to make use of quite short similes, e.g. *his mood was as dark as night*, but as you saw in Chapter 14, Classical poetry often involves a much more extended comparison.

If you go on to read more Greek and Roman epic, you will find that extended similes are frequent within this genre, creating mini scenes which connect with the main scene in some aspects and sometimes offer contrast in other aspects.

The more concise nature of the shorter poems in this chapter, however, make more use of **metaphor**, **personification** or **image**.

Notice how Catullus mourns his brother in an intensely personal way but uses the extended image of the funeral rites to create a moment where his grief becomes representative of mourning for loved ones through the ages. In the Horace poem below, notice how the power of the gods to change someone's circumstances is presented through the extended image of Jupiter's lightning bolt and the depiction of Fortuna as a bird of prey. These images create a chilling way to understand human weakness and impermanence.

TEST YOURSELF!

Can you explain what each of these literary terms means? If not, there is a glossary available on the *scripta in Latin* section of the Companion Website.

1. simile
2. metaphor
3. personification
4. epic simile
5. chiasmus
6. alliteration
7. hexameter
8. elegiac couplet

Chapter 16 Catullus, Horace, Tibullus, Martial – Shorter Poems

> ### scripta 16.4: Death, grief and fear
>
> The most famous of Rome's poets show a remarkable versatility of style and topic. Many of the poems are playful or provocative, but some focus on pain and suffering. In the poems below, Catullus mourns the death of a brother, and Horace explores the terror of the changeability of Fortune. One of the most famous Latin quotations of all time – carpe diem – savour the day – is from another of Horace's poems. A recurring theme in his poetry is the advice to make the most of what is available today in recognition that tomorrow might be very different.

Brother, I have travelled through many countries and over many seas and now I have arrived at these wretched rites for the dead so that I might give you one last offering in death and so that I might speak in vain to your silent ashes. This is all because fortune has taken you, you yourself, from me. Alas, wretched brother, taken undeservedly from me, now even so receive these things which, by the ancient custom of our ancestors, are handed over as a grim gift for the funeral rites. Receive them soaked with a brother's tears. O my brother, goodbye and farewell forever.

multas per gentes et multa per aequora vectus
   advenio has miseras, frater, ad inferias,
ut te postremo donarem munere mortis
   et mutam nequiquam alloquerer cinerem.
quandoquidem fortuna mihi tete abstulit ipsum.
   heu miser indigne frater adempte mihi,
nunc tamen interea haec, prisco quae more parentum
   tradita sunt tristi munere ad inferias,
accipe fraterno multum manantia fletu,
   atque in perpetuum, frater, ave atque vale.

Catullus 101

aequor, aequoris, n	sea
vectus -a -um	having travelled
inferiae, inferiarum, f pl	offerings in honour of the dead
postremus -a -um	last
dono, donare	bestow, present with
munus, muneris, n	gift, duty
nequiquam	in vain
cinis, cineris, m	ashes
quandoquidem	since indeed
heu	alas
indigne	undeservingly
ademptus -a -um	taken away
priscus -a -um	ancient
mos, moris, m	custom
manans, manantis	dripping
fletus, fletus, m	weeping
perpetuus -a- um	everlasting
ave	'goodbye'
vale	'farewell'

I used to be a grudging and infrequent worshipper of the gods, while I was getting it wrong, paying heed to a mad wisdom. Now I am forced to turn my sails backwards and to renew an abandoned course.

For **Jupiter**, cleaving the clouds on a huge scale with his flashing lightning, has driven his thundering horses and flying chariot through the pure air,

a chariot with which the brute earth and the wandering rivers, the Styx and the horrible home of hateful **Taenarum**, and the Atlantean territory is shaken. He has the power to swap the lowest with the highest

and – as a god – he makes the lofty insignificant, raising up the lowly. With a piercing screech, rapacious Fortune snatches up a man of the highest rank from over there and delights to have put him down over here.

parcus deorum cultor et infrequens,
insanientis dum sapientiae
   consultus erro, nunc retrorsum
   vela dare atque iterare cursus

cogor relictos: namque **Diespiter**
igni corusco nubila dividens
   plerumque, per purum tonantis
   egit equos volucremque currum,

quo bruta tellus et vaga flumina,
quo Styx et invisi horrida **Taenari**
   sedes Atlanteusque finis
   concutitur. valet ima summis

mutare et insignem attenuat deus,
obscura promens; hinc apicem rapax
   Fortuna cum stridore acuto
   sustulit, hic posuisse gaudet.
                   Horace 1.34

Diespiter was another name for Jupiter.

Taenarum was a town in the South of Greece; the Romans believed it was near to the entrance to the Underworld.

parcus -a -um	thrifty, meagre
consultus -a -um (+ genitive)	experienced in
retrorsum	backwards
velum, veli, n	sail
itero, iterare	renew, do again
coruscus -a -um	flashing
nubila, nubilorum, n pl	clouds
plerumque	for the most part
purum, puri, n	clear sky
tonans, tonantis	thundering
volucer, volucris	winged
currus, currus, m	chariot
tellus, telluris, f	earth
vagus -a -um	wandering
invisus -a -um	hateful
finis, finis, m	boundary, territory
concutio, concutere	shake
valeo, valere (+ infinitive)	be strong enough to
imus -a -um	lowest
muto, mutare	change
attenuo, attenuare	reduce, weaken
promo, promere	promote, bring forwards
apex, apicis, m	top
stridor, stridoris, m	screech
acutus -a -um	sharp, shrill

Chapter 16 Catullus, Horace, Tibullus, Martial – Shorter Poems

> **DERIVATIONS**
>
> This task builds skills in deducing the meaning of one word by using a word.
>
> The words below derive from words in the passages above which have not been glossed.
>
> Can you find the Latin words from which these English words derive? Can you use either the Latin or the English word to help you explain the meaning of the other?
>
> Remember that you will need to think about the part of speech of both the Latin and English words and – if they are different – you will need to consider how to adjust the meaning to move from one part of speech to the other.
>
> *mute, fortunate, fraternal, infrequent, insanity, error, cursive, dividend, brutal, summation, rapacious, gaudy*

Reading original Latin note 13: Cultural values and symbols

The personal nature of shorter Roman poetry makes it one of the most accessible genres of Latin literature, but it was written in the context of a society with its own cultural values. These cultural values shape both **content** and **style**.

The **content** of these poems can be surprising because our modern-day society has developed different expectations about what might be written in a poem. You may find some of the **explicit sexual references** in the poems below surprising. In the final section of texts, you might find the **insults** shocking.

Cultural values impact **style** because they shape the **symbols** available to writers. Roman society was originally built around farming and fighting: as a result, **agricultural metaphors** are common (see, for example, the metaphor of crops and harvest which runs through Catullus 48 below). In addition, poets often take metaphors from **military campaigns** to explore ideas of power and conquest in other settings, such as love affairs. Writers often make use of **slavery** as a symbol for the power dynamic between lover and beloved.

It is also interesting to look for symbolism which carries over to the modern-day, such as **fire** as a symbol for passion, or **storms** as a symbol for disagreements and pain.

Exploring the symbolism used in these poems will help deepen your understanding of each poem. It will help you explore cultural values and consider the differences and similarities between Roman society and societies today.

scripta 16.5: Love poetry

Love poetry is perhaps the most famous type of shorter poem, and poets often wrote of the joy and pain found in the changing tides of love affairs. Frequently sexually explicit, many of the poems focus on the pain of betrayal and separation, and the powerlessness often felt by a lover.

Catullus is perhaps the most famous Roman writer of love poetry: some of his love poems are addressed to a man and some are addressed to a woman. The most famous of his lovers is a woman he calls Lesbia. The Lesbia poems convey the range of feelings within this long-lasting affair, from powerless devotion to bitter contempt and resentment.

This section ends with an extract from a much longer poem by Tibullus: Tibullus' writing is more expansive in style and rich in descriptive detail, but covers similar themes of pain and betrayal.

Juventius, if anyone were to let me keep kissing your honeyed eyes, I would keep kissing them right up to 300,000 kisses but don't think that I would be satisfied – never! – not even if the harvest of our kissing were greater than harvested corn.

mellitos oculos tuos, Iuventi,
si quis me sinat usque basiare,
usque ad milia basiem trecenta
nec numquam videar satur futurus,
non si densior aridis aristis
sit nostrae seges osculationis.

Catullus 48

mellitus -a -um	honeyed
oculus, oculi, m	eye
si quis . . . sinat	'if anyone were to allow'
usque	continuously
basio, basiare	kiss
basiem	'I would keep kissing'
videar	'I would seem'
satur, satura, saturum	full, satisfied
si . . . sit	'if there were to be'
arista, aristaae, f	ear of corn, harvest
seges, segetis, f	crop
osculatio, osculationis, f	kissing

I hate and I love. Perhaps you ask why I do this. I do not know, but I feel it happen and I am tormented.

odi et amo. quare id faciam, fortasse requiris.
nescio, sed fieri sentio et excrucior.

Catullus 85

odi, odisse	hate
quare . . . faciam	'why I do . . .'
fio, fieri	become, happen

Chapter 16 Catullus, Horace, Tibullus, Martial – Shorter Poems

Caelius, my own Lesbia, that Lesbia of mine, that Lesbia, the one girl whom Catullus loved more than himself and all the rest of his family, now, at the crossroads and in the alleyways, she gives sexual thrills to the descendants of great-hearted Remus.

Caeli, Lesbia nostra, Lesbia illa,
illa Lesbia, quam Catullus unam
plus quam se atque suos amavit omnes,
nunc in quadriviis et angiportis
glubit magnanimi Remi nepotes.

Catullus 58

quadrivium, quadrivii, n	crossroad
angiportum, angiporti, n	narrow street
glubo, glubere	peel, pull back the bark (a metaphor)
nepos, nepotis, m	grandson, descendant

Lesbia says very many mean things to me when her husband is there: this is a great source of joy to him, idiot that he is. You fool, don't you understand anything? If, forgetful of me, she were silent, she would be in her right mind. As it is, because she snarls and contradicts me, not only am I on her mind, but – something which cuts deeper by far – she is angry. This is what it is: she burns and she talks.

Lesbia mi praesente viro mala plurima dicit:
   haec illi fatuo maxima laetitia est.
mule, nihil sentis? si nostri oblita taceret,
   sana esset: nunc quod gannit et obloquitur,
non solum meminit, sed, quae multo acrior est res,
irata est. hoc est: uritur et loquitur.

Catullus 83

mi = mihi	
fatuus -a -um	idiotic
mulus, muli, m	mule, ass
si . . . taceret	'if she were silent'
oblitus -a -um (+ genitive)	forgetful of
esset	'she would be'
gannio, ganniire	snarl, growl
memini, meminisse	remember
acer, acris, acre	bitter, painful
uro, urere	burn

No woman is able to say truly that she has been loved as much as my Lesbia has been loved by me. No faithfulness ever existed in any pledge as great as mine has been proven to be, for my part, in my love for you.

nulla potest mulier tantum se dicere amatam
   vere, quantum a me Lesbia amata mea est.
nulla fides ullo fuit umquam foedere tanta,
   quanta in amore tuo ex parte reperta mea est.

Catullus 87

tantum . . . quantum	'to the extent to which'
vere	truly
foedus, foederis, n	treaty, pact
reperio, reperire, repperi, repertum	find, discover

I was brusque and kept saying that I bore our separation well, but now that bold boast is far away from me. For I am sent flying just as a fast spinning top is driven with a strike over flat ground, a spinning top which a fast-moving boy spins with practised skill. Burn your wild lover, and torture him; let it not please him to say anything grand after this. Tame his horrid words. But be gentle to me, please, I beg you, because of the pact of our secret love-making, because of our love and because of the head you laid next to mine.

. . .

Often I tried to drive off my pains with wine, but grief had turned all the alcohol into tears. Often I embraced another girl, but at the very moment when I was coming close to joy, Venus reminded me of my mistress and abandoned me.

asper eram et bene discidium me ferre loquebar,
   at mihi nunc longe gloria fortis abest.
namque agor ut per plana citus sola verbere turben,
   quem celer adsueta versat ab arte puer.
ure ferum et torque, libeat ne dicere quicquam
   magnificum post haec: horrida verba doma.
parce tamen, per te furtivi foedera lecti,
   per venerem quaeso conpositumque caput.

. . .

saepe ego temptavi curas depellere vino,
   at dolor in lacrimas verterat omne merum.
saepe aliam tenui, sed iam cum gaudia adirem,
   admonuit dominae deseruitque Venus.

Tibullus 1.5 (lines 1–9; 37–40)

asper, aspera, asperum	harsh, rough
discidium, discidii, n	tearing apart, separation
at	but
planus -a -um	flat, level
citus -a -um	quick
solum, soli, n	ground
verber, verberis, n	whip, lash
turben, turbinis, m	spinning top
adsuetus -a -um	usual, customary
verso, versare	twist and turn, turn about
uro, urere	burn
ferus -a -um	wild
torqueo, torquere	twist, torture
libeat ne	'may it not please him'
quisquam, quaequam, quicquam	anyone, anything
domo, domare	tame
parco, parcere (+ dative)	spare, hold back from injuring
foedus, foederis, n	treaty, pact
lectus, lecti, m	bed
dolor, doloris, m	pain
merum, meri, n	undiluted wine
desero, deserere, deserui	abandon

Chapter 16 Catullus, Horace, Tibullus, Martial – Shorter Poems

DERIVATIONS

This task builds skills in deducing the meaning of one word by using an elated word.

The words below derive from words in the passages above which have not been glossed.

Can you find the Latin words from which these English words derive? Can you use either the Latin or the English word to help you explain the meaning of the other?

Remember that you will need to think about the part of speech of both the Latin and English words and – if they are different – you will need to consider how to adjust the meaning to move from one part of speech to the other.

millimetre, dense, arid, requisition, excruciating, magnanimous, present, sanity, accelerate, magnificent, furtive, venereal, admonish

Reading original Latin note 14: Power play

As discussed in Chapter 8, ambitious Romans could win personal power through their skill in debate. This could be displayed in discussions in the senate, in public elections or in the open-air law-courts watched by citizens at large. Rome did not have a central prosecution service; trials were brought by individuals who were either looking to address a wrong done to them or who were keen to humiliate a political rival.

Using words to insult or criticise others publicly, therefore, was a significant ingredient in the power play that went on in Rome at this time. It is no surprise that it features in Roman poetry too.

In the poems below, it is interesting to look for the **power-dynamics** which feed the poem's energy. It is useful to consider who is being insulted and what this shows us about Roman cultural values. At the same time, it is interesting to explore **how the poet is promoting their own worth** via the cleverness of their writing. You will see that some of the most scandalous insults are delivered via the most elegant phrasing: think about the impact of the contrast created between the poet's literary finesse and the coarse way in which the poem's victim is characterised.

scripta 16.6: Insults

As you read in Chapter 8, Romans often insulted each other publicly. The directness of the insults can seem shocking to a modern-day audience, as can the ribald content of the poems, especially in the context of a literary form as elegant and refined as this type of poem. Such poetry is a useful example of how cultural values change over time.

Rufus, don't wonder why no woman wants to place her smooth thigh under you: she won't do it, not even if you work on her with the gift of a rare dress or with the delights of shimmering jewellery. There's a bad rumour which harms you – it's spreading the idea that a rough goat lives in your armpit. Everyone fears this – no surprise! It's a really bad beast and no pretty girl will lie near it. For this reason, either get rid of the cruel plague on our noses or stop wondering why girls run from you.

noli admirari, <u>quare</u> tibi femina nulla,
   Rufe, <u>velit</u> <u>tenerum</u> supposuisse <u>femur</u>,
non si illam rarae <u>labefactes</u> <u>munere</u> <u>vestis</u>
   <u>aut</u> perluciduli <u>deliciis</u> <u>lapidis</u>.
<u>laedit</u> te quaedam mala fabula, qua tibi <u>fertur</u>
   <u>valle</u> sub <u>alarum</u> <u>trux</u> habitare <u>caper</u>.
hunc <u>metuunt</u> omnes, neque mirum: nam mala <u>valde</u> est
   bestia, nec <u>quicum</u> bella puella <u>cubet</u>.
quare aut crudelem nasorum interfice pestem,
   aut admirari <u>desine</u> cur fugiunt.

Catullus 69

quare	why, for which reason
velit	'wants'
tener, tenera, tenerum	delicate, soft
femur, femoris, n	thigh
labefactes	'you shake [her]', 'you weaken [her]'
munus, muneris, n	gift
vestis, vestis, f	clothing
aut	or
deliciae, deliciarum, f pl	delights
lapis, lapidis, m	stone, gemstone
laedo, laedere	hurt, harm
fertur	'[it] is said'
valles, vallis, f	valley
ala, alae, f	armpit
trux, trucis	rough, savage
caper, capri, m	goat
metuo, metuere	fear
valde	very much
quicum = cum + quo	
cubet	'[she] might lie down'
desine (+ infinitive)	stop . . .

There was no-one in the whole city who wanted to touch your wife for free, Caecilianus, while it was allowed. But, now you have put guards all around, there is a huge queue of lovers. You really are a very clever man.

nullus in urbe fuit tota qui <u>tangere</u> <u>vellet</u>
   uxorem gratis, Caeciliane, tuam,
dum <u>licuit</u>: sed nunc positis custodibus ingens
   turba <u>fututorum</u> est: ingeniosus homo es.

Martial 1.73

tango, tangere	touch
vellet	'[who] wanted'
licuit	'it was allowed'
fututor, fututoris, m	lover, sexual partner

Chapter 16 Catullus, Horace, Tibullus, Martial – Shorter Poems

When she is alone, Gellia does not weep that her father is dead. If anyone is present, her tears spring forth on command. Someone who is looking for praise, Gellia, is not really mourning; the person who grieves without a witness is the person who truly grieves.

amissum non flet cum sola est Gellia patrem,
 si quis adest iussae prosiliunt lacrimae.
non luget quisquis laudari, Gellia, quaerit,
 ille dolet vere qui sine teste dolet.

Martial 1.33

fleo, flere	weep
si quis	'if anyone'
prosilio, prosilire	spring up, leap forth
lugeo, lugere	mourn
quisquis	whoever
doleo, dolere	feel pain, grieve
vere	truly

Candidus, you are the only one to have country estates and you are the only one to have piles of money, you are the only one to have golden objects, you are the only one to have lots of myrrh, you are the only one to have Massic wines, and you are the only one to have Caecuban wines of Opimian vintage, you are the only one to have a heart and you alone are clever. You alone have everything – don't think that I wish to deny it – but you share your wife, Candidus, with everyone else.

praedia solus habes et solus, Candide, nummos,
 aurea solus habes, murrina solus habes,
Massica solus habes et Opimi Caecuba solus,
 et cor solus habes, solus et ingenium.
omnia solus habes nec me puta velle negare
 uxorem sed habes, Candide, cum populo.

Martial 3.26

praedium, praedii, n	country estate
nummus, nummi, m	coin
murrinus -a -um	of myrrh
Massicum, Massici, n	Massican wine
Opimi	'of Opimian vintage'
Caecubum, Caecubi, n	Caecuban wine
cor, cordis, n	heart
ingenium, ingenii, n	natural talent, intelligence
nego, negare	deny

DERIVATIONS

This task builds skills in deducing the meaning of one word by using a related word.

The words below derive from words in the passages above which have not been glossed.

Can you find the Latin words from which these English words derive? Can you use either the Latin or the English word to help you explain the meaning of the other?

Remember that you will need to think about the part of speech of both the Latin and English words and – if they are different – you will need to consider how to adjust the meaning to move from one part of speech to the other.

admiration, supposition, lucid, bestial, nasal, pestilence, testimony, uxorious, custody, ingenious, tincture, compute, popular

QUESTIONS FOR DISCUSSION

1 Catullus and Tibullus are both famous for the emotional power of their poetry: which of the poems in this chapter do you think is the most emotionally evocative? Which emotions does it evoke and how does it do this?

2 Some of the poems in this chapter are shocking in their content: which poem do you find most shocking and why?

3 Some of the poems in this chapter focus on ideas or feelings which still feel familiar today; others reveal how different Roman society was in its attitudes and power-structures. What have you observed in these poems that is similar or different to modern-day societies?

4 Many of Martial's epigrams read as private comments to people who we no longer know anything about: does this diminish their appeal?

5 Literary finesse is central to Roman poetry: explore the patterns of word order and sound in one of the poems in this chapter.

Chapter 16: Additional Language

SECTION A16: CHAPTER 16 VOCABULARY

Exercise A16.1: Derivations

This exercise explores derivations from the vocabulary list for Chapter 16.

Each of the words below derives from a Latin word. Find this Latin word and use it to help you explain the meaning of the English word. You may not know some of these words; think about what part of speech they might be and see if you can work out their meaning based on the Latin.

	derivation	Latin word and translation	meaning of the English derivation
1	summit		
2	quality		
3	proximity		
4	invert		
5	vital		
6	custody		
7	exhortation		
8	mode		
9	tempestuous		
10	imperative		

Exercise A16.2: Parts of speech

Sort the following words from the vocabulary list for Chapter 16 into the correct categories and write the meaning next to each word.

quot   custos   qualis   consul   tantus   summus   oro
quomodo   quantus   inimicus   num   conficio   talis

noun	verb	adjective	question word

Exercise A16.3: Case endings (nouns and adjectives)

Circle the stem and identify the declension of the following nouns and adjectives from Chapter 16. Then give the case requested.

	Latin	declension	
1	consul, consulis, m		nominative pl =
2	custos, custodis, m/f		accusative sg =
3	vita, vitae, f		genitive sg =
4	inimicus, inimici, m		accusative pl =
5	tempestas, tempestatis, f		ablative sg =
6	modus, modi, m		dative sg =
7	ianua, ianuae, f		dative pl =
8	tantus, tanta, tantum		nominative neuter pl =
9	qualis, quale?		accusative masculine pl =
10	talis, tale		accusative feminine sg =

Exercise A16.4: Verbs

The following verbs are from the vocabulary list for Chapter 16. Circle each of the stems of each verb: present, perfect and supine. Remember, not all verbs have all three stems.

Give the meaning of each verb and its conjugation.

	principal parts	meaning	conjugation
1	verto, vertere, verti, versum		
2	hortor, hortari, hortatus sum		
3	impero, imperare, imperavi, imperatum (+ dative)		
4	reddo, reddere, reddidi, redditum		
5	conficio, conficere, confeci, confectum		
6	oro, orare, oravi, oratum		
7	cogo, cogere, coegi, coactum		
8	surgo, surgere, surrexi		

Chapter 16 Catullus, Horace, Tibullus, Martial – Shorter Poems

Exercise A16.5: Cognates

In the table below are pairs of words: the first in each pair is a word from the vocabulary list for Chapter 16 and below it is a cognate word, i.e. a word which is related to it. You may not have met the cognate word before and it will not be listed in the vocabulary list at the back of this book.

Identify the part of speech of each Latin word and then give the meaning; you will have to work out the meaning of the second word by thinking about its part of speech and how it relates in meaning to the first word in each pair.

	Latin	part of speech	meaning
1	vita, vitae, f		
	vitalis, vitale		
2	hortor, hortari, hortatus sum		
	hortamen, hortaminis, n		
3	inimicus, inimici, m		
	inimicus, inimica, inimicum		
4	consul, consulis, m		
	consulo, consulere, consului, consultum		
5	ianua, ianuae, f		
	ianitor, ianitoris, m		
6	custos, custodis, m / f		
	custodia, custodiae, f		
7	summus, summa, summum		
	summa, summae, f		
8	proximus, proxima, proximum		
	proxime		
9	quantus? quanta? quantum?		
	quantitas, quantitatis, f		
10	verto, vertere, verti, versum		
	reverto, revertere, reverti, reversum		

SECTION B16: WORD ENDINGS

Exercise B16.1: Verbs: tense, time and aspect

This exercise practises the different tenses of verbs from the vocabulary list for Chapter 16. It focuses on identifying the time and aspect of different finite verb tenses.

Complete the table below.

		tense	translation	time (past, present, future)	aspect (viewed as not-yet finished or finished)
1	surrexi				
2	hortabamur				
3	orabunt				
4	vertistis				
5	conficiebat				
6	coactae sunt				
7	reddunt				
8	imperavisti				
9	coegerat				
10	hortantur				
11	orabamus				
12	reddentur				
13	surrexeras				
14	imperabo				
15	cogimini				

Chapter 16 Catullus, Horace, Tibullus, Martial – Shorter Poems

Exercise B16.2: Subjunctive verbs (Latin into English)

This exercise practises recognising imperfect and pluperfect subjunctive forms for the verbs you have met in Chapter 16.

Sort the verbs into the correct category in the table below and identify the person of each one. You do not need to translate the verb into English, since a subjunctive verb's translation will depend on its context.

orarem   imperavisses   hortareris
   conficeret   surrexissemus   redderemus
coactus esset   hortatae essemus   verterentur   confecta essent

imperfect subjunctive active	imperfect subjunctive passive	imperfect subjunctive deponent

pluperfect subjunctive active	pluperfect subjunctive passive	pluperfect subjunctive deponent

Exercise B16.3: Forming the imperfect subjunctive

This exercise practises forming the imperfect active subjunctive of the verbs from the vocabulary lists for Chapters 15 and 16.

Remember that because the imperfect subjunctive uses the present stem, its endings will depend upon a verb's conjugation:

- 1st conjugation: **amo**, **amare** – imperfect active subjunctive = **amarem**, **amares** etc.
- 2nd conjugation: **terreo**, **terrere** – imperfect active subjunctive = **terrerem**, **terreres** etc.
- 3rd conjugation: **rego**, **regere** – imperfect active subjunctive = **regerem**, **regeres** etc.
- 4th conjugation: **audio**, **audire** – imperfect active subjunctive = **audirem**, **audires** etc.

Identify the conjugation of each verb below, and write out the 1st person sg of its imperfect active subjunctive.

	principal parts	conjugation	imperfect active subjunctive
1	impero, imperare, imperavi, imperatum (+ dative)		
2	oro, orare, oravi, oratum		
3	surgo, surgere, surrexi		
4	iaceo, iacere, iacui		
5	verto, vertere, verti, versum		
6	reddo, reddere, reddidi, redditum		
7	cogo, cogere, coegi, coactum		
8	conficio, conficere, confeci, confectum		
9	resisto, resistere, restiti (+ dative)		
10	accido, accidere, accidi		

Chapter 16 Catullus, Horace, Tibullus, Martial – Shorter Poems

Exercise B16.4: Forming the pluperfect subjunctive

This exercise practises forming the pluperfect subjunctive of the verbs from the vocabulary lists for Chapters 14–16.

The pluperfect active subjunctive uses the perfect active stem (e.g. **rex**issem).

The pluperfect passive subjunctive uses the PPP + *essem* (e.g. **rectus** *essem*).

Complete the table below, giving the 1st person sg of the pluperfect active and passive subjunctives.

	principal parts	pluperfect subjunctive active	pluperfect subjunctive passive
1	oro, orare, oravi, oratum		
2	reddo, reddere, reddidi, redditum		
3	verto, vertere, verti, versum		
4	conficio, conficere, confeci, confectum		
5	cogo, cogere, coegi, coactum		
6	opprimo, opprimere, oppressi, oppressum		
7	pello, pellere, pepuli, pulsum		
8	ago, agere, egi, actum		
9	celo, celare, celavi, celatum		
10	sentio, sentire, sensi, sensum		

Exercise B16.5: Forming the imperfect and pluperfect subjunctive for deponent verbs

This exercise practises the imperfect and pluperfect subjunctive forms for the deponent verbs from Chapters 13–16.

Remember that deponent verbs use passive forms. Write out the subjunctive forms in full for all persons of the verb. The 1st person sg form is given for you for each subjunctive.

	deponent verb	imperfect subjunctive	pluperfect subjunctive
1	hortor, hortari, hortatus sum	hortarer	hortatus essem
2	videor, videri, visus sum	viderer	visus essem
3	loquor, loqui, locutus sum	loquerer	locutus essem
4	regredior, regredi, regressus sum	regrederer	regressus essem

Chapter 16 Catullus, Horace, Tibullus, Martial – Shorter Poems

Exercise B16.6: Subordinating conjunctions, question words and prepositions

This exercise focuses on small words from the vocabulary lists for Chapters 13–16. It is easy to forget or confuse the meaning of these words.

Below are some of the subordinating conjunctions, question words and prepositions you have met in Chapters 13–16. Give the meaning of each word.

	Latin word	meaning
1	sine	
2	dum	
3	nisi	
4	si	
5	ut (+ indicative)	
6	ut (+ subjunctive)	
7	-ne	
8	ne (+ subjunctive)	
9	qualis	
10	quantus	
11	quot	
12	cur	
13	quomodo	
14	num	
15	cum (+ subjunctive)	
16	cum (+ ablative)	

Chapter 16 Additional Language

SECTION C16: ENGLISH TO LATIN SENTENCES

Exercise C16.1: Identifying subordinate clauses in English

Each of the sentences below contains a subordinate clause. Identify the words which form this subordinate clause and then specify whether it conveys purpose, a command, fear or result.

1. The commander urged the soldiers that they should fight more fiercely.
2. The chief begged the consuls that they should not attack the ships.
3. The consul was afraid that the citizens were fighting in the streets.
4. The army set out so that they might arrive at the camp of the enemy.
5. We captured so many enemies that the general rejoiced loudly.
6. The consul returned home so that he might conceal the crime.
7. I begged the general to such an extent that I did not suffer greatly.
8. The soldiers stayed in the camp so that they might not be wounded by the enemy.
9. The guards were afraid that the captives had escaped.
10. You fought so violently that the enemy did not resist.

Exercise C16.2: Indirect questions: question words

The English sentences below contain indirect questions. For each English quest on word in bold, choose the correct Latin question word from those given below.

quis	cur	quomodo	quot	num
ubi	quantus	qualia	quo	quem

1. The children were amazed at **how many** books they ought to read.
2. The teacher taught the boys **how** a senator used to speak in the forum.
3. The messenger announced **who** the consul had defeated.
4. The daughter of the consul realised at last **why** they had set out.
5. The commander of the enemy did not know **where** the army had advanced **to**.
6. The inhabitants wanted to know **whether** their children were alive.
7. The woman wanted to know **what sort of** wounds her husband was going to suffer.
8. Everyone was asking **where** the gold had been hidden.
9. No one noticed **who** had stolen the weapons.
10. The citizens were afraid because they did not know **how big** the army was.

Exercise C16.3: Sentences using the subjunctive

Each of the sentences below contains a subordinate clause which would need a subjunctive verb in Latin. The conjunction introducing each subordinate clause has been underlined and the verb in the clause is in bold.

Identify the Latin conjunction and the tense of the subjunctive needed. You will need to think about what type of subordinate clause it is and how the subjunctive behaves in that type of clause.

1. The consuls feared <u>that</u> the citizens **would die.**
2. The guard feared <u>that</u> the captives **had escaped**.
3. The army set out <u>so that</u> **they might arrive** at the camp before night.
4. The senators fled <u>so that</u> **they might not be captured**.
5. The commander ordered the army <u>that</u> **they should advance** towards the sea.
6. The woman begged her sons <u>that</u> **they should not fight** with weapons against the citizens.
7. This consul was so wicked <u>that</u> everyone **supported** that consul.
8. The father had so many enemies <u>that</u> his children **wanted** to escape.
9. <u>When</u> the enemy **had attacked** the camp, the captives were terrified.
10. <u>Since</u> the weapons **had been hidden**, no one was killed on that day.
11. We wanted to know <u>whether</u> the consul **was praising** the commander.
12. The soldiers asked <u>why</u> great rewards **had not been promised** to them.

Exercise C16.4: Sentences to translate into Latin

1. With the town occupied, the inhabitants despaired because they feared they would be killed.
2. The leaders, since they had fought with weapons for a long time, were worn out.
3. The soldiers carried their swords for many hours so that they might attack the enemy who were staying in the woods.
4. The women, carrying many things, went out quickly so that their husbands would not hear them.
5. The senators, who were standing near the door of the temple, asked who was going to speak to the citizens.
6. You announced that our friend had died. We didn't know whether he had suffered greatly.
7. The weeping daughter begged her father not to set out from Rome.
8. Were you afraid of danger? I was afraid that evil enemies were approaching.
9. After the cruel master arrived home, the slave suffered dreadful wounds.
10. The storm was so great that the army wanted to return to the camp.

APPENDIX 1: ADVANCED SYNTAX

In this section you will find a brief summary of the most important remaining principles of Latin sentence structure and grammar. You have encountered examples of these forms or constructions in some of the Latin texts in this book. Students keen to progress beyond this will find further detail in an advanced Latin grammar reference book.

GERUNDS

In Chapter 15 you met the gerundive but Latin has another verb form which looks very similar to this; this form is known as a **gerund**.

Gerunds are verbal nouns and refer to an action in abstract form. They are formed from the present stem and decline as a 2nd declension neuter noun. For example:

- am**andum** -i, n   (the action of) loving
- terr**endum** -i, n   (the action of) terrifying
- reg**endum** -i, n   (the action of) ruling
- aud**iendum** -i, n   (the action of) hearing

Confusion can arise because their English equivalent shares the same spelling as the English present participle. It is important to distinguish between a gerund (which is a noun) and a participle (which is an adjective). For example:

- I hear the sound of **fighting**.   gerund
- I hear the **fighting** children.   present participle

The gerund is used in Latin after prepositions and when a verbal noun is needed in the genitive, dative or ablative cases. When a verbal noun acts as subject or object of a finite verb, it is more idiomatic in Latin to use an infinitive. For example:

- pugnare volo.   I want to fight.
- pugnare est difficile.   Fighting is difficult. / It is difficult to fight.
- adsumus ad pugnandum.   We are here for the purpose of fighting.
- arte pugnandi vicimus.   Through skill in fighting we won.
- fortiter pugnando vicimus.   By fighting bravely we won.

FUTURE PERFECT INDICATIVES

As mentioned in Chapter 16, Latin has a future perfect indicative. This form of the verb is used for actions in future time which are viewed as complete. Like all verb forms with the perfect aspect, Latin uses the perfect active stem for the active voice and the PPP + part of the verb *to be* for the passive voice. The same endings are used in all conjugations (including irregular verbs).

An example of a future perfect indicative is given below.

future perfect indicative (active)		future perfect indicative (passive)	
amav**ero**	I will have loved	amatus ero	I will have been loved
amav**eris**	you (sg) will have loved	amatus eris	you (sg) will been have loved
amav**erit**	he / she / it will have loved	amatus erit	he / she / it will have been loved
amav**erimus**	we will have loved	amati erimus	we will have been loved
amav**eritis**	you (pl) will have loved	amati eritis	you (pl) will have been loved
amav**erint**	they will have loved	amati erunt	they will have been loved

Like all verb forms which include the PPP, the PPP has to agree with the subject of the verb in number and gender.

The future perfect indicative is fairly rare and it is used mainly in subordinate clauses that refer to a future time action which will have been completed before the main clause action takes place. Notice, however, that English idiom typically uses a present tense verb instead. For example:

si templum magnum aedificaveris, dei laeti erunt.　　　　　　If you build a big temple, the gods will be happy.

FUTURE PASSIVE INFINITIVES

In addition to the infinitives you met in Chapter 14, Latin also has a future passive infinitive but it is very rarely used. All verbs form their future passive infinitive in the same way, using the supine + *iri*. For example:

- amatum iri　　　　to be about to be loved
- territum iri　　　　to be about to be terrified
  etc.

Note that deponent verbs do not use this form for their future infinitives. Instead, their future infinitives are active in form, e.g. *secuturus esse* – *to be about to follow*.

THE IMPERSONAL PASSIVE

As discussed in Chapter 9, not all actions can be expressed in the passive. Only **transitive** verbs can move straightforwardly into the passive. This is because it is the direct object of the active voice which becomes the subject of the passive voice. For example:

- pater filium punivit.　　　　The father punished his son.
- filius a patre punitus est.　　　　The son was punished by his father.

A surprising number of verbs in Latin are **intransitive.** Sometimes this is because no direct object is involved (e.g. *hostes fugerunt* – *the enemy fled*) but sometimes it is because they take the dative (for example, *persuadeo* + dative). This means that they are technically intransitive even though their English equivalent is transitive.

Latin is able, however, to form the passive of these intransitive verbs, but only if the action itself is used as the subject. This means that the verb has to be 3rd person sg in form and neuter in gender. For example:

- filio persuasum est.
    A persuading was persuaded to the son.
    → The son was persuaded.

The impersonal passive construction appears very unwieldy when viewed from an English perspective, but in fact it can create drama and emphasis because it focuses entirely on the action itself, rather than dividing its attention between subject and action. To match this focus, it is often best translated with a noun in English.

Compare the following sentences:

- fortiter pugnaverunt.   They fought bravely.
- fortiter pugnatum est.   A fighting was fought bravely.
                             →There was brave fighting. / There was a brave battle.

PRESENT AND PERFECT TENSE SUBJUNCTIVES

In Chapter 16 you met the imperfect and pluperfect tenses of the subjunctive. Two more tenses exist: the present and the perfect. Like the imperfect and pluperfect subjunctive, the translation of the present and perfect subjunctive depends upon context and is explained further below.

The present subjunctive uses the present stem and is used for actions which are viewed as incomplete or continuous. The vowels used depend upon conjugation and the standard active / passive person endings are used.

	present active subjunctive	present passive subjunctive
1st conjugation	amem ames amet amemus ametis ament	amer ameris ametur amemur amemini amentur
2nd conjugation	terream terreas etc.	terrear terrearis etc.
3rd conjugation	regam regas etc.	regar regaris etc.
4th conjugation	audiam audias etc.	audiar audiaris etc.

Appendix 1: Advanced Syntax

The perfect tense subjunctive uses the perfect active stem for the active voice and the PPP plus a bit of the verb *to be* for the passive voice. All verbs (including irregular verbs) form their perfect subjunctives in the same way.

	perfect active subjunctive	perfect passive subjunctive
1st conjugation	amav**erim** amav**eris** amav**erit** amav**erimus** amav**eritis** amav**erint**	amatus **sim** amatus **sis** amatus **sit** amatus **simus** amatus **sitis** amatus **sint**
2nd conjugation	terru**erim** etc.	territus **sim** etc.
3rd conjugation	rex**erim** etc.	rectus **sim** etc.
4th conjugation	audiv**erim** etc.	auditus **sim** etc.

PRESENT AND PERFECT SUBJUNCTIVES IN SUBORDINATE CLAUSES: SEQUENCE OF TENSE

In Chapter 16, you learned that imperfect and pluperfect subjunctives are used in subordinate clauses in two different ways:

- in subordinate clauses where the action is in some way 'in the mind' of the subject of the main clause (such as purpose clauses, fearing clauses and indirect commands), the tense of the subjunctive depends upon the aspect of the action (as viewed from the standpoint of the subject of the main clause);
- in subordinate clauses where the action is not 'in the mind' of the subject of the main clause (such as result clauses), the subjunctive tenses behave in a way which is very similar to indicative tenses.

In subordinate clauses, the present and perfect subjunctives behave in a very similar way, but whereas the imperfect and pluperfect subjunctives are used in subordinate clauses attached to main clauses that are **in the past**, the present and perfect subjunctives are used in subordinate clauses which are attached to a main clause which is **not in the past**.

The principle that the tense of a verb in a subordinate clause is affected by whether or not the main clause is in the past is known as the principle of **sequence of tense**. A past time main clause will be followed by **historic sequence** subjunctives (i.e. the imperfect / pluperfect subjunctive) and a non-past time main clause will be followed by **primary sequence** subjunctives (i.e. the present / perfect subjunctive).

	historic sequence (i.e. past time main clause)	primary sequence (i.e. non-past time main clause)
subordinate clause action viewed as ongoing / incomplete	imperfect subjunctive	present subjunctive
subordinate clause action viewed as finished	pluperfect subjunctive	perfect subjunctive

Over time, the subjunctive gradually became a default verb form for subordinate clauses and it was used in more and more clauses; this means that the rules for its tenses gradually blurred with the rules for indicative tenses. You should not be surprised if you meet subjunctives which need to be translated as if they were indicatives.

MAIN CLAUSE SUBJUNCTIVES

The subjunctive can be used as the finite verb in a main clause when the action expressed is something imagined or hypothetical. For example:

- **wishes**, e.g. 'Would that the Romans had won! / If only the Romans had won!'
- **suggestions / exhortations**, e.g. 'Let's fight bravely tomorrow!'
- **potential actions**: these are actions which may have / may be / might be happening or which would have / would be / would happen, e.g. 'I would have run away'.

For a main clause subjunctive, tense denotes **aspect** and **time** as follows:

time of the action in the main clause	action viewed as ongoing / continuous	action viewed as finished
future time	present tense subjunctive	perfect tense subjunctive
present time	imperfect tense subjunctive	n/a
past time	imperfect tense subjunctive	pluperfect tense subjunctive

EXTENDED INDIRECT SPEECH

As discussed in Chapter 15, Roman writers often reported (or imagined) the words and thoughts of others. You have already met indirect statements, indirect questions and indirect commands: each of these constructions takes a piece of direct speech and embeds it as a subordinate phrase or clause within a sentence. Extended indirect speech is not embedded within another sentence: it stands free and is made up of a series of main clauses and subordinate clauses. Extended indirect speech is known as **oratio obliqua**.

The most important principles of oratio obliqua are:

- a main clause which is a statement will be conveyed as the accusative + infinitive construction.
- a main clause which is a question will follow the rules for indirect questions.
- a main clause which is a command will take the subjunctive; unlike indirect commands; however, the conjunction *ut* will not be used. This is because *ut* is only used when an indirect command is a subordinate clause.
- any subordinate clauses within oratio obliqua will take the subjunctive; the tense used will depend upon **sequence of tense** and **aspect**. The sequence of tense for the oratio obliqua is dictated by the verb which introduced the whole speech.

English, however, does not construct extended indirect speech in the same way. In English you will need to keep subordinating the indirect speech by adding main clauses such as 'He said ...', 'He added....', 'Furthermore he thought ...'.

Appendix 1: Advanced Syntax

For example:

dux ita locutus est. hostes progredi ut castra oppugnarent. milites suos optimos esse quod iam contra hostes alios pugnavissent. fortiter pugnarent.

The leader spoke as follows. He said that the enemy were advancing to attack the camp. He added that his own soldiers were excellent because they had already fought against other enemies. He urged them to fight bravely.

SEQUENCE OF TENSE IN ENGLISH

The principles of sequence of tense apply to English, too, and affect the English indicative as well as the English subjunctive. Compare the following examples and see how the tense in the subordinate clause changes when the main clause moves from non-past time to past time.

- I see the woman who is sitting over there.
    - I saw the woman who was sitting over there
- I say that the soldiers are fleeing.
    - I said that the soldiers were fleeing.
- I go to the shops so that I may buy milk.
    - I went to the shops so that I might buy milk.

You have already met the principle that when an ablative absolute or an indirect statement is translated idiomatically into a clause, the tense of the finite verb depends partly on the tense of the main clause. This is because of sequence of tense.

THE SUBJUNCTIVE IN CONDITIONAL SENTENCES

A sentence which contains an if-clause is known as a conditional sentence. You met these in Chapter 15.

When a conditional sentence contains a main clause that is a potential statement (i.e. it deals with something that would have happened, would be happening or might / would happen in the future), notice that the 'if' clause also takes a subjunctive. In these if-clauses, the tense of subjunctive used observes the principles for a main clause subjunctive (see table above).

For example,

si milites fortiter pugnavissent, vicissent.   If the soldiers had fought bravely, they would have won.
si iam milites fortiter pugnarent, vincerent. If the soldiers were fighting bravely now, they would be winning.
si cras milites fortiter pugnent, vincant.   If the soldiers were to fight bravely tomorrow, they would win.

APPENDIX 2: LATIN METRE

As discussed in Chapter 14, the rhythm of Latin poetry is based around patterns of long and short syllables. These are sometimes referred to as 'heavy' and 'light' syllables.

A syllable is long if it contains a long vowel, a diphthong or if the vowel is followed by two consonants. These consonants do not need to be in the same word, for example, the first syllable of *et Venus* is long because the vowel *e* is followed by the consonants *t* and then *V*.

A syllable is short if it contains a short vowel followed by only one consonant.

In addition to these principles:

- if the second of two consonants is the letter *l* or *r* then the syllable could be short or long;
- *x* counts as two consonants.

When annotating the rhythm of a poem, the following annotations are used:

long / heavy syllable	–
short / light syllable	U

The two most important patterns in Latin verse are known as **spondees** and **dactyls**. A spondee contains two long syllables and a dactyl contains a long syllable followed by two short syllables. Spondees and dactyls are annotated as follows:

spondee	– –
dactyl	– U U

In addition, when Latin poetry is read aloud, words will merge together when one word ending in a vowel (or a vowel + *m*) is followed by a word which begins with a vowel (or *h* + vowel). This is known as **elision**.

The two most common metres in Latin poetry are the hexameter metre (used for epic poetry) and the elegiac couplet (often used in shorter poems).

The hexameter metre is made up of six units (known as **feet**) as follows:

1st foot	2nd foot	3rd foot	4th foot	5th foot	6th foot
spondee or dactyl	spondee or dactyl	spondee or dactyl	spondee or dactyl	dactyl	two syllable foot (anceps)
– – – U U	– – – U U	– – – U U	– – – U U	– U U	– X

The very last syllable of a line could be either long or short; this is why it is marked as *x*. The name for this symbol is **anceps**.

Appendix 2: Latin Metre

The elegiac couplet is made up of a line of hexameter followed by a line of pentameter. The pentameter metre looks like this:

1st foot	2nd foot	half-foot	3rd foot	4th foot	half-foot
spondee or dactyl	spondee or dactyl	single long syllable	dactyl	dactyl	single syllable
– – – U U	– – – U U	–	– U U	– U U	X

Latin poetry is a delicate mixture of balance and imbalance: the patterns of the metre create balance and this is offset by the imbalance of where pauses fall in a line. A pause in the rhythm is called a **caesura**.

The Latin texts in Chapter 14 are all written in the hexameter metre. In Chapter 16, many are composed in elegiac couplets; it is easy to see which are in elegiac couplets because the convention is to print the second line of the couplet indented from the first.

Some Latin poetry uses different metres altogether. These are often based on earlier Greek poetry.

Below are some extracts from the Latin texts with the rhythm annotated. The process of marking up the rhythm of a line of verse is known as **scansion**. In the examples below, the hexameter metre has been marked in blue and the pentameter in green. The caesuras are marked in purple.

Latin text 14.1 – Hexameter

```
–    UU|– UU  |–‖ U U| –   –  |– UU | – X
saucius ille tamen 'fer opem, matertera' dixit

–    UU|–‖ U U|– UU  | – – |– UU |–   X
'Autonoe! moveant animos Actaeonis umbrae!'

– U U | – – | –‖ – | –   – | –   U   U| – X
illa quis Actaeon, nescit dextramque precanti

–    UU|  – – |–‖U U|– –    | – UU| – X
abstulit, Inoo lacerata est altera raptu.
```

Latin text 16.1 – Elegiac couplets

```
–    U U| – UU|–‖U U|– UU | – U    U|– X
hic mihi servitium video dominamque paratam:

   –    UU | – – |–‖– U U | – U    U|X
   iam mihi, libertas illa paterna, vale.

– UU|–   – | – U   U| –‖UU|–   U   U|– X
servitium sed triste datur, teneorque catenis,

    –    – | –    UU|–‖ –   U U |–UU| X
    et numquam misero vincla remittit Amor,

– – | –     UU|–‖ – | –   – | – UU | – X
et seu quid merui seu nil peccavimus, urit.

   – U U| – U   U| –‖– U  U|– UU | X
   uror, io, remove, saeva puella, faces.
```

REFERENCE GRAMMAR

SECTION 1: GRAMMATICAL FORMS

NOUNS

Cases

Latin uses different case endings to show a noun's role in a sentence. The main roles are as follows:

nominative	• the subject of a finite verb, e.g. The **father** loves his daughter / The **general** is killed by the soldier.
vocative	• a noun which is directly addressed, e.g. O **king**, do not punish us!
accusative	• the object of an active verb, e.g. The father loves his **daughter**. • after certain prepositions • in time phrases to show time how long, e.g. **for three hours** • for the subject of an infinitive • for the names of towns to show motion towards that town
genitive	• used to show that one noun is connected to another: most typically it shows possession, e.g. the **father's** daughter • often best translated as *of*
dative	• the indirect object, used to mean *to* or *for* • after certain verbs such as *persuādeō* • to show possession
ablative	• used without a preposition to mean *by, with, from* and sometimes *in* or *because of* • after certain prepositions • in time phrases to show time when, e.g. **in the second year** • with the names of towns to show motion away from that town • within a comparison to mean *than* • in a noun and participle phrase as an **ablative absolute** (see p60)

Latin has one more case – the **locative** case – which is used mainly for the names of towns and small islands. The locative case shows that someone or something is in or at that place. The locative case looks identical to the ablative case, with the exception of singular 1st and 2nd declension nouns; for these, the locative looks the same as the genitive.

e.g. **Rōmae** senātōrem clārissimum cōnspexī. – **At Rome** I saw a very famous senator.

Reference Grammar

Declensions

There are five groups of Latin nouns; nouns in each group (declension) share the same spellings for their endings.

You can identify the declension of a noun by looking at how it is listed in a dictionary or word list. The nominative and genitive singular forms are given, together with the gender.

The genitive singular allows us to work out the declension of the noun and its stem.

fēmina, **fēminae**, f	1st declension feminine	stem = fēmin-
deus, **deī**, m	2nd declension masculine	stem = de-
bellum, **bellī**, n	2nd declension neuter	stem = bell-
rēx, **rēgis**, m	3rd declension masculine	stem = rēg-
flūmen, **flūminis**, n	3rd declension neuter	stem = flūmin-
exercitus, **exercitūs**, m	4th declension masculine	stem = exercit-
rēs, **reī**, f	5th declension feminine	stem = r-

N.B. Neuter nouns have slightly different endings from masculine / feminine nouns in the same declension.

1st declension	
nominative sg	fēmin-a
accusative sg	fēmin-am
genitive sg	fēmin-ae
dative sg	fēmin-ae
ablative sg	fēmin-ā
nominative pl	fēmin-ae
accusative pl	fēmin-ās
genitive pl	fēmin-ārum
dative pl	fēmin-īs
ablative pl	fēmin-īs

- *fēmina* is a feminine noun; masculine first declension nouns (e.g. *agricola*) have exactly the same endings. There are no neuter nouns in the 1st declension.
- in the 1st declension, vocative endings are the same as the nominative

Reference Grammar

2nd declension		neuter nouns
nominative sg	de-us	bell-um
accusative sg	de-um	bell-um
genitive sg	de-ī	bell-ī
dative sg	de-ō	bell-ō
ablative sg	de-ō	bell-ō
nominative pl	de-ī	bell-a
accusative pl	de-ōs	bell-a
genitive pl	de-ōrum	bell-ōrum
dative pl	de-īs	bell-īs
ablative pl	de-īs	bell-īs

- *deus* is a masculine noun; feminine second declension nouns are extremely rare and have exactly the same endings
- second declension nouns have a separate vocative singular ending as follows:
  - for nouns such as *servus, servī, m* the vocative is *serve*
  - for nouns such as *filius, filiī, m* the vocative is *filī*
  - *deus* has an irregular vocative singular form *deus*
- for the vocative plural, the ending is the same as the nominative plural
- some second declension masculine nouns have a nominative ending in *-er*, e.g. *puer, puerī* and *ager, agrī*

3rd declension		neuter nouns
nominative sg	(rēx)	(flūmen)
accusative sg	rēg-em	(flūmen)
genitive sg	rēg-is	flūmin-is
dative sg	rēg-ī	flūmin-ī
ablative sg	rēg-e	flūmin-e
nominative pl	rēg-ēs	flūmin-a
accusative pl	rēg-ēs	flūmin-a
genitive pl	rēg-um	flūmin-um
dative pl	rēg-ibus	flūmin-ibus
ablative pl	rēg-ibus	flūmin-ibus

Reference Grammar

- *rēx* is a masculine noun; feminine and masculine 3rd declension nouns have the same endings
- there is no uniform ending for the nominative singular (or for neuter nouns the nominative and accusative singular). This is why *rēx* and *flūmen* are written in brackets: they can not serve as a template for another 3rd declension nominative singular.
- vocative endings in the 3rd declension are the same as the nominative
- some nouns in the 3rd declension have *-ium* as their genitive plural ending: typically these are nouns such as *hostis* (where the genitive singular and the nominative singular are the same) or nouns such as *mōns* (where the nominative singular ends in two consonants). The nouns you have met of this type in *de Romanis* are as follows: *mōns, urbs, cīvis, hostis, mors, nāvis, pars, gēns*. In addition, *mare* has unusual endings; these are listed in full on p255.

4th declension		neuter nouns
nominative sg	exercit-us	corn-ū
accusative sg	exercit-um	corn-ū
genitive sg	exercit-ūs	corn-ūs
dative sg	exercit-uī	corn-ū
ablative sg	exercit-ū	corn-ū
nominative pl	exercit-ūs	corn-ua
accusative pl	exercit-ūs	corn-ua
genitive pl	exercit-uum	corn-uum
dative pl	exercit-ibus	corn-ibus
ablative pl	exercit-ibus	corn-ibus

- *exercitus* is a masculine noun; feminine and masculine 4th declension nouns have the same endings.
- 4th declension neuter nouns are very rare (*cornū* – *horn, wing (of an army)* – is given here as an example; notice that – unusually – the dative sg endings (as well as the nominative and accusative endings) are spelled differently from the masculine / feminine nouns in their declension.
- vocative endings in the 4th declension are the same as the nominative.
- there are lots of 4th declension nouns which share the same stem as their cognate verb's PPP, e.g. *exitus, exitūs,* m – *a going forth, an outcome*.

5th declension	
nominative sg	r-ēs
accusative sg	r-em
genitive sg	r-eī
dative sg	r-eī
ablative sg	r-ē

Reference Grammar

nominative pl	r-ēs
accusative pl	r-ēs
genitive pl	r-ērum
dative pl	r-ēbus
ablative pl	r-ēbus

- *rēs* is a feminine noun; feminine and masculine 4th declension nouns have the same endings; most 5th declension nouns are feminine
- there are no neuter 5th declension nouns
- vocative endings in the 5th declension are the same as the nominative

ADJECTIVES

There are two main types of adjectives: those with a mixture of 2nd / 1st declension endings, and those with 3rd declension endings.

Adjectives must agree with the noun they describe in case, gender and number.

It is fairly common for an adjective to be used without a noun: in these circumstances the gender and number of the adjective should guide its translation.

e.g. *īrātī rēgem interfēcērunt.* The angry men killed the king.

2-1-2 adjectives

	masculine	feminine	neuter
nominative sg	īrāt-us	īrāt-a	īrāt-um
accusative sg	īrāt-um	īrāt-am	īrāt-um
genitive sg	īrāt-ī	īrāt-ae	īrāt-ī
dative sg	īrāt-ō	īrāt-ae	īrāt-ō
ablative sg	īrāt-ō	īrāt-ā	īrāt-ō
nominative pl	īrāt-ī	īrāt-ae	īrāt-a
accusative pl	īrāt-ōs	īrāt-ās	īrāt-a
genitive pl	īrāt-ōrum	īrāt-ārum	īrāt-ōrum
dative pl	īrāt-īs	īrāt-īs	īrāt-īs
ablative pl	īrāt-īs	īrāt-īs	īrāt-īs

N.B. As with some 2nd declension nouns, some 2-1-2 adjectives have a nominative masculine sg form ending in *-er*, for example *pulcher, pulchra, pulchrum* and *miser, misera, miserum*.

Reference Grammar

3rd declension adjectives

There are two main types of 3rd declension adjectives: those with a separate neuter nominative sg ending, and those without. Each type is listed slightly differently in a word list, and the stem can be found as follows:

    fortis, **fort**e   brave, strong   (nominative forms only given)

    ingens, **ingent**is   huge   (nominative & genitive given)

	masculine / feminine	neuter	masculine / feminine	neuter
nominative sg	fort-is	fort-e	(ingēns)	(ingēns)
accusative sg	fort-em	fort-e	ingent-em	(ingēns)
genitive sg	fort-is	fort-is	ingent-is	ingent-is
dative sg	fort-ī	fort-ī	ingent-ī	ingent-ī
ablative sg	fort-ī	fort-ī	ingent-ī	ingent-ī
nominative pl	fort-ēs	fort-ia	ingent-ēs	ingent-ia
accusative pl	fort-ēs	fort-ia	ingent-ēs	ingent-ia
genitive pl	fort-ium	fort-ium	ingent-ium	ingent-ium
dative pl	fort-ibus	fort-ibus	ingent-ibus	ingent-ibus
ablative pl	fort-ibus	fort-ibus	ingent-ibus	ingent-ibus

N.B. Adjectives like *celer, celeris, celere* are an exception. They have three different nominative forms: *celer* (nominative masculine sg), *celeris* (nominative feminine sg) and *celere* (nominative neuter sg). For all other cases the endings are the same as *fortis*.

Comparative adjectives

Comparative adjectives are formed by adding the following endings to a noun's stem. These endings are used for all types of adjectives. They are very similar to the usual 3rd declension adjective endings.

A comparative adjective means *more . . . / rather . . . / too . . .*

	masculine / feminine	neuter
nominative sg	laet-ior	laet-ius
accusative sg	laet-iōrem	laet-ius
genitive sg	laet-iōris	laet-iōris
dative sg	laet-iōrī	laet-iōrī
ablative sg	laet-iōre	laet-iōre
nominative pl	laet-iōrēs	laet-iōra
accusative pl	laet-iōrēs	laet-iōra
genitive pl	laet-iōrum	laet-iōrum
dative pl	laet-iōribus	laet-iōribus
ablative pl	laet-iōribus	laet-iōribus

Latin has two ways of comparing nouns:

- the ablative of comparison: e.g. *rēx cīvibus laetior erat.* The king was happier than the citizens.
- using *quam* to mean *than*: e.g. *rēx laetior quam cīvēs erat.* The king was happier than the citizens.

Superlative adjectives

A superlative adjective means *very . . . / the most . . .*

Superlative adjectives are easy to recognise. The different types of adjectives you have met form their superlative in the following ways:

fortis, forte – strong	fortissimus, fortissima, fortissimum – very strong
audāx, audācis – bold	audācissimus, audācissima, audācissimum – very bold
celer, celeris, celere – quick	celerrimus, celerrima, celerrimus – very quick
pulcher, pulchra, pulchrum – beautiful	pulcherrimus, pulcherrima, pulcherrimum – very beautiful
facilis, facile – easy	facillimus, facillima, facillimum – very easy
difficilis, difficile – difficult	difficillimus, difficillima, difficillimum – very difficult

Superlative adjectives have 2-1-2 endings.

	masculine	feminine	neuter
nominative sg	īrātissim-us	īrātissim-a	īrātissim-um
accusative sg	īrātissim-um	īrātissim-am	īrātissim-um
for the other 2-1-2 case endings see p221			

Common irregular comparative and superlative adjectives

Some of Latin's most common adjectives have irregular comparative and superlative stems; the case endings used with these stems, however, are the same as for any other comparative or superlative adjective.

	comparative	superlative
bonus, bona, bonum – good	melior, melius – better	optimus, optima, optimum – best
malus, mala, malum – bad	peior, peius – worse	pessimus, pessima, pessimum – worst
magnus, magna, magnum – big	maior, maius – bigger	maximus, maxima, maximum – largest
parvus, parva, parvum – small	minor, minus – smaller	minimus, minima, minimum – smallest, least
multus, multa, multum – much / many	plūs – more *	plūrimus, plūrima, plūrimum – most, very many

*N.B. *plūs* is unusual in the way it is used: for more details see p257

Reference Grammar

PRONOUNS

Pronouns are words which can be used instead of nouns or to emphasise them. Pronouns change their endings according to the gender and number of the noun they represent, and they take the case that is right for their role in the sentence.

is, ea, id

is, ea, id usually means *he, she, it, they*; used with a noun (rather than on its own) it can mean *that, those*.

    e.g. *eum timēbam.*   I feared him.
        eum rēgem timēbam. I feared that king.

he / she / it	masculine	feminine	neuter		masculine	feminine	neuter
nominative sg	is	ea	id	nominative pl	eī	eae	ea
accusative sg	eum	eam	id	accusative pl	eōs	eās	ea
genitive sg	eius	eius	eius	genitive pl	eōrum	eārum	eōrum
dative sg	eī	eī	eī	dative pl	eīs	eīs	eīs
ablative sg	eō	eā	eō	ablative pl	eīs	eīs	eīs

īdem, eadem, idem

īdem, eadem, idem usually means *the same*. Its forms are very similar to *is, ea, id* but notice that it is the start of the word that changes.

the same	masculine	feminine	neuter		masculine	feminine	neuter
nominative sg	īdem	eadem	idem	nominative pl	eīdem	eaedem	eadem
accusative sg	eundem	eandem	idem	accusative pl	eōsdem	eāsdem	eadem
genitive sg	eiusdem	eiusdem	eiusdem	genitive pl	eōrumdem	eārumdem	eōrumdem
dative sg	eīdem	eīdem	eīdem	dative pl	eīsdem	eīsdem	eīsdem
ablative sg	eōdem	eādem	eōdem	ablative pl	eīsdem	eīsdem	eīsdem

hic, haec, hoc & ille, illa, illud

hic, haec, hoc usually means *this* or *these*. *ille, illa, illud* usually means *that* or *those*.

Sometimes *ille, illa, illud* is used to mean *he, she, it*, especially when there is a change in subject.

e.g. *pater fīlium pūnīvit: ille trīstis erat.*   The father punished the son: he was sad.

Both these pronouns are often used on their own to mean *that man*, or *those women*, or *these things* etc.
e.g. *haec audīvit.*   He heard these things.

this / these	masculine	feminine	neuter		masculine	feminine	neuter
nominative sg	hic	haec	hoc	nominative pl	hī	hae	haec
accusative sg	hunc	hanc	hoc	accusative pl	hōs	hās	haec
genitive sg	huius	huius	huius	genitive pl	hōrum	hārum	hōrum
dative sg	huic	huic	huic	dative pl	hīs	hīs	hīs
ablative sg	hōc	hāc	hōc	ablative pl	hīs	hīs	hīs

that / those	masculine	feminine	neuter		masculine	feminine	neuter
nominative sg	ille	illa	illud	nominative pl	illī	illae	illa
accusative sg	illum	illam	illud	accusative pl	illōs	illās	illa
genitive sg	illīus	illīus	illīus	genitive pl	illōrum	illārum	illōrum
dative sg	illī	illī	illī	dative pl	illīs	illīs	illīs
ablative sg	illō	illā	illō	ablative pl	illīs	illīs	illīs

ipse, ipsa, ipsum

ipse, ipsa, ipsum means *himself, herself* etc. It is an emphatic pronoun, often used to add a tone of surprise.

himself, herself etc	masculine	feminine	neuter		masculine	feminine	neuter
nominative sg	ipse	ipsa	ipsum	nominative pl	ipsī	ipsae	ipsa
accusative sg	ipsum	ipsam	ipsum	accusative pl	ipsōs	ipsās	ipsa
genitive sg	ipsius	ipsius	ipsius	genitive pl	ipsōrum	ipsārum	ipsōrum
dative sg	ipsī	ipsī	ipsī	dative pl	ipsīs	ipsīs	ipsīs
ablative sg	ipsō	ipsā	ipsō	ablative pl	psīs	ipsīs	ipsīs

Reference Grammar

quī, quae, quod

quī, quae, quod means *who* or *which*. It is known as the relative pronoun, because it introduces a subordinate clause which relates to a noun in the sentence.

Like any other pronoun it takes its gender and number from the noun it represents, and its case from its role in the sentence. Because the relative pronoun is used in a different clause from the noun it relates to, it may have a different role in its own clause and so it may need a different case.

who / which	masculine	feminine	neuter		masculine	feminine	neuter
nominative sg	quī	quae	quod	nominative pl	quī	quae	quae
accusative sg	quem	quam	quod	accusative pl	quōs	quās	quae
genitive sg	cuius	cuius	cuius	genitive pl	quōrum	quārum	quōrum
dative sg	cui	cui	cui	dative pl	quibus	quibus	quibus
ablative sg	quō	quā	quō	ablative pl	quibus	quibus	quibus

quis, quis, quid

The question word *quis, quis, quid* – *who? what? which?* looks very similar to the relative pronoun; it is only different in its nominative sg (and neuter accusative sg) forms.

who? / which? / what?	masculine	feminine	neuter		masculine	feminine	neuter
nominative sg	quis	quis	quid	nominative pl	quī	quae	quae
accusative sg	quem	quam	quid	accusative pl	quōs	quās	quae
genitive sg	cuius	cuius	cuius	genitive pl	quōrum	quārum	quōrum
dative sg	cui	cui	cui	dative pl	quibus	quibus	quibus
ablative sg	quō	quā	quō	ablative pl	quibus	quibus	quibus

quīdam, quaedam, quoddam

quīdam, quaedam, quoddam means *a certain, some*.

Its forms are very similar to *quī, quae, quod*, but notice that it is the start of the word which changes.

who / which	masculine	feminine	neuter		masculine	feminine	neuter
nominative sg	quīdam	quaedam	quoddam	nominative pl	quīdam	quaedam	quaedam
accusative sg	quendam	quandam	quoddam	accusative pl	quōsdam	quāsdam	quaedam
genitive sg	cuiusdam	cuiusdam	cuiusdam	genitive pl	quōrumdam	quārumdam	quōrumdam
dative sg	cuidam	cuidam	cuidam	dative pl	quibuscam	quibusdam	quibusdam
ablative sg	quōdam	quādam	quōdam	ablative pl	quibuscam	quibusdam	quibusdam

Personal pronouns

Like other pronouns, personal pronouns have different case endings, and like other pronouns their case depends upon their role in their clause.

	I	you (sg)	we	you (pl)	(him / her / it) -self (sg)	themselves (pl)
nominative	ego	tū	nōs	vōs		
accusative	mē	tē	nōs	vōs	sē	sē
genitive	meī	tuī	nostrum	vestrum	suī	suī
dative	mihī	tibī	nōbis	vōbis	sibi	sibi
ablative	mē	tē	nōbis	vōbis	sē	sē

Unlike other pronouns, personal pronouns do not have different forms for different genders.

sē is known as the reflexive pronoun; this means that it has to refer to the subject of the sentence. This is why it has no nominative form: it has to refer to the subject and so can never be used as the subject. Unlike all other pronouns, *sē* does not have different singular and plural forms.

e.g. *rēx sē interfēcit.*   The king killed himself.
    cīvēs sē interfēcērunt.   The citizens killed themselves.
    rēx eum interfēcit.   The king killed him.

Reference Grammar

ADVERBS

Like English, Latin can turn adjectives into adverbs by changing their endings.

The two main adverb endings are *-ē* and *-ter*

e.g. laetus, laeta, laetum   happy   laetē   happily
    fortis, forte   brave, strong   fortiter   bravely, strongly

Latin also has lots of adverbs which do not use these endings; examples of these are:

etiam	also; even	semper	always
saepe	often	iterum	again
tum	then	magnopere	greatly; very much
fortiter	bravely; strongly	mox	soon
nōn	not	nunc	now
celeriter	quickly	hīc	here
diū	for a long time	iam	now; already
ōlim	once; some time ago	ibi	there
subitō	suddenly	numquam	never
tandem	at last; finally	sīc	thus; in this way

Sometimes adjectives are used instead of adverbs. For example:

- *līberī prīmī fūgērunt.*   The children were the first to flee.
- *māter īrāta fīliōs pūnīvit.*   The mother punished her sons angrily.

Comparative and superlative adverbs

Adverbs also have comparative and superlative forms: as for normal adverbs, the endings for each of these do not change.

Here are some examples:

adverb	comparative adverb	superlative adverb
fortiter – bravely	fortius – more bravely	fortissimē – most bravely
celeriter – quickly	celerius – more quickly	celerrimē – most quickly
ferōciter – fiercely	ferōcius – more fiercely	ferōcissimē – most fiercely
saepe – often	saepius – more often	saepissimē – most often
diū – for a long time	diūtius – for rather a long time	diūtissimē – for a very long time
magnopere – greatly	magis – more	maximē – very greatly

If *quam* is used with a superlative adverb, it means *as . . . as possible*. e.g. *quam celerrimē cucurrī.* – I ran as quickly as possible.

PREPOSITIONS

A preposition is a word which is positioned before a noun and shows its relationship to something else in the sentence.

In Latin, each preposition has to be followed by a particular case: this is usually the accusative or the ablative. The case required by a preposition is listed in a dictionary or word list, for example:

ad + accusative	to; towards; at
contrā + accusative	against
in + accusative	into
ā, ab + ablative	from; away from; by
ē, ex + ablative	from; out of; out from
in + ablative	in; on

QUESTION WORDS

Like English, Latin has several words which are used to ask a question. It is usual for the question word to be the first word in the sentence.

There are three different words used to introduce questions which have *yes* or *no* as their answer.

-ne	invites the answer *yes* or *no*
nōnne . . . ?	invites the answer *yes*
num . . . ?	invites the answer *no*

-ne is used at the end of the first word in the question, which typically will be a verb.

   e.g. *tulistīne ad templum dōna?*   Did you bring gifts to the temple?

There are different question words for questions which do not have *yes* or *no* as their answers. These include:

cūr?	why?
quandō?	when?
ubi?	where?
quis / quis / quid?	who? what?
quō?	to where?
unde?	from where?

quis, quis, quid is a pronoun and so it changes its endings: it takes the number and gender of the noun it represents and the case needed for its own role in the sentence.

NUMBERS

ūnus, ūna, ūnum	1
duo, duae, duo	2
trēs, tria	3
quattuor	4
quīnque	5
sex	6
septem	7
octō	8
novem	9
decem	10
centum	100
mīlle	1000
mīlia, mīlium	1000s

In Latin, *ūnus*, *duo* and *trēs* change their endings, but the Latin words for 4–100 do not change.

mīlle is an exception: it does not change in the singular (1000), but its plural form (*mīlia* - 1000s) does change its endings and behaves like a 3rd declension neuter noun. *mīlia* is often followed by a genitive noun: e.g. *Rōmānī duo mīlia hostium interfēcērunt*. – The Romans killed 2000 enemy.

one	masculine	feminine	neuter	two	masculine	feminine	neuter
nominative	ūnus	ūna	ūnum	nominative	duo	duae	duo
accusative	ūnum	ūnam	ūnum	accusative	duōs	duās	duo
genitive	ūnīus	ūnīus	ūnīus	genitive	duōrum	duārum	duōrum
dative	ūnī	ūnī	ūnī	dative	duōbus	duābus	duōbus
ablative	ūnō	ūnā	ūnō	ablative	duōbus	duābus	duōbus

three	masculine	feminine	neuter
nominative	trēs	trēs	tria
accusative	trēs	trēs	tria
genitive	trium	trium	trium
dative	tribus	tribus	tribus
ablative	tribus	tribus	tribus

Latin also has adjectives for 'first', 'second', 'third' etc.

prīmus, prīma, prīmum	first
secundus, secunda, secundum	second
tertius, tertia, tertium	third
quārtus, quārta, quārtum	fourth
quīntus, quīnta, quīntum	fifth
sextus, sexta, sextum	sixth
septimus, septima, septimum	seventh
octāvus, octāva, octāvum	eighth
nōnus, nōna, nōnum	ninth
decimus, decima, decimum	tenth

NEGATIVES

Latin has several negative words. These include:

nōn	not
nihil	nothing
nēmō, nūllius	no-one; nobody
neque, nec	and not; nor; neither
nōlō, nōlle, nōluī	not want; refuse
nūllus, nūlla, nūllum	not any; no
num . . .?	surely not . . .? (invites the answer *no*)
numquam	never

nihil, nēmō, nōlō and *nūllus* all have unusual forms. The endings for *nōlō* are listed on p250; details of *nihil, nēmō* and *nūllus* are on p256.

Reference Grammar

VERBS

Verbs are the most complex part of speech. They have many different forms. Each form belongs to one of the following categories:

- finite verb forms (i.e. indicatives, subjunctives and imperatives): these are forms with a person and a tense
- verbal adjectives (i.e. participles, gerundives): these are forms of the verb which function as adjectives
- verbal nouns (i.e. infinitives, gerunds): these often refer to the action in abstract form.

Latin verbs have multiple stems; as discussed in Chapter 16 (p162), different verb stems convey different **aspects** of the verb (i.e. whether or not an action is viewed as finished or not-yet finished).

Latin verbs belong to **conjugations**; the spelling of a Latin verb's ending depends partly on which conjugation it is in.

Principal parts

The principal parts of a verb show the verb's conjugation and stems.

amō	amāre	**amāv**ī	**amāt**um
I love	to love	I loved	supine
present tense	infinitive	perfect tense	
present stem		**perfect stem**	**supine stem**

The present stem is used for the present, imperfect and future tenses; it signals that the action's aspect is viewed as not-yet finished.

The perfect stem is used for the perfect and pluperfect active tenses; it signals that the action's aspect is viewed as finished.

The supine stem is used for the perfect passive participle (PPP); the PPP is used on its own as a participle and also as part of all perfect and pluperfect passive verb forms. The supine stem signals that the action's aspect is viewed as finished.

Deponent verbs (i.e. those verbs which are passive in form, but active in meaning) only have three principal parts because they do not have a perfect active stem.

cōnor	cōnārī	**cōnāt**us sum
I try	to try	I tried
present tense	infinitive	perfect tense
present stem		**supine stem**

Conjugations

There are four main groups of Latin verbs. Verbs in each group (conjugation) share the same endings.

The first two principal parts show which conjugation a verb is in:

amō	amāre	amāvī	amātum	– 1st conjugation
terreō	terrēre	terruī	territum	– 2nd conjugation
regō	regere	rēxī	rēctum	– 3rd conjugation
audiō	audīre	audīvī	audītum	– 4th conjugation

Some verbs are a mixture of the 3rd and 4th conjugations.

| capiō | capere | cēpī | captum | – mixed conjugation |

The first two principal parts for a deponent verb can be used to identify conjugation in the same way:

cōnor	cōnārī	cōnātus sum	– 1st conjugation
videor	vidērī	vīsus sum	– 2nd conjugation
loquor	loquī	locūtus sum	– 3rd conjugation
orior	orīrī	ortus sum	– 4th conjugation
ēgredior	ēgredī	ēgressus sum	– mixed conjugation

Active and passive

A verb form is either active or passive.

- The subject of an active verb does the action: e.g. **The senator** heard the citizens.
- The subject of a passive verb suffers or experiences the action: e.g. **The citizens** were heard by the senator.

Remember, the subject of a finite verb will be nominative, whether or not the verb is active or passive.

Latin also has a group of verbs which take passive forms but are active in meaning; these verbs are known as **deponent verbs**. In addition, there are a small number of **semi-deponent** verbs which are non-deponent for their present-stem forms but deponent for all perfect and pluperfect verb forms. See further Chapter 14, p56.

FINITE FORMS OF THE VERB

All finite forms of the verb have a **person ending**. Latin has three different **moods** of finite verbs: **indicatives**, **subjunctives** and **imperatives**.

The **nominative case** is used for the subject of all finite verb forms.

Reference Grammar

INDICATIVE VERBS

Indicative finite verbs are used to indicate an action which took place in past, present or future time.

Present indicative (active)

Verbs in the present indicative use the present stem and the following endings; the vowel depends on a verb's conjugation.

The present active indicative can be translated as follows: *amō – I love* or *I am loving*.

present indicative (active)	1st conjugation	2nd conjugation	3rd conjugation	4th conjugation	mixed conjugation
I	amō	terreō	regō	audiō	capiō
you (sg)	amās	terrēs	regis	audīs	capis
he / she / it	amat	terret	regit	audit	capit
we	amāmus	terrēmus	regimus	audīmus	capimus
you (pl)	amātis	terrētis	regitis	audītis	capitis
they	amant	terrent	regunt	audiunt	capiunt

Present indicative (passive)

Verbs in the present indicative use the present stem and the following endings; the vowel used depends on a verb's conjugation:

The present passive indicative can be translated as follows: *amor – I am loved* or *I am being loved*.

present indicative (passive)	1st conjugation	2nd conjugation	3rd conjugation	4th conjugation	mixed conjugation
I	amor	terreor	regor	audior	capior
you (sg)	amāris	terrēris	regeris	audīris	caperis
he / she / it	amātur	terrētur	regitur	audītur	capitur
we	amāmur	terrēmur	regimur	audīmur	capimur
you (pl)	amāminī	terrēminī	regiminī	audīminī	capiminī
they	amantur	terrentur	reguntur	audiuntur	capiuntur

Present indicative (deponent)

Verbs in the present indicative use the present stem and the following endings; the vowel depends on a verb's conjugation.

The present indicative for a deponent verb is passive in form but active in meaning; it can be translated as follows: *cōnor* – *I try* or *I am trying*.

present indicative (deponent)	1st conjugation	2nd conjugation	3rd conjugation	4th conjugation	mixed conjugation
I	cōn**or**	vid**eor**	loqu**or**	or**ior**	ēgred**ior**
you (sg)	cōn**āris**	vid**ēris**	loqu**eris**	or**īris**	ēgred**eris**
he / she / it	cōn**ātur**	vid**ētur**	loqu**itur**	or**ītur**	ēgred**itur**
we	cōn**āmur**	vid**ēmur**	loqu**imur**	or**īmur**	ēgred**imur**
you (pl)	cōn**āminī**	vid**ēminī**	loqu**iminī**	or**īminī**	ēgred**iminī**
they	cōn**antur**	vid**entur**	loqu**untur**	or**iuntur**	ēgred**iuntur**

Imperfect indicative (active)

Verbs in the imperfect indicative use the present stem; the vowel which comes before the imperfect endings depends on the verb's conjugation.

The imperfect indicative is used in Latin for past actions that are viewed as ongoing, or lasting quite a long time.

The imperfect indicative active can be translated in three main ways:

    regēbam   I was ruling / I used to rule / I began to rule

N.B. Although in Latin the imperfect is used for actions which typically last for some time, in English we are often more likely to use the perfect tense. This means that sometimes the best translation for a Latin imperfect indicative is an English perfect indicative.

    e.g. *diū rēx regēbat.*   The king ruled for a long time.

imperfect indicative (active)	1st conjugation	2nd conjugation	3rd conjugation	4th conjugation	mixed conjugation
I	am**ābam**	terr**ēbam**	reg**ēbam**	aud**iēbam**	cap**iēbam**
you (sg)	am**ābās**	terr**ēbās**	reg**ēbās**	aud**iēbās**	cap**iēbās**
he / she / it	am**ābat**	terr**ēbat**	reg**ēbat**	aud**iēbat**	cap**iēbat**
we	am**ābāmus**	terr**ēbāmus**	reg**ēbāmus**	aud**iēbāmus**	cap**iēbāmus**
you (pl)	am**ābātis**	terr**ēbātis**	reg**ēbātis**	aud**iēbātis**	cap**iēbātis**
they	am**ābant**	terr**ēbant**	reg**ēbant**	aud**iēbant**	cap**iēbant**

Imperfect indicative (passive)

Verbs in the imperfect indicative use the present stem; the vowel which comes before the imperfect endings depends on the verb's conjugation.

The imperfect indicative passive can be translated as follows: *amābar – I was being loved* or *I used to be loved* or *I began to be loved*.

N.B. Although in Latin the imperfect is used for actions which typically last for some time, in English we are often more likely to use the perfect tense. This means that sometimes the best translation for a Latin imperfect indicative is an English perfect indicative.

    e.g. *diū cīvēs regēbantur.*   The citizens were ruled for a long time.

imperfect indicative (passive)	1st conjugation	2nd conjugation	3rd conjugation	4th conjugation	mixed conjugation
I	amābar	terrēbar	regēbar	audiēbar	capiēbar
you (sg)	amābāris	terrēbāris	regēbāris	audiēbāris	capiēbāris
he / she / it	amābātur	terrēbātur	regēbātur	audiēbātur	capiēbātur
we	amābāmur	terrēbāmur	regēbāmur	audiēbāmur	capiēbāmur
you (pl)	amābāminī	terrēbāminī	regēbāminī	audiēbāminī	capiēbāminī
they	amābantur	terrēbantur	regēbantur	audiēbantur	capiēbantur

Imperfect indicative (deponent)

Verbs in the imperfect indicative use the present stem; the vowel which comes before the imperfect endings depends on the verb's conjugation.

The imperfect indicative for a deponent verb is passive in form but active in meaning; it can be translated as follows: *cōnābar - I was trying* or *I used to try* or *I began to try*.

N.B. Although in Latin the imperfect is used for actions which typically last for some time, in English we are often more likely to use the perfect tense. This means that sometimes the best translation for a Latin imperfect indicative is an English perfect indicative.

    e.g. *diū cīvēs cōnābantur.*   The citizens were trying for a long time.

Reference Grammar

imperfect deponent	1st conjugation	2nd conjugation	3rd conjugation	4th conjugation	mixed conjugation
I	cōnābar	vidēbar	loquēbar	oriēbar	ēgrediēbar
you (sg)	cōnābāris	vidēbāris	loquēbāris	oriēbāris	ēgrediēbāris
he / she / it	cōnābātur	vidēbātur	loquēbātur	oriēbātur	ēgrediēbātur
we	cōnābāmur	vidēbāmur	loquēbāmur	oriēbāmur	ēgrediēbāmur
you (pl)	cōnābāminī	vidēbāminī	loquēbāminī	oriēbāminī	ēgrediēbāminī
they	cōnābantur	vidēbantur	loquēbantur	oriēbantur	ēgrediēbantur

Future indicative (active)

Verbs in the future indicative use the present stem and the following endings.

There are two sets of endings depending on the verb's conjugation. The 1st and 2nd conjugations share the same endings, and the 3rd and 4th conjugations share a different set of endings. The vowel used before the endings depends on the verb's conjugation.

The future indicative active can be translated as follows: *amābō* – *I shall love*.

future indicative (active)	1st conjugation	2nd conjugation	3rd conjugation	4th conjugation	mixed conjugation
I	amābō	terrēbō	regam	audiam	capiam
you (sg)	amābis	terrēbis	regēs	audiēs	capiēs
he / she / it	amābit	terrēbit	reget	audiet	capiet
we	amābimus	terrēbimus	regēmus	audiēmus	capiēmus
you (pl)	amābitis	terrēbitis	regētis	audiētis	capiētis
they	amābunt	terrēbunt	regent	audient	capient

Future indicative (passive)

Verbs in the future indicative use the present stem and the following endings.

There are two sets of endings depending on the verb's conjugation. The 1st and 2nd conjugations share the same endings, and the 3rd and 4th conjugations share a different set of endings. The vowel used before the endings depends on the verb's conjugation.

The future indicative passive can be translated as follows: *amābor* – *I shall be loved*.

Reference Grammar

future indicative (passive)	1st conjugation	2nd conjugation	3rd conjugation	4th conjugation	mixed conjugation
I	amābor	terrēbor	regar	audiar	capiar
you (sg)	amāberis	terrēberis	regēris	audiēris	capiēris
he / she / it	amābitur	terrēbitur	regētur	audiētur	capiētur
we	amābimur	terrēbimur	regēmur	audiēmur	capiēmur
you (pl)	amābiminī	terrēbiminī	regēminī	audiēminī	capiēminī
they	amābuntur	terrēbuntur	regentur	audientur	capientur

Future indicative (deponent)

Verbs in the future indicative use the present stem and the following endings.

There are two sets of endings depending on the verb's conjugation. The 1st and 2nd conjugations share the same endings, and the 3rd and 4th conjugations share a different set of endings. The vowel used before the endings depends on the verb's conjugation.

The future indicative for a deponent verb is passive in form but active in meaning; it can be translated as follows: *cōnābor – I shall try*.

future indicative (deponent)	1st conjugation	2nd conjugation	3rd conjugation	4th conjugation	mixed conjugation
I	cōnābor	vidēbor	loquar	oriar	ēgrediar
you (sg)	cōnāberis	vidēberis	loquēris	oriēris	ēgrediēris
he / she / it	cōnābitur	vidēbitur	loquētur	oriētur	ēgrediētur
we	cōnābimur	vidēbimur	loquēmur	oriēmur	ēgrediēmur
you (pl)	cōnābiminī	vidēbiminī	loquēminī	oriēminī	ēgrediēminī
they	cōnābuntur	vidēbuntur	loquentur	orientur	ēgredientur

Perfect indicative (active)

All verbs in Latin use the same set of endings for the perfect indicative active; these endings are added to the perfect active stem.

The perfect indicative active can be translated as follows: *amāvī – I loved* or *I have loved*.

Reference Grammar

perfect indicative (active)	1st conjugation	2nd conjugation	3rd conjugation	4th conjugation	mixed conjugation
I	amāvī	terruī	rēxī	audīvī	cēpī
you (sg)	amāvistī	terruistī	rēxistī	audīvistī	cēpistī
he / she / it	amāvit	terruit	rēxit	audīvit	cēpit
we	amāvimus	terruimus	rēximus	audīvimus	cēpimus
you (pl)	amāvistis	terruistis	rēxistis	audīvistis	cēpistis
they	amāvērunt	terruērunt	rēxērunt	audīvērunt	cēpērunt

Perfect indicative (passive)

The perfect indicative passive uses two words: the perfect passive participle + *sum, es, est, sumus, estis, sunt*.

The perfect indicative passive can be translated as follows: *amātus sum* – *I was loved* or *I have been loved*.

perfect indicative (passive)	1st conjugation	2nd conjugation	3rd conjugation	4th conjugation	mixed conjugation
I	amātus sum	territus sum	rēctus sum	audītus sum	captus sum
you (sg)	amātus es	territus es	rēctus es	audītus es	captus es
he / she / it	amātus est	territus est	rēctus est	audītus est	captus est
we	amātī sumus	territī sumus	rēctī sumus	audītī sumus	captī sumus
you (pl)	amātī estis	territī estis	rēctī estis	audītī estis	captī estis
they	amātī sunt	territī sunt	rēctī sunt	audītī sunt	captī sunt

Remember that the PPP changes its endings to agree with the noun it describes, which – for the perfect indicative passive – will be its nominative subject:

The boy was loved.	puer amāt**us** est.
The girl was loved.	puella amāt**a** est.
The gold was seized.	aurum rapt**um** est.

Perfect indicative (deponent)

As with the perfect indicative passive, the perfect tense for a deponent verb uses two words: the perfect participle + *sum, es, est, sumus, estis, sunt*.

The perfect tense for a deponent verb is passive in form but active in meaning: it can be translated as follows: *cōnātus sum* – *I tried* or *I have tried*.

Reference Grammar

Pluperfect indicative (active)

All verbs in Latin use the same set of endings for the pluperfect indicative active; these endings are added to the perfect active stem.

The pluperfect indicative active can be translated as follows: *amāveram – I had loved.*

pluperfect indicative (active)	1st conjugation	2nd conjugation	3rd conjugation	4th conjugation	mixed conjugation
I	amāv**eram**	terru**eram**	rēx**eram**	audīv**eram**	cēp**eram**
you (sg)	amāv**erās**	terru**erās**	rēx**erās**	audīv**erās**	cēp**erās**
he / she / it	amāv**erat**	terru**erat**	rēx**erat**	audīv**erat**	cēp**erat**
we	amāv**erāmus**	terru**erāmus**	rēx**erāmus**	audīv**erāmus**	cēp**erāmus**
you (pl)	amāv**erātis**	terru**erātis**	rēx**erātis**	audīv**erātis**	cēp**erātis**
they	amāv**erant**	terru**erant**	rēx**erant**	audīv**erant**	cēp**erant**

Pluperfect indicative (passive)

The pluperfect indicative passive uses two words: the perfect passive participle + *eram, erās, erat, erāmus, erātis, erant.*

The pluperfect indicative passive can be translated as follows: *amātus eram – I had been loved.*

pluperfect indicative (passive)	1st conjugation	2nd conjugation	3rd conjugation	4th conjugation	mixed conjugation
I	amātus eram	territus eram	rēctus eram	audītus eram	captus eram
you (sg)	amātus erās	territus erās	rēctus erās	audītus erās	captus erās
he / she / it	amātus erat	territus erat	rēctus erat	audītus erat	captus erat
we	amātī erāmus	territī erāmus	rēctī erāmus	audītī erāmus	captī erāmus
you (pl)	amātī erātis	territī erātis	rēctī erātis	audītī erātis	captī erātis
they	amātī erant	territī erant	rēctī erant	audītī erant	captī erant

Remember that the PPP changes its endings to agree with the noun it describes, which – for the pluperfect indicative passive – will be its nominative subject:

The boy had been loved.	puer amāt**us** erat.
The girl had been loved.	puella amāt**a** erat.
The gold had been seized.	aurum rapt**um** erat.
The citizens had been captured.	cīvēs capt**ī** erant.

Pluperfect tense (deponent)

As with the pluperfect indicative passive, the pluperfect indicative for a deponent verb uses two words: the perfect participle + *eram, erās, erat, erāmus, erātis, erant*.

The pluperfect indicative for a deponent verb is passive in form but active in meaning; it can be translated as follows: *cōnātus eram* – *I had tried.*

SUBJUNCTIVES

The subjunctive originally was a form of the verb which was used for actions which were thought about / imagined rather than 'real'; over time, however, its use evolved and it became the form of the verb used in many types of subordinate clause.

There are only four tenses of the subjunctive: the present and imperfect subjunctive are used for actions with continuous aspect (i.e. actions viewed as not-yet finished) and the perfect and pluperfect subjunctive are used for actions with completed aspect (i.e. actions viewed as finished).

The translation of the subjunctive depends on how it is used: see Chapter 16 and Appendix 1: Advanced Syntax (pp209–214) for more details.

Active subjunctives

All active forms of the subjunctive use the active person endings (*-m, -s, -t, -mus, -tis, -nt*) and so only the 1st and 2nd person sg forms are listed in the table below.

Like all other not-yet finished aspect forms of the verb, the present and imperfect subjunctive use the present stem and so the vowels vary by conjugation.

Like all other finished aspect active forms of the verb, the perfect and pluperfect subjunctive use the perfect active stem.

	present subjunctive	imperfect subjunctive	perfect subjunctive	pluperfect subjunctive
1st conjugation	amem amēs etc.	amārem amārēs etc.	amāverim amāveris etc.	amāvissem amāvissēs etc.
2nd conjugation	terream terreās etc.	terrērem terrērēs etc.	terruerim terrueris etc.	terruissem terruissēs etc.
3rd conjugation	regam regās etc.	regerem regerēs etc.	rēxerim rēxeris etc.	rēxissem rēxissēs etc.
4th conjugation	audiam audiās etc.	audīrem audīrēs etc.	audīverim audīveris etc.	audīvissem audīvissēs etc.
mixed conjugation	capiam capiās etc.	caperem caperēs etc.	cēperim cēperis etc.	cēpissem cēpissēs etc.

Reference Grammar

Passive / deponent subjunctives

Like all other finished aspect forms of the verb, the present and imperfect subjunctive use the present stem and so the vowels vary by conjugation. These forms use the passive person endings (*-r, -ris, -tur, -mur, -mini, -ntur*) and so only the 1st and 2nd person sg forms are listed in the table below.

Like all other finished-aspect passive forms of the verb, the perfect and pluperfect subjunctive use the PPP + part of *esse*. The subjunctive forms of *esse* are listed in full on p247.

	present subjunctive	imperfect subjunctive	perfect subjunctive	pluperfect subjunctive
1st conjugation	amer ameris etc.	amarer amareris etc.	amatus sim amatus sis etc.	amatus essem amatus esses etc.
2nd conjugation	terrear terrearis etc.	terrerer terrereris etc.	territus sim territus sis etc.	territus essem territus esses etc.
3rd conjugation	regar regaris etc.	regerer regereris etc.	rectus sim rectus sis etc.	rectus essem rectus esses etc.
4th conjugation	audiar audiaris etc.	audirer audireris etc.	rectus sim rectus sis etc.	rectus essem rectus esses etc.
mixed conjugation	capiar capiaris etc.	caperer capereris etc.	captus sim captus sis etc.	captus essem captus esses etc.

IMPERATIVES

An imperative is the part of the verb used to give a command or an order directly to someone.

The imperative can be translated as follows: *ama – love!*

Imperatives use the present stem of the verb, and so the endings are slightly different in each of the different conjugations.

	1st conjugation	2nd conjugation	3rd conjugation	4th conjugation	mixed conjugation
imperative (sg)	ama	terre	rege	audi	cape
imperative (pl)	amate	terrete	regite	audite	capite

To tell someone not to do something, *nōlī* (sg), *nōlīte* (pl) is used with the infinitive:

e.g. *ō rēx, nōlī rēgīnam interficere!*   O king, do not kill the queen!
    ō līberī, nōlīte clāmāre!   Children, do not shout!

nōlī / nōlīte are the imperatives of *nōlō*.

NON-FINITE FORMS OF THE VERB

PARTICIPLES

A participle behaves like an adjective: it must agree with the noun it describes in case, gender and number.

The tenses for participles denote time relative to the finite verb in its clause:

- a present participle denotes an action taking place at the same time as the finite verb in its clause
- a perfect participle denotes an action taking place prior to the finite verb in its clause
- a future participle denotes an action yet to take place at the time of the finite verb in its clause.

The case of the noun it describes will depend on its role in its clause. Sometimes the noun described by a participle will be grammatically separate from the rest of this sentence. In this instance, the noun and participle will be in the ablative case; this construction is known as the **ablative absolute** construction (see further Chapter 14, p60).

e.g. *vīllīs incēnsīs, incolae effūgērunt.*   (With) their houses having been burned, the inhabitants fled.

In an ablative absolute, it is usual for an ablative singular present participle to use the alternative ablative ending -*e*, e.g. *regēnte*.

Present participles

The present participle describes a noun as *doing* an action. Like any adjective, the present participle must agree with the noun it describes.

e.g. *puerōs rīdentēs videō.*   I see the laughing boys.

1st conjugation	am**ā**ns, am**antis** – loving
2nd conjugation	terr**ē**ns, terr**entis** – terrifying
3rd conjugation	reg**ē**ns, reg**entis** – ruling
4th conjugation	aud**iē**ns, aud**ientis** – listening
mixed conjugation	cap**iē**ns, cap**ientis** – taking

Deponent verbs form their present participles in the same way as non-deponent verbs in their conjugation, e.g. *cōn**ā**ns, cōn**antis** – trying*, *loqu**ē**ns loqu**entis** – speaking*.

All present participles use 3rd declension adjective endings and decline like *ingēns, ingentis*.

Reference Grammar

	masculine / feminine	neuter
nominative sg	regēns	regēns
accusative sg	regent-em	regēns
genitive sg	regent-is	regent-is
dative sg	regent-ī	regent-ī
ablative sg	regent-ī	regent-ī
nominative pl	regent-ēs	regent-ia
accusative pl	regent-ēs	regent-ia
genitive pl	regent-ium	regent-ium
dative pl	regent-ibus	regent-ibus
ablative pl	regent-ibus	regent-ibus

In some circumstances (e.g. an ablative absolute), present participles use *-e* for their ablative sg ending, e.g. *regente*.

Perfect passive participles (PPP)

The perfect passive participle (PPP) is formed from the supine stem of the verb. It declines like a 2-1-2 adjective, such as *īrātus*.

rēct-us, rēct-a, rēct-um   having been ruled

1st conjugation	amātus, amāta, amātum – having been loved
2nd conjugation	territus, territa, territum – having been frightened
3rd conjugation	rēctus, rēcta, rēctum – having been ruled
4th conjugation	audītus, audīta, audītum – having been heard
mixed conjugation	captus, capta, captum – having been captured

The literal translation is often unwieldy, and it can be better to translate the participle phrase with a clause.

e.g. *dux vulnerātus mortuus est.*   The having been wounded commander is dead.
→ The commander, who has been wounded, is dead.

epistulam scrīptam lēgī.   I read the having been written letter
→ I read the letter, which had been written.

Deponent verbs have a perfect participle which is active in meaning (e.g. *having followed*). The perfect participle form is listed in the 3rd principal part of the verb, for example:

loquor, loquī, **locūtus** sum

Like all other perfect participles, a deponent verb's perfect participle declines like a 2-1-2 adjective.

Future participles

All verbs (including deponent verbs) form their future participle the same way. The future participle is built upon the supine stem and declines like a 2-1-2 adjective.

e.g. amāt**ūrus**, amāt**ūra**, amāt**ūrum**   being about to love
 locūt**ūrus**, locūt**ūra**, locūt**ūrum**   being about to speak

Note the unusual stem of the following future participles:

- moritūrus, moritūra, moritūrum   being about to die
- futūrus, futūra, futūrum   being about to be

INFINITIVES

Infinitives are often used in Latin just like in English, e.g. *Rōmulus Rōmānōs pugnāre iūssit.* – Romulus ordered the Romans to fight.

If an adjective is used with an infinitive it will be neuter in gender, e.g. *difficile erat pugnāre.* – It was difficult to fight.

Sometimes an infinitive is used with a noun, e.g. *tempus erat fugere.* – It was time to flee.

If the infinitive has a subject, it will be in the accusative case, e.g. *volō puellās audīre.* – I want the girls to listen.

It is very common for an infinitive and its accusative subject to follow a verb of saying / thinking / knowing.

e.g. *dīxī Rōmānōs pugnāre.*   I said that the Romans were fighting.

The accusative + infinitive construction after a verb of saying / thinking / knowing is often referred to as an **indirect statement**. This is one of Latin's most important constructions; see further Chapter 14 (pp62–66).

Infinitive tenses denote time relative to the finite verb in its clause:

- a present infinitive denotes an action taking place at the same time as the finite verb in its clause
- a perfect infinitive denotes an action taking place prior to the finite verb in its clause
- a future infinitive denotes an action yet to take place at the time of the finite verb in its clause.

Present infinitives

The present infinitives use the present stem and so the vowel used depends on the verb's conjugation.

	present active	present passive	deponent
1st conjugation	am**ā**re – to love	am**ā**rī – to be loved	cōn**ā**rī – to try
2nd conjugation	terr**ē**re	terr**ē**rī	vid**ē**rī
3rd conjugation	reg**e**re	reg**ī**	loqu**ī**
4th conjugation	aud**ī**re	aud**ī**rī	or**ī**rī
mixed conjugation	cap**e**re	cap**ī**	ēgred**ī**

Reference Grammar

Perfect infinitives

All verbs form their perfect infinitives in the same way:

- the perfect active infinitive uses the perfect active stem
- the perfect passive infinitive uses the PPP + *esse*; if the infinitive has a subject, the PPP will need to agree with that subject in case, gender and number
- deponent verbs have perfect infinitives which are passive in form but active in meaning.

perfect active	perfect passive	perfect deponent
am**āv**isse – *to have loved*	am**āt**us esse – *to have been loved*	c**ōnāt**us esse – *to have tried*

Future infinitives

All verbs form their future infinitives the same way:

- future active infinitive = future participle + *esse*
- future infinitive (deponent) = future participle + *esse*
- future passive infinitive = supine + *īrī*

When the infinitive has a subject, the future participle has to agree with that subject in case, number and gender, but – for the future passive infinitive – the supine is not an adjective and so does not change its endings to agree with its subject.

future active	future passive	future deponent
amātūrus esse – *to be about to love*	amātum īrī – *to be about to be loved*	conātūrus esse – *to be about to try*

GERUNDIVES AND GERUNDS

Gerundives are adjectives. They are formed from the present stem of the verb and so the vowels used vary across the conjugations. Gerundives take the endings of a 2-1-2 adjective and they are passive in meaning.

	non-deponent verbs
1st conjugation	am**a**ndus, am**a**nda, am**a**ndum – *needing to be loved*
2nd conjugation	terr**e**ndus, terr**e**nda, terr**e**ndum – *needing to be terrified*
3rd conjugation	reg**e**ndus, reg**e**nda, reg**e**ndum – *needing to be ruled*
4th conjugation	aud**ie**ndus, aud**ie**nda, aud**ie**ndum – *needing to be heard*
mixed conjugation	cap**ie**ndus, cap**ie**nda, cap**ie**ndum – *needing to be taken*

Deponent verbs use these endings too and have the same passive meaning.

See further Chapter 15, pp118–119.

Gerunds look very similar to gerundives but they are 2nd declension neuter nouns, not adjectives, and refer to the action itself, e.g. *amandum -ī, n – (the action of fighting)*. Unfortunately, the spelling of the English gerund is identical to the English present participle and it can be easy to get confused: remember that a gerund is a noun and a participle is an adjective. See further Appendix 1: Advanced Syntax, p209.

IRREGULAR VERBS

sum, esse, fuī – *be*

indicatives	present – *I am, etc.*	imperfect – *I was, etc.*	future – *I shall be, etc.*
I	sum	eram	erō
you (sg)	es	erās	eris
he / she / it	est	erat	erit
we	sumus	erāmus	erimus
you (pl)	estis	erātis	eritis
they	sunt	erant	erunt

As for all Latin verbs, the perfect tense is formed from the perfect stem with the usual perfect endings: *fuī* (*I have been*) etc.

The pluperfect tense is formed from the perfect stem with the usual pluperfect endings: *fueram* (*I had been*) etc.

It is unusual, however, to meet the perfect and pluperfect tenses of *sum*. This is because Latin typically uses the imperfect tense for the past tense of verbs referring to actions which naturally last for some time.

The subjunctive forms of *sum* are listed in the table below. All forms use the active person endings (*-m, -s, -t, -mus, -tis, -nt*) and so only the 1st person sg form is given.

present subjunctive	imperfect subjunctive	perfect subjunctive	pluperfect subjunctive
sim	essem	fuerim	fuissem

present participle	the present participle of *sum* exists only in compound verbs such as *absēns, absentis* – *being absent*
future participle	futūrus, futūra, futūrum – *being about to be*

Reference Grammar

present infinitive	esse – *to be*
future infinitive	futūrus esse / fore – *to be about to be*
perfect infinitive	fuisse – *to have been*

possum, posse, potuī – *can, be able*

indicatives	present – *I am able, etc.*	imperfect – *I was able, etc.*	future – *I shall be able, etc.*
I	possum	poteram	poterō
you (sg)	potes	poterās	poteris
he / she / it	potest	poterat	poterit
we	possumus	poterāmus	poterimus
you (pl)	potestis	poterātis	poteritis
they	possunt	poterant	poterunt

As for all Latin verbs, the perfect tense is formed from the perfect stem with the usual perfect endings: *potuī* (*I have been able*) etc.

The pluperfect tense is formed from the perfect stem with the usual pluperfect endings: *potueram* (*I had been able*) etc.

It is comparatively unusual, however, to meet the perfect and pluperfect tenses of *possum*. This is because Latin typically uses the imperfect tense for the past tense of verbs referring to actions which naturally last for some time.

The subjunctive forms of *possum* are listed in the table below. All forms use the active person endings *(-m, -s, -t, -mus, -tis, -nt)* and so only the 1st person sg form is given.

present subjunctive	imperfect subjunctive	perfect subjunctive	pluperfect subjunctive
possim	possem	potuerim	potuissem

present infinitive	posse – *to be able*
perfect infinitive	potuisse – *to have been able*

eō, īre, īvī (or iī) – go

indicatives	present – I go, etc.	imperfect – I was going, etc.	future – I shall go, etc.
I	eō	ībam	ībō
you (sg)	īs	ībās	ībis
he / she / it	it	ībat	ībit
we	īmus	ībāmus	ībimus
you (pl)	ītis	ībātis	ībitis
they	eunt	ībant	ībunt

As for all Latin verbs, the perfect tense is formed from the perfect stem with the usual perfect endings: *īvī* (*I have gone*) etc.

The pluperfect tense is formed from the perfect stem with the usual pluperfect endings: *īveram* (*I had gone*) etc.

In compound verbs (e.g. *abeō*) it is more usual for the alternative perfect stem to be used: *abiī* (*I have gone away*) etc.

The subjunctive forms of *possum* are listed in the table below. All forms use the active person endings (*-m, -s, -t, -mus, -tis, -nt*) and so only the 1st person sg form is given.

present subjunctive	imperfect subjunctive	perfect subjunctive	pluperfect subjunctive
eam	īrem	ierim	iissem

imperative sg	ī – *go!*
imperative pl	īte – *go!*

present participle	iēns, euntis – *going*
future participle	itūrus, itūra, itūrum – *being about to go*

present infinitive	ire – *to go*
future infinitive	itūrus esse – *to be about to go*
perfect infinitive	iisse – *to have gone*

Reference Grammar

volō, velle, voluī – *want*

indicatives	present – *I want, etc.*	imperfect – *I wanted, etc.*	future – *I shall want, etc.*
I	volō	volēbam	volam
you (sg)	vīs	volēbās	volēs
he / she / it	vult	volēbat	volet
we	volumus	volēbāmus	volēmus
you (pl)	vultis	volēbātis	volētis
they	volunt	volēbant	volent

As for all Latin verbs, the perfect tense is formed from the perfect stem with the usual perfect endings: *voluī* (*I wanted*) etc.

The pluperfect tense is formed from the perfect stem with the usual pluperfect endings: *volueram* (*I had wanted*) etc.

It is comparatively unusual, however, to meet the perfect and pluperfect tenses of *volō*. This is because Latin typically uses the imperfect tense for the past tense of verbs referring to actions which naturally last for some time.

The subjunctive forms of *volō* are listed in the table below. All forms use the active person endings (*-m, -s, -t, -mus, -tis, -nt*) and so only the 1st person sg form is given.

present subjunctive	imperfect subjunctive	perfect subjunctive	pluperfect subjunctive
velim	vellem	voluerim	voluissem

present participle	volēns, volentis – *wanting*

present infinitive	velle – *to want*
perfect infinitive	voluisse – *to have gone*

nōlō, nolle, nōluī – *not want; refuse*

indicatives	present – *I do not want, etc.*	imperfect – *I did not want, etc.*	future – *I shall not want, etc.*
I	nōlō	nōlebam	nōlam
you (sg)	nōn vīs	nōlebās	nōlēs
he / she / it	nōn vult	nōlebat	nōlet
we	nōlumus	nōlebāmus	nōlēmus
you (pl)	nōn vultis	nōlebātis	nōlētis
they	nōlunt	nōlebant	nōlent

As for all Latin verbs, the perfect tense is formed from the perfect stem with the usual perfect endings: *nōluī* (*I did not want*) etc.

The pluperfect tense is formed from the perfect stem with the usual pluperfect endings: *nōlueram* (*I had not wanted*) etc.

It is unusual, however, to meet the perfect and pluperfect tenses of *nōlō*. This is because Latin typically uses the imperfect tense for the past tense of verbs referring to actions which naturally last for some time.

The subjunctive forms of *nōlō* are listed in the table below. All forms use the active person endings (*-m, -s, -t, -mus, -tis, -nt*) and so only the 1st person sg form is given.

present subjunctive	imperfect subjunctive	perfect subjunctive	pluperfect subjunctive
nōlim	nōllem	nōluerim	nōluissem

present participle	nōlēns, nōlentis – *not wanting*

present infinitive	nōlle – *to not want*
perfect infinitive	nōluisse – *to have not wanted*

imperative sg	nōlī – *don't want!*
imperative pl	nōlīte – *don't want!*

mālō, mālle, māluī – *prefer*

indicatives	present – *I prefer etc.*	imperfect – *I preferred, etc.*	future – *I shall prefer, etc.*
I	mālō	mālēbam	mālam
you (sg)	māvīs	mālēbās	mālēs
he / she / it	māvult	mālēbat	mālet
we	mālumus	mālēbāmus	mālēmus
you (pl)	māvultis	mālēbātis	mālētis
they	mālunt	mālēbant	mālent

As for all Latin verbs, the perfect tense is formed from the perfect stem with the usual perfect endings: *māluī* (*I did not want*) etc.

The pluperfect tense is formed from the perfect stem with the usual pluperfect endings: *mālueram* (*I had not wanted*) etc.

It is unusual, however, to meet the perfect and pluperfect tenses of *mālō*. This is because Latin typically uses the imperfect tense for the past tense of verbs referring to actions which naturally last for some time.

Reference Grammar

The subjunctive forms of *mālō* are listed in the table below. All forms use the active person endings (*-m, -s, -t, -mus, -tis, -nt*) and so only the 1st person sg form is given.

present subjunctive	imperfect subjunctive	perfect subjunctive	pluperfect subjunctive
mālim	māllem	māluerim	māluissem

present participle	mālēns, mālentis – *preferring*

present infinitive	mālle – *to prefer*
perfect infinitive	māluisse – *to have preferred*

ferō, ferre, tulī, lātum – *carry; bear*

active indicatives	present active I carry, etc.	imperfect active I was carrying, etc.	future active I shall carry, etc.	perfect active I carried, etc.	pluperfect active I had carried, etc.
I	ferō	ferēbam	feram	tulī	tuleram
you (sg)	fers	ferēbās	ferēs	tulistī	tulerās
he / she / it	fert	ferēbat	feret	tulit	tulerat
we	ferimus	ferēbāmus	ferēmus	tulimus	tulerāmus
you (pl)	fertis	ferēbātis	ferētis	tulistis	tulerātis
they	ferunt	ferēbant	ferent	tulērunt	tulerant

passive indicatives	present passive I am carried, etc.	imperfect passive I was being carried, etc.	future passive I shall be carried, etc.	perfect passive I was carried, etc.	pluperfect passive I had been carried, etc.
I	feror	ferēbar	ferar	lātus sum	lātus eram
you (sg)	ferris	ferēbāris	ferēris	lātus es	lātus erās
he / she / it	fertur	ferēbātur	ferētur	lātus est	lātus erat
we	ferimur	ferēbāmur	ferēmur	lātī sumus	lātī erāmus
you (pl)	feriminī	ferēbāminī	ferēminī	lātī estis	lātī erātis
they	feruntur	ferēbantur	ferentur	lātī sunt	lātī erant

The subjunctive forms of *ferō* are listed in the table below. All active forms use the active person endings (*-m, -s, -t, -mus, -tis, -nt*) and so only the 1st person sg form is given. The present and imperfect passive forms use the passive person endings (*-r, -ris, -tur, -mur, -minī, -ntur*) and the perfect and pluperfect passive forms use the PPP + a subjunctive form of *esse*, just like regular verbs.

	present subjunctive	imperfect subjunctive	perfect subjunctive	pluperfect subjunctive
active	feram	ferrem	tulerim	tulissem
passive	ferar	ferrer	lātus sim	lātus essem

imperative sg	fer – *bring!*
imperative pl	ferte – *bring!*

present participle	ferēns, ferentis – *carrying*
perfect passive participle	lātus, lāta, lātum – *having been carried*
future participle	lātūrus, lātūrus, lātūrus – *being about to carry*

	active	passive
present infinitive	ferre – *to carry*	ferrī – *to be carried*
future infinitive	lātūrus esse – *to be about to go*	lātum īrī – *to be about to be carried*
perfect infinitive	tulisse – *to have carried*	lātus esse – *to have been carried*

Semi-deponent verbs: **gaudeō** – *be pleased; rejoice*

gaudeō follows the patterns for a 2nd conjugation verb within each tense and so only its 1st person sg forms are listed below.

	present active *I rejoice, etc.*	**imperfect active** *I was rejoicing, etc.*	**future active** *I shall rejoice, etc.*	**perfect active** *I rejoiced, etc.*	**pluperfect active** *I had rejoiced, etc.*
indicatives	gaudeō	gaudēbam	gaudēbō	gāvīsus sum	gāvīsus eram
subjunctives	gaudeam	gaudērem		gāvīsus sim	gāvīsus essem

imperative sg	gaudē – *rejoice!*
imperative pl	gaudēte – *rejoice!*

present participle	gaudēns, gaudentis – *rejoicing*
perfect participle	gāvīsus, gāvīsa, gāvīsum – *having rejoiced*
future participle	gāvīsūrus, gāvīsūra, gāvīsūrum – *being about to rejoice*

present infinitive	gaudēre – *to rejoice*
perfect infinitive	gāvīsus esse – *to have rejoiced*
future infinitive	gāvīsūrus esse – *to be about to rejoice*

SECTION 2: WORDS WITH UNUSUAL ENDINGS

You have learned the following words in the vocabulary checklists, but each has slightly unusual forms or is used in a slightly unusual way:

- alius; alter, altera, alterum
- domus
- inquit
- mare
- nēmō
- necesse
- nihil
- nūllus, ūllus, ūnus, sōlus, tōtus
- plūs
- satis

alius, alia, aliud – *other, another*; alter, altera, alterum – *the other, another, one (of two)*

alius is very like a 2-1-2 adjective, but for the nominative and accusative neuter sg, and all genders of the genitive and dative sg different endings are used.

	masculine	feminine	neuter		masculine	feminine	neuter
nominative sg	alius	alia	aliud	nominative pl	aliī	aliae	alia
accusative sg	alium	aliam	aliud	accusative pl	aliōs	aliās	alia
genitive sg	alīus	alīus	alīus	genitive pl	aliōrum	aliārum	aliōrum
dative sg	aliī	aliī	aliī	dative pl	aliīs	aliīs	aliīs
ablative sg	aliō	aliā	aliō	ablative pl	aliīs	aliīs	aliīs

In the plural, *aliī . . . aliī* is often used to mean *some . . . others*, e.g. *aliī pugnābant sed aliī fugiēbant.* – Some men were fighting, but others were fleeing.

Notice also the following idiom: *aliī alia faciunt.* – Different men do different things.

The endings for *alter, altera, alterum* follow the same pattern as *alius,* with the exception of their neuter nominative sg and accusative sg forms.

domus – *home*

domus takes its endings from both the 2nd and the 4th declension. The possible forms for *domus* are listed in full in the table below.

In addition, *domus* does not need a preposition to express *motion towards*, *away from*, or *position at*. Instead its accusative form is used for *motion towards*, its ablative for *motion away from* and its locative for *position at*: *domī – at home*.

	singular	plural
nominative	dom-us	dom-ūs
accusative	dom-um	dom-ūs / dom-ōs
genitive	dom-ūs	dom-uum / dom-ōrum
dative	dom-uī	dom-ibus
ablative	dom-ō	dom-ibus

inquit – *he / she / it says / said*

inquit is known as a defective verb, i.e. not all its forms remain. In this course you have met only two of its forms:

inquit – he / she / it says (/ said)
inquiunt – they say (/ said)

It is the verb most often used after direct speech and, although technically present tense in form, it is usually best translated into English as a past tense.

e.g. *'omnēs līberōs amāmus,' inquiunt parentēs laetī.*   'We love all our children,' said the happy parents.

mare – *sea*

A small number of 3rd declension nouns have endings which resemble 3rd declension adjective endings; *mare* is one of these nouns.

nominative sg	mare	nominative pl	mar-ia
accusative sg	mare	accusative pl	mar-ia
genitive sg	mar-is	genitive pl	mar-(i)um
dative sg	mar-ī	dative pl	mar-ibus
ablative sg	mar-ī	ablative pl	mar-ibus

Reference Grammar

nēmō – no one

nēmō is extremely irregular. Naturally enough, it has no plural forms.

nominative sg	nēmō
accusative sg	nēminem
genitive sg	nūllīus
dative sg	nēminī
ablative sg	nūllō

necesse – *necessary*

necesse is indeclinable; this means that it never changes its endings.

It is often used with a dative noun and an infinitive.

    e.g. *necesse est līberīs audīre.*   It is necessary for the children to listen.

nihil – *nothing*

nihil is usually met only in the nominative and accusative case. Because *nihil* is neuter, it has the same form for both these cases.

nūllus, nūlla, nūllum – *not any, none*

nūllus is very similar to a 2-1-2 adjective, but it has different genitive and dative singular endings.

	masculine	**feminine**	**neuter**		**masculine**	**feminine**	**neuter**
nominative sg	nūll-us	nūll-a	nūll-um	nominative pl	nūll-i	nūll-ae	nūll-a
accusative sg	nūll-um	nūll-am	nūll-um	accusative pl	nūll-ōs	nūll-ās	nūll-a
genitive sg	nūll-īus	nūll-īus	nūll-īus	genitive pl	nūll-ōrum	nūll-ārum	nūll-ōrum
dative sg	nūll-ī	nūll-ī	nūll-ī	dative pl	nūll-īs	nūll-īs	nūll-īs
ablative sg	nūll-ō	nūll-ā	nūll-ō	ablative pl	nūll-īs	nūll-īs	nūll-īs

ūllus, sōlus, ūnus and *tōtus* all follow the same pattern as *nūllus*.

plūs – *more*

plūs in the singular is a neuter noun and it is often followed by a genitive – e.g. *plūs cibī mihī dā!* – Give me more food!

In the plural it is a 3rd declension adjective: e.g. *plūrēs Rōmānī pugnābant quam incolae.* – More Romans were fighting than inhabitants.

				masculine / feminine	neuter
nominative sg	plūs	nominative pl		plūr-ēs	plūr-a
accusative sg	plūs	accusative pl		plūr-ēs	plūr-a
genitive sg	plūr-is	genitive pl		plūr-ium	plūr-ium
dative sg	plūr-ī	dative pl		plūr-ibus	plūr-ibus
ablative sg	plūr-e	ablative pl		plūr-ibus	plūr-ibus

satis – *enough*

satis is often used as an indeclinable noun, i.e. it does not change its form.

Like *plūs*, it is often followed by a genitive, e.g. *satis pecūniae habeō.* – I have enough money.

SECTION 3: SENTENCE STRUCTURE

In this course you have met the following key principles for sentence structure.

1. **Clauses v. phrases**: a unit of sense that contains a finite verb is known as a **clause**; a unit of sense which does not contain a finite verb is a **phrase**. The distinction between clauses and phrases is an important one because whenever there is a new finite verb the case structure re-sets.

2. **Verb tenses** give information about the **time** and **aspect** of an action.

   - Latin has two **aspects**, and parts of the verb which share the same stem share the same aspect: the present stem is used for parts of the verb where the action is viewed as **continuous / not-yet finished**, and the perfect stem / PPP is used for parts of the verb where the action is viewed as **finished**.
   - the tenses of **indicative verbs** locate the action in past, present or future time, but the tenses of **non-finite** forms of the verb (such as participles and infinitive) indicate a time which is relative to the main finite verb.
   - the tenses of **subjunctive verbs** denote aspect; their connection to **time** depends on whether or not the subjunctive is used as a main verb or a in a subordinate clause. The subjunctive behaves differently in different subordinate clauses.

3. All **subordinate clauses** are introduced by a **subordinating conjunction** and contain a **finite verb**. Some subordinate clauses use the subjunctive rather than the indicative. Further notes are given on this in Chapter 16 and in Appendix 1: Advanced Syntax. Subordinate clauses take their name from their relationship with the main clause; a purpose clause expresses the purpose of the main clause and so on.

Reference Grammar

4. The tense of a finite verb in a subordinate clause depends partly on the tense of the finite verb in the main clause: this is known as **sequence of tense**. See further Appendix 1: Advanced Syntax, p212.

5. Sometimes Latin and English do not align in their grammatical structures. The most important examples of these are the **ablative absolute** and **indirect statement** (see further Chapter 14). In these constructions, Latin subordinates information using a phrase; idiomatic English will often change this to a clause. This means that the form of the verb used has to change from non-finite to finite and its tense in English will be affected by **sequence of tense**, see p214.

SECTION 4: WORD ORDER

Latin word order is more flexible than English word order, but the following key principles apply:

- the subject is often the first word in the sentence and the verb is often the last word. This means that it is very common for the object to be written before the verb.
- adjectives are typically next to their nouns: it is common for adjectives of size / quantity to be written before their nouns, and for other adjectives to be after their nouns.
- adverbs are typically before the word they describe, which is often the verb. If the adverb applies to the whole sentence then it is usual for it to be at the very start of the sentence.
- prepositions are positioned before their nouns or at least one word from their phrase.
- clauses often follow temporal order, i.e. the first event comes first in the sentence, then the second, and so on.

It is common, however, for Latin to break from these principles in order to emphasise important words within a sentence or to form patterns in a way that creates literary finesse. Key words can be placed at the start or end of a sentence or line of verse for emphasis, or they can be arranged in elegant patterns. Latin's most famous pattern is known as a chiasmus: in a chiasmus Latin uses word order which creates a mirror image.

e.g. *audāx dux laudāvit mīlitēs fortēs*.
adjective noun verb noun adjective

For certain words stricter rules apply: *enim, igitur* and *tamen* are typically second word in their sentence.

ENGLISH-TO-LATIN VOCABULARY LIST

	Chapter		
accept; receive take in	11	accipiō	accipere, accēpī, acceptum
across	2	trāns	+ accusative
advance	13	prōgredior	prōgredī, prōgressus sum
advance; proceed	14	prōcēdō	prōcēdere, prōcessī
advise; warn	6	moneō	monēre, monuī, monitum
after; behind	10	post	+ accusative
after; when (conjunction)	7	postquam	
afterwards (adverb)	11	posteā	
again	5	iterum	
against	2	contrā	+ accusative
all; every	7	omnis	omne
ally	11	socius	sociī, m
almost; nearly	14	paene	
alone; lonely; only; on one's own	13	sōlus	sōla, sōlum
along; through	2	per	+ accusative
also; even	1	etiam	
also; too	7	quoque	
although	7	quamquam	
always	4	semper	
among; between	10	inter	+ accusative
and	14	ac, atque	
and	10	-que	
and; even	1	et	
anger	4	īra	īrae, f
angry	1	īrātus	īrāta, īrātum
announce; report	11	nūntiō	nūntiāre, nūntiāvī, nūntiātum
approach; come near to	8	appropinquō	appropinquāre, appropinquāvī, appropinquātum (+ dative)
arms; weapons	2	arma	armōrum, n pl
army	13	exercitus	exercitūs, m
around	10	circum	+ accusative
arrive	11	adveniō	advenīre, advēnī, adventum
arrow	2	sagitta	sagittae, f
art; skill	14	ars	artis, f
as . . . as possible	8	quam	+ superlative
as soon as	15	simulac, simulatque	
as; when	15	ut	+ indicative
ask; ask for	6	rogō	rogāre, rogāvī, rogātum
at last; finally	3	tandem	

English-to-Latin Vocabulary List

	Chapter		
at the same time	15	simul	
at; to; towards	2	ad	+ accusative
attack	9	oppugnō	oppugnāre, oppugnāvī, oppugnātum
battle	9	proelium	proeliī, n
be	1	sum	esse, fuī
be absent; be away; be distant from	5	absum	abesse, āfuī
be accustomed	14	soleō	solere, solītus sum
be here; be present	5	adsum	adesse, adfuī
be silent; be quiet	11	taceō	tacēre, tacuī, tacitum
beautiful; handsome	1	pulcher	pulchra, pulchrum
because	4	quod	
before (adverb)	15	anteā	
before (conjunction)	7	antequam	
beg	16	ōrō	ōrāre, ōrāvī, ōrātum
beg/ask for; make for; seek	3	petō	petere, petīvī, petītum
began	13	coepī	coepisse
believe; trust	4	crēdō	crēdere, crēdidī, crēditum (+ dative)
best	8	optimus	optima, optimum
better	8	melior	melius
big; large; great	3	magnus	magna, magnum
bigger; larger; greater	8	maior	maius
blood	14	sanguis	sanguinis, m
body	2	corpus	corporis, n
bold; daring	2	audāx	audācis
book	8	liber	librī, m
both . . . and	7	et . . . et	
boy	6	puer	puerī, m
brave; strong	2	fortis	forte
bravely; strongly	2	fortiter	
bring; carry; bear	4	ferō	ferre, tulī, lātum
bring/carry back; report; tell	13	referō	referre, rettulī, relātum
brother	12	frāter	frātris, m
build	4	aedificō	aedificāre, aedificāvī, aedificātum
burn; set on fire	9	incendō	incendere, incendī, incēnsum
but	1	sed	
but; however	11	autem	
buy	6	emō	emere, ēmī, ēmptum
by chance	10	forte	
call	5	vocō	vocāre, vocāvī, vocātum
camp	15	castra	castrōrum, n pl
can; be able	3	possum	posse, potuī
captive; prisoner	15	captīvus	captīvī, m
care; worry	14	cūra	cūrae, f
careful	15	dīligens	dīligēntis

English	Chapter	Latin	Principal Parts
carry; bear; take	12	portō	portāre, portāvī, portātum
catch sight of; notice	3	cōnspiciō	cōnspicere, cōnspexī, cōnspectum
chief; emperor	15	prīnceps	prīncipis, m
children	1	līberī	līberōrum, m pl
choose; read	8	legō	legere, lēgī, lēctum
citizen	7	cīvis	cīvis, m / f
city	5	urbs	urbis, f
climb	3	ascendō	ascendere, ascendī, ascēnsum
come	5	veniō	venīre, vēnī, ventum
come together; gather; meet	8	conveniō	convenīre, convēnī, conventum
comrade; companion	9	comes	comitis, m / f
conquer; win; be victorious; defeat	2	vincō	vincere, vīcī, victum
consul	16	cōnsul	cōnsulis, m
country; homeland	9	patria	patriae, f
courage; virtue	14	virtūs	virtūtis, f
crime	15	scelus	sceleris, n
crowd	10	turba	turbae, f
cruel	4	crūdēlis	crūdēle
crush; overwhelm	15	opprimō	opprimere, oppressī, oppressum
cry; weep	1	lacrimō	lacrimāre, lacrimāvī, lacrimātum
danger	2	perīculum	perīculī, n
dare	14	audeō	audēre, ausus sum
daughter	1	fīlia	fīliae, f
day	13	diēs	diēī, m
dead	5	mortuus	mortua, mortuum
dear; beloved	11	cārus	cāra, cārum
death	9	mors	mortis, f
decide	12	cōnstituō	cōnstituere, cōnstituī, cōnstitūtum
deep; high	6	altus	alta, altum
defend	9	dēfendō	dēfendere, dēfendī, dēfēnsum
depart; leave	11	discēdō	discēdere, discessī, discessum
despair	12	dēspērō	dēspērāre, dēspērāvī, dēspērātum
destroy	9	dēleō	dēlēre, dēlēvī, dēlētum
die	13	morior	morī, mortuus sum
die; perish	8	pereō	perīre, periī, peritum
difficult	3	difficilis	difficile
dinner; meal	5	cēna	cēnae, f
do; act; drive	14	agō	agere, ēgī, āctum
don't . . .	6	nōlī / nōlīte	+ infinitive
door	16	iānua	iānuae, f
drag	12	trahō	trahere, trāxī, tractum
dreadful	14	dīrus	dīra, dīrum
drink	5	bibō	bibere, bibī
drive	15	pellō	pellere, pepulī, pulsum
easy	3	facilis	facile

English-to-Latin Vocabulary List

	Chapter		
eat	5	cōnsūmō	cōnsūmere, cōnsūmpsī, cōnsūmptum
educated	10	doctus	docta, doctum
eighth	6	octāvus	octāva, octāvum
emperor; general; leader	15	imperātor	imperātōris, m
empire; power; command	15	imperium	imperiī, n
enemy	9	hostis	hostis, m
enemy (personal)	16	inimīcus	inimīcī, m
enough	10	satis	
enter	13	ingredior	ingredī, ingressus sum
enter	11	intrō	intrāre, intrāvī, intrātum
escape	12	effugiō	effugere, effūgī
ever	15	umquam	
evil; bad	3	malus	mala, malum
faithful; loyal	14	fidēlis	fidēle
fall	12	cadō	cadere, cecidī, cāsum
famous; clear	7	clārus	clāra, clārum
famous; well-known	8	nōtus	nōta, nōtum
farmer	5	agricola	agricolae, m
father	1	pater	patris, m
favour; support	15	faveō	favēre, fāvī, fautum (+ dative)
fear; be afraid	2	timeō	timēre, timuī, timitum
feel; notice	14	sentiō	sentīre, sēnsī, sēnsum
few; a few	7	paucī	paucae, pauca
field	4	ager	agrī, m
fierce; ferocious	8	ferōx	ferōcis
fifth	6	quīntus	quīnta, quīntum
fight	3	pugnō	pugnāre, pugnāvī, pugnātum
find	10	inveniō	invenīre, invēnī, inventum
finish; wear out	16	cōnficiō	cōnficere, cōnfēcī, cōnfectum
first	6	prīmus	prīma, prīmum
flee; run away	10	fugiō	fugere, fūgī, fugitum
follow	13	sequor	sequi, secūtus sum
food	5	cibus	cibī, m
foot	14	pēs	pedis, m
for	8	enim	
for	12	nam	
for a long time	3	diū	
force; compel	16	cōgō	cōgere, coēgī, coāctum
forces; troops	9	cōpiae	cōpiārum, f pl
fortunate; happy; lucky	3	fēlīx	fēlīcis
forum; market place	7	forum	forī, n
fourth	6	quārtus	quārta, quārtum
freedman; ex-slave	7	lībertus	lībertī, m
friend	6	amīcus	amīcī, m
frighten; terrify	1	terreō	terrēre, terruī, territum

English-to-Latin Vocabulary List

English	Chapter	Latin	
from where?	11	unde?	
from; away from; by	3	ā, ab	+ ablative
from; down from; about	3	dē	+ ablative
from; out of; out from	3	ē, ex	+ ablative
garden	7	hortus	hortī, m
gate	11	porta	portae, f
gather together; collect	12	colligō	colligere, collēgī, collēctum
get to know; find out	14	cognōscō	cognōscere, cognōvī, cognitum
get up; stand up; rise	16	surgō	surgere, surrēxī
gift; present	4	dōnum	dōnī, n
girl	6	puella	puellae, f
give	4	dō	dare, dedī, datum
give back; restore	16	reddō	reddere, reddidī, redditum
go	2	eō	īre, iī / īvī, itum
go away	8	abeō	abīre, abiī, abitum
go back; come back; return	8	redeō	redīre, rediī, reditum
go back; return	13	regredior	regredī, regressus sum
go down; come down	3	dēscendō	dēscendere, dēscendī, dēscēnsum
go into; enter	8	ineō	inīre, iniī, initum
go out	13	ēgredior	ēgredī, ēgressus sum
go out from; go away	8	exeō	exīre, exiī, exitum
go over; cross	8	trānseō	trānsīre, trānsiī, trānsitum
go to; approach	8	adeō	adīre, adiī, aditum
god	1	deus	deī, m
goddess	1	dea	deae, f
gold	4	aurum	aurī, n
good	3	bonus	bona, bonum
greatest; largest; biggest	8	maximus	maxima, maximum
greatly; very much	5	magnopere	
Greek	2	Graecus	Graeca, Graecum
greet	7	salūtō	salūtāre, salūtāvī, salūtātum
ground; land; country	3	terra	terrae, f
group of people; hand	13	manus	manūs, f
guard	9	custōdiō	custōdīre, custōdīvī, custōdītum
guard	16	custōs	custōdis, m / f
hand over; hand down	9	trādō	trādere, trādidī, trāditum
hand; group of people	13	manus	manūs, f
handsome; beautiful	1	pulcher	pulchra, pulchrum
happen	15	accidō	accidere, accidī
happy	1	laetus	laeta, laetum
hasten; march; compete	12	contendō	contendere, contendī, contentum
have; hold	4	habeō	habēre, habuī, habitum
he / she says / said; they say / said	2	inquit	inquiunt
he; she; it; that; those	7	is	ea, id
head	12	caput	capitis, n

English-to-Latin Vocabulary List

English	Chapter	Latin	
hear; listen to	3	audiō	audīre, audīvī, audītum
heavy; serious	12	gravis	grave
help	3	auxilium	auxiliī, n
here	6	hīc	
hide	14	cēlō	cēlāre, cēlavi, cēlātum
high; deep	6	altus	alta, altum
highest; greatest; top (of)	16	summus	summa, summum
himself; herself; itself; themselves	8	sē	suī
his / her / its / their (own)	6	suus	sua, suum
hold	10	teneō	tenēre, tenuī, tentum
home	13	domus	domūs, f
at home	13	domī	
hope	13	spēs	speī, f
hope; expect	14	spērō	spērāre, spērāvī, spērātum
horse	3	equus	equī, m
hour	6	hōra	hōrae, f
house; country villa	5	vīlla	vīllae, f
how big? how much?	16	quantus?	quanta? quantum?
how many?	16	quot?	
how?	16	quōmodō?	
however	4	tamen	
huge	2	ingēns	ingentis
hurry	5	festīnō	festīnāre, festīnāvī, festīnātum
husband	10	marītus	marītī, m
husband / wife	10	coniūnx	coniugis, m / f
I; me	8	ego	meī
if	15	sī	
if . . . not; unless; except	15	nisi	
immediately; at once	10	statim	
in front of; for; on behalf of	11	prō	+ ablative
in this way; to such an extent; so	16	ita	
in vain	8	frūstrā	
in; on	3	in	+ ablative
inhabitant	9	incola	incolae, m / f
into; onto	2	in	+ accusative
invite	9	invītō	invītāre, invītāvī, invītātum
island	12	īnsula	īnsulae, f
journey	10	iter	itineris, n
joy; pleasure	14	gaudium	gaudiī, n
kill	2	interficiō	interficere, interfēcī, interfectum
kill	9	necō	necāre, necāvī, necātum
kill	9	occīdō	occīdere, occīdī, occīsum
king	1	rēx	rēgis, m
kingdom	12	rēgnum	rēgnī, n
know	14	sciō	scīre, scīvī, scītum

English-to-Latin Vocabulary List

	Chapter		
laugh; smile; laugh at	5	rīdeō	rīdēre, rīsī, rīsum
lead back; bring back	11	redūcō	redūcere, redūxī, reductum
lead; take	9	dūcō	dūcere, dūxī, ductum
leader	9	dux	ducis, m
leave; leave behind	11	relinquō	relinquere, relīquī, relictum
legion	15	legiō	legiōnis, f
letter	8	epistula	epistulae, f
lie (down)	15	iaceō	iacēre, iacuī
life	16	vīta	vītae, f
light; daylight	10	lūx	lūcis, f
live	7	habitō	habitāre, habitāvī, habitātum
live; be alive	14	vīvō	vīvere, vīxī
long	8	longus	longa, longum
look at; watch	5	spectō	spectāre, spectāvī, spectātum
look!	11	ecce!	
love	10	amor	amōris, m
love; like	1	amō	amāre, amāvī, amātum
lucky; fortunate; happy	3	fēlīx	fēlīcis
make a mistake; stray	12	errō	errāre, errāvī, errātum
make for; seek; beg/ask for	3	petō	petere, petīvī, petītum
make; do	4	faciō	facere, fēcī, factum
man; human being	1	homō	hominis, m
man; husband	8	vir	virī, m
manner; way; kind	16	modus	modī, m
master	7	dominus	dominī, m
meanwhile	15	intereā	
messenger	7	nūntius	nūntiī, m
middle	8	medius	media, medium
miserable; wretched; sad	4	miser	misera, m serum
mistress	7	domina	dominae, f
money	4	pecūnia	pecūniae, f
more (adverb)	8	magis	
more (adjective)	8	plūrēs	plūra
more (noun)	8	plūs	+ genitive
most; very many	8	plūrimus	plūrima, plūrimum
mother	1	māter	mātris, f
mountain	3	mōns	montis, m
move	9	moveō	movēre, mōvī, mōtum
much; many	1	multus	multa, multum
my	6	meus	mea, meum
myself; yourself; himself; herself; itself etc.	13	ipse	ipsa, ipsum
name	4	nōmen	nōminis, n
near	2	prope	+ accusative
nearest; next to	16	proximus	proxima, proximum

English-to-Latin Vocabulary List

English	Chapter	Latin	
necessary	10	necesse	
never	6	numquam	
new	6	novus	nova, novum
night	12	nox	noctis, f
ninth	6	nōnus	nōna, nōnum
no one; nobody	12	nēmō	nūllīus
noble; renowned; of noble birth	8	nōbilis	nōbile
nor; neither; and not	11	neque, nec	
not	2	nōn	
not any; no	12	nūllus	nūlla, nūllum
not know	14	nesciō	nescīre, nescīvī
not want; refuse	4	nōlō	nōlle, nōluī
nothing	10	nihil	
now	5	nunc	
now; already	6	iam	
O	6	ō	+ vocative
offer	13	offerō	offerre, obtulī, oblatum
often	1	saepe	
old man	8	senex	senis, m
on account of; because of	11	propter	+ accusative
on behalf of; in front of; for	11	prō	+ ablative
on the next day	15	postrīdiē	
once; some time ago	3	ōlim	
one; a certain; some	13	quīdam	quaedam, quoddam
order	3	iubeō	iubēre, iūssī, iūssum
order; command	16	imperō	imperāre, imperāvī, imperātum (+ dative)
other; another	10	alius	alia, aliud
our	6	noster	nostra, nostrum
overcome; overpower	9	superō	superāre, superāvī, superātum
owe; ought; should; must	11	dēbeō	dēbēre, dēbuī, dēbitum
parent	10	parēns	parentis, m / f
part	10	pars	partis, f
pay the penalty; be punished	14	poenās dō	
peace	11	pāx	pācis, f
people; tribe; family	12	gēns	gentis, f
perhaps	12	fortasse	
persuade	4	persuādeō	persuādēre, persuāsī, persuāsum (+ dative)
place	6	locus	locī, m
plan; idea; advice	11	cōnsilium	cōnsiliī, n
poet	11	poēta	poētae, m
praise	1	laudō	laudāre, laudāvī, laudātum
prefer	13	mālō	mālle, māluī
prepare; provide	5	parō	parāre, parāvī, parātum
prize; reward; profit	15	praemium	praemiī, n
promise	14	prōmittō	prōmittere, prōmīsī, prōmissum

English-to-Latin Vocabulary List

	Chapter		
punish	1	pūniō	pūnīre, pūnīvī, pūnītum
punishment	14	poena	poenae, f
put; place; set up	4	pōnō	pōnere, posuī, positum
queen	1	rēgīna	rēgīnae, f
quick; fast	12	celer	celeris, celere
quickly	3	celeriter	
raise; lift up; hold up	13	tollō	tollere, sustulī, sublātum
read; choose	8	legō	legere, lēgī, lēctum
receive; accept; take in	11	accipiō	accipere, accēpī, acceptum
rejoice; be pleased	14	gaudeō	gaudēre, gāvīsus sum
remain; stay	2	maneō	manēre, mānsī, mānsum
reply	6	respondeō	respondēre, respondī, respōnsum
resist	15	resistō	resistere, restitī (+ dative)
river	2	flūmen	flūminis, n
Roman	1	Rōmānus	Rōmāna, Rōmānum
Rome	7	Rōma	Rōmae, f
at Rome	*7*	*Rōmae*	
rule	1	regō	regere, rēxī, rēctum
run	2	currō	currere, cucurrī, cursum
sacred	5	sacer	sacra, sacrum
sad	4	trīstis	trīste
safe	10	tūtus	tūta, tūtum
sail	10	nāvigō	nāvigāre, nāvigāvī, nāvigātum
sailor	10	nauta	nautae, m
savage; cruel	1	saevus	saeva, saevum
save; protect; keep	11	servō	servāre, servāvī, servātum
say; speak; tell	7	dīcō	dīcere, dīxī, dictum
school; game; public games / festival (pl)	5	lūdus	lūdī, m
sea	3	mare	maris, n
search for; look for; ask	10	quaerō	quaerere, quaesīvī, quaesītum
second	6	secundus	secunda, secundum
see	6	videō	vidēre, vīdī, vīsum
seem; appear	13	videor	vidērī, vīsus sum
seize; grab	9	rapiō	rapere, rapuī, raptum
sell	12	vēndō	vēndere, vēndidī, vēnditum
senator	7	senātor	senātōris, m
send	9	mittō	mittere, mīsī, missum
serious; heavy	12	gravis	grave
set free	7	līberō	līberāre, līberāvī, līberātum
set out	13	proficīscor	proficīscī, profectus sum
seventh	6	septimus	septima, septimum
shield	9	scūtum	scūtī, n
ship	10	nāvis	nāvis, f
shop; inn	5	taberna	tabernae, f

English-to-Latin Vocabulary List

English	Chapter	Latin	
short; brief	14	brevis	breve
shout	5	clāmō	clāmāre, clāmāvī, clāmātum
shout; shouting; noise	8	clāmor	clāmōris, m
show	6	ostendō	ostendere, ostendī, ostentum
since; when; although	16	cum	+ subjunctive
sister	12	soror	sorōris, f
sit	12	sedeō	sedēre, sēdī, sessum
sixth	6	sextus	sexta, sextum
sky; heaven	3	caelum	caelī, n
slave (male)	5	servus	servī, m
slave (female)	5	ancilla	ancillae, f
sleep	6	dormiō	dormīre, dormīvī, dormītum
slow	15	lentus	lenta, lentum
small	6	parvus	parva, parvum
smaller; less	8	minor	minus
smallest; least	8	minimus	minima, minimum
so	16	tam	
so great; such a great	16	tantus	tanta, tantum
so many	16	tot	
so much; so greatly; to such an extent	16	adeō	
soldier	9	mīles	mīlitis, m
some . . . others	10	aliī . . . aliī . . .	
some; several	13	nōnnūllī	nōnnūllae, nōnnūlla
son	1	fīlius	fīliī, m
soon	5	mox	
speak; talk	13	loquor	loquī, locūtus sum
spear	2	hasta	hastae, f
spirit; soul; mind	14	animus	animī, m
stand	11	stō	stāre, stetī, statum
storm	16	tempestās	tempestātis, f
street; road; way	7	via	viae, f
strong	11	validus	valida, validum
stupid; foolish	8	stultus	stulta, stultum
such; of such a kind	16	tālis	tāle
suddenly	3	subitō	
suffer; endure	13	patior	patī, passus sum
surely . . . ?	4	nōnne . . . ?	
surely . . . not?	4	num . . . ?	
sword	2	gladius	gladiī, m
take away; carry off; steal	13	auferō	auferre, abstulī, ablātum
take possession of; occupy	9	occupō	occupāre, occupāvī, occupātum
take; catch; capture; make (a plan)	2	capiō	capere, cēpī, captum
teach	10	doceō	docēre, docuī, doctum
teacher	8	magister	magistrī, m
tell; relate	12	nārrō	nārrāre, nārrāvī, nārrātum

English-to-Latin Vocabulary List

English	Chapter	Latin	
temple	4	templum	templī, n
tenth	6	decimus	decima, decimum
terrified	4	perterritus	perterrita, perterritum
than; how	8	quam	
that . . . not; so that . . . not; that; lest	16	ne	+ subjunctive
that; so that; in order that	16	ut	+ subjunctive
that; those; he; she; it	7	ille	illa, illud
the other; another; one (of two); the second (of two)	13	alter	altera, alterum
the rest; the others	5	cēterī	cēterae, cētera
the same	13	īdem	eadem, idem
then	9	deinde	
then	1	tum	
there	6	ibi	
therefore; and so	12	igitur	
therefore; and so	6	itaque	
thing; matter; event	13	rēs	reī, f
think	11	putō	putāre, putāvī, putātum
think; consider	14	cōgitō	cōgitāre, cōgitavi, cōgitātum
third	6	tertius	tertia, tertium
this; these	7	hic	haec, hoc
through; along	2	per	+ accusative
throw	2	iaciō	iacere, iēcī, iactum
thus; in this way	6	sīc	
time	11	tempus	temporis, n
tired	5	fessus	fessa, fessum
to where?	11	quō?	
to; towards; at	2	ad	+ accusative
today	12	hodiē	
tomorrow	12	crās	
town	9	oppidum	oppidī, n
troops; forces	9	cōpiae	cōpiārum, f pl
trust; beleive	4	crēdō	crēdere, crēdidī, crēditum (+ dative)
try	13	cōnor	cōnārī, cōnātus sum
turn	16	vertō	vertere, vertī, versum
under; beneath	13	sub	+ accusative / ablative
understand; realise	11	intellegō	intellegere, intellēxī, intellēctum
unlucky; unhappy	14	īnfēlīx	īnfēlīcis
urge; encourage	16	hortor	hortārī, hortātus sum
very greatly	8	maximē	
victory	15	victōria	victōriae, f
violently; loudly	15	vehementer	
voice; shout	14	vōx	vōcis, f
wage (war); wear (clothes)	9	gerō	gerere, gessī, gestum
wait for; expect	10	exspectō	exspectāre, exspectāvī, exspectātum

English-to-Latin Vocabulary List

English	Chapter	Latin	
walk	7	ambulō	ambulāre, ambulāvī, ambulātum
wall	7	mūrus	mūrī, m
want; desire	8	cupiō	cupere, cupīvī, cupītum
want; wish; be willing	4	volō	velle, voluī
war	2	bellum	bellī, n
warn; advise	6	moneō	monēre, monuī, monitum
water	5	aqua	aquae, f
wave	11	unda	undae, f
we; us	8	nōs	nostrum
weapons; arms	2	arma	armōrum, n pl
wear out; finish	16	cōnficiō	cōnficere, cōnfēcī, cōnfectum
weep; cry	1	lacrimō	lacrimāre, lacrimāvī, lacrimātum
well (adverb)	9	bene	
what sort of?	16	quālis?	quāle
when; since; although	16	cum	+ subjunctive
when; where	7	ubi	
when?	4	quandō?	
where?	4	ubi?	
whether	16	num	
while; until	15	dum	
who; which	7	quī	quae, quod
who? what? which?	7	quis?	quis? quid?
whole	13	tōtus	tōta, tōtum
why?	4	cūr?	
wicked	15	scelestus	scelesta, scelestum
wife	1	uxor	uxōris, f
willingly; gladly	15	libenter	
wind	12	ventus	ventī, m
wine	5	vīnum	vīnī, n
with	3	cum	+ ablative
without	13	sine	+ ablative
woman	1	fēmina	fēminae, f
woman; wife	10	mulier	mulieris, f
wonder at; admire	13	mīror	mīrārī, mīrātus sum
wonderful; extraordinary	10	mīrābilis	mīrābile
wood	2	silva	silvae, f
word	6	verbum	verbī, n
work; toil	14	labor	labōris, m
work; toil	8	labōrō	labōrāre, labōrāvī, labōrātum
worse	8	peior	peius
worst	8	pessimus	pessima, pessimum
wound	14	vulnus	vulneris, n
wound; injure	9	vulnerō	vulnerāre, vulnerāvī, vulnerātum
write	8	scrībō	scrībere, scrīpsī, scrīptum
year	6	annus	annī, m

English-to-Latin Vocabulary List

	Chapter		
yesterday	12	herī	
you (pl)	8	vōs	vestrum
you (sg)	8	tū	tuī
young man	6	iuvenis	iuvenis, m
your (pl); yours	6	vester	vestra, vestrum
your (sg); yours	6	tuus	tua, tuum
1	6	ūnus	ūna, ūnum
2	6	duo	duae, duo
3	6	trēs	tria
4	6	quattuor	
5	6	quīnque	
6	6	sex	
7	6	septem	
8	6	octō	
9	6	novem	
10	6	decem	
100	6	centum	
1000	6	mīlle	
1000s	6	mīlia	mīlium
(introduces question)	4	-ne	

LATIN-TO-ENGLISH VOCABULARY LIST

		Chapter	
ā, ab	+ ablative	3	from; away from; by
abeō	abīre, abiī, abitum	8	go away
absum	abesse, āfuī	5	be absent; be away; be distant from
ac, atque		14	and
accidō	accidere, accidī	15	happen
accipiō	accipere, accēpī, acceptum	11	receive; accept; take in
ad	+ accusative	2	to; towards; at
adeō		16	so much; so greatly; to such an extent
adeō	adīre, adiī, aditum	8	go to; approach
adsum	adesse, adfuī	5	be here; be present
adveniō	advenīre, advēnī, adventum	11	arrive
aedificō	aedificāre, aedificāvī, aedificātum	4	build
ager	agrī, m	4	field
agō	agere, ēgī, āctum	14	do; act; drive
agricola	agricolae, m	5	farmer
aliī . . . aliī . . .		10	some . . . others
alius	alia, aliud	10	other; another
alter	altera, alterum	13	the other; another; one (of two); the second (of two)
altus	alta, altum	6	high; deep
ambulō	ambulāre, ambulāvī, ambulātum	7	walk
amīcus	amīcī, m	6	friend
amō	amāre, amāvī, amātum	1	love; like
amor	amōris, m	10	love
ancilla	ancillae, f	5	slave (female)
animus	animī, m	14	spirit; soul; mind
annus	annī, m	6	year
anteā		15	before (adverb)
antequam		7	before (conjunction)
appropinquō	appropinquāre, appropinquāvī, appropinquātum (+ dative)	8	approach; come near to
aqua	aquae, f	5	water
arma	armōrum, n pl	2	arms; weapons
ars	artis, f	14	art; skill
ascendō	ascendere, ascendī, ascēnsum	3	climb
audāx	audācis	2	bold; daring
audeō	audēre, ausus sum	14	dare
audiō	audīre, audīvī, audītum	3	hear; listen to
auferō	auferre, abstulī, ablātum	13	take away; carry off; steal
aurum	aurī, n	4	gold

Latin-to-English Vocabulary List

		Chapter	
autem		11	but; however
auxilium	auxiliī, n	3	help
bellum	bellī, n	2	war
bene		9	well
bibō	bibere, bibī	5	drink
bonus	bona, bonum	3	good
brevis	breve	14	short; brief
cadō	cadere, cecidī, cāsum	12	fall
caelum	caelī, n	3	sky; heaven
capiō	capere, cēpī, captum	2	take; catch; capture; make (a plan)
captīvus	captīvī, m	15	captive; prisoner
caput	capitis, n	12	head
cārus	cāra, cārum	11	dear; beloved
castra	castrōrum, n pl	15	camp
celer	celeris, celere	12	quick; fast
celeriter		3	quickly
cēlō	cēlāre, cēlavi, cēlātum	14	hide
cēna	cēnae, f	5	dinner; meal
centum		6	100
cēterī	cēterae, cētera	5	the rest; the others
cibus	cibī, m	5	food
circum	+ accusative	10	around
cīvis	cīvis, m / f	7	citizen
clāmō	clāmāre, clāmāvī, clāmātum	5	shout
clāmor	clāmōris, m	8	shout; shouting; noise
clārus	clāra, clārum	7	famous; clear
coepī	coepisse	13	began
cōgitō	cōgitāre, cōgitavi, cōgitātum	14	think; consider
cognōscō	cognōscere, cognōvī, cognitum	14	get to know; find out
cōgō	cōgere, coēgī, coāctum	16	force; compel
colligō	colligere, collēgī, collēctum	12	gather together; collect
comes	comitis, m / f	9	comrade; companion
cōnficiō	cōnficere, cōnfēcī, cōnfectum	16	finish; wear out
coniūnx	coniugis, m / f	10	husband / wife
cōnor	cōnāri, cōnātus sum	13	try
cōnsilium	cōnsiliī, n	11	plan; idea; advice
cōnspiciō	cōnspicere, cōnspexī, cōnspectum	3	catch sight of; notice
cōnstituō	cōnstituere, cōnstituī, cōnstitūtum	12	decide
cōnsul	cōnsulis, m	16	consul
cōnsūmō	cōnsūmere, cōnsūmpsī, cōnsūmptum	5	eat
contendō	contendere, contendī, contentum	12	hasten; march; compete
contrā	+ accusative	2	against
conveniō	convenīre, convēnī, conventum	8	come together; gather; meet
cōpiae	cōpiārum, f pl	9	forces; troops
corpus	corporis, n	2	body
crās		12	tomorrow
crēdō	crēdere, crēdidī, crēditum (+ dative)	4	believe; trust

Latin-to-English Vocabulary List

		Chapter	
crūdēlis	crūdēle	4	cruel
cum	+ subjunctive	16	when; since; although
cum	+ ablative	3	with
cupiō	cupere, cupīvī, cupītum	8	want; desire
cūr?		4	why?
cūra	cūrae, f	14	care; worry
currō	currere, cucurrī, cursum	2	run
custōdiō	custōdīre, custōdīvī, custōdītum	9	guard
custōs	custōdis, m / f	16	guard
dē	+ ablative	3	from; down from; about
dea	deae, f	1	goddess
dēbeō	dēbēre, dēbuī, dēbitum	11	owe; ought; should; must
decem		6	10
decimus	decima, decimum	6	tenth
dēfendō	dēfendere, dēfendī, dēfēnsum	9	defend
deinde		9	then
dēleō	dēlēre, dēlēvī, dēlētum	9	destroy
dēscendō	dēscendere, dēscendī, dēscēnsum	3	go down; come down
dēspērō	dēspērāre, dēspērāvī, dēspērātum	12	despair
deus	deī, m	1	god
dīcō	dīcere, dīxī, dictum	7	say; speak; tell
diēs	diēī, m	13	day
difficilis	difficile	3	difficult
dīligens	dīligēntis	15	careful
dīrus	dīra, dīrum	14	dreadful
discēdō	discēdere, discessī, discessum	11	depart; leave
diū		3	for a long time
dō	dare, dedī, datum	4	give
doceō	docēre, docuī, doctum	10	teach
doctus	docta, doctum	10	educated
domina	dominae, f	7	mistress
dominus	dominī, m	7	master
domus	domūs, f	13	home
domī		13	locative: *at home*
dōnum	dōnī, n	4	gift; present
dormiō	dormīre, dormīvī, dormītum	6	sleep
dūcō	dūcere, dūxī, ductum	9	lead; take
dum		15	while; until
duo	duae, duo	6	2
dux	ducis, m	9	leader
ē, ex	+ ablative	3	from; out of; out from
ecce!		11	look!
effugiō	effugere, effūgī	12	escape
ego	meī	8	I; me
ēgredior	ēgredī, ēgressus sum	13	go out
emō	emere, ēmī, ēmptum	6	buy

Latin-to-English Vocabulary List

		Chapter	
enim		8	for
eō	īre, iī / īvī, itum	2	go
epistula	epistulae, f	8	letter
equus	equī, m	3	horse
errō	errāre, errāvī, errātum	12	stray; make a mistake
et		1	and; even
et . . . et		7	both . . . and
etiam		1	also; even
exeō	exīre, exiī, exitum	8	go out from; go away
exercitus	exercitūs, m	13	army
exspectō	exspectāre, exspectāvī, exspectātum	10	wait for; expect
facilis	facile	3	easy
faciō	facere, fēcī, factum	4	make; do
faveō	favēre, fāvī, fautum (+ dative)	15	favour; support
fēlīx	fēlīcis	3	fortunate; happy; lucky
fēmina	fēminae, f	1	woman
ferō	ferre, tulī, lātum	4	bring; carry; bear
ferōx	ferōcis	8	fierce; ferocious
fessus	fessa, fessum	5	tired
festīnō	festīnāre, festīnāvī, festīnātum	5	hurry
fidēlis	fidēle	14	faithful; loyal
fīlia	fīliae, f	1	daughter
fīlius	fīliī, m	1	son
flūmen	flūminis, n	2	river
fortasse		12	perhaps
forte		10	by chance
fortis	forte	2	brave; strong
fortiter		2	bravely; strongly
forum	forī, n	7	forum; market place
frāter	frātris, m	12	brother
frūstrā		8	in vain
fugiō	fugere, fūgī, fugitum	10	run away; flee
gaudeō	gaudēre, gāvīsus sum	14	be pleased; rejoice
gaudium	gaudiī, n	14	joy; pleasure
gēns	gentis, f	12	family; tribe; people
gerō	gerere, gessī, gestum	9	wear (clothes); wage (war)
gladius	gladiī, m	2	sword
Graecus	Graeca, Graecum	2	Greek
gravis	grave	12	heavy; serious
habeō	habēre, habuī, habitum	4	have; hold
habitō	habitāre, habitāvī, habitātum	7	live
hasta	hastae, f	2	spear
herī		12	yesterday
hic	haec, hoc	7	this; these
hīc		6	here
hodiē		12	today
homō	hominis, m	1	man; human being

Latin-to-English Vocabulary List

		Chapter	
hōra	hōrae, f	6	hour
hortor	hortārī, hortātus sum	16	encourage; urge
hortus	hortī, m	7	garden
hostis	hostis, m	9	enemy
iaceō	iacēre, iacuī	15	lie (down)
iaciō	iacere, iēcī, iactum	2	throw
iam		6	now; already
iānua	iānuae, f	16	door
ibi		6	there
īdem	eadem, idem	13	the same
igitur		12	therefore; and so
ille	illa, illud	7	that; those; he; she; it
imperātor	imperātōris, m	15	emperor; general; leader
imperium	imperiī, n	15	empire; power; command
imperō	imperāre, imperāvī, imperātum (+ dative)	16	order; command
in	+ accusative	2	into; onto
in	+ ablative	3	in; on
incendō	incendere, incendī, incēnsum	9	burn; set on fire
incola	incolae, m / f	9	inhabitant
ineō	inīre, iniī, initum	8	go into; enter
īnfēlīx	īnfēlīcis	14	unlucky; unhappy
ingēns	ingentis	2	huge
ingredior	ingredī, ingressus sum	13	enter
inimīcus	inimīcī, m	16	(personal) enemy
inquit	inquiunt	2	he / she says / said; they say / said
īnsula	īnsulae, f	12	island
intellegō	intellegere, intellēxī, intellēctum	11	understand; realise
inter	+ accusative	10	among; between
intereā		15	meanwhile
interficiō	interficere, interfēcī, interfectum	2	kill
intrō	intrāre, intrāvī, intrātum	11	enter
inveniō	invenīre, invēnī, inventum	10	find
invītō	invītāre, invītāvī, invītātum	9	invite
ipse	ipsa, ipsum	13	myself; yourself; himself; herself; itself etc.
īra	īrae, f	4	anger
īrātus	īrāta, īrātum	1	angry
is	ea, id	7	he; she; it; that; those
ita		16	in this way; to such an extent; so
itaque		6	and so; therefore
iter	itineris, n	10	journey
iterum		5	again
iubeō	iubēre, iūssī, iūssum	3	order
iuvenis	iuvenis, m	6	young man
labor	labōris, m	14	work; toil
labōrō	labōrāre, labōrāvī, labōrātum	8	work; toil
lacrimō	lacrimāre, lacrimāvī, lacrimātum	1	weep; cry
laetus	laeta, laetum	1	happy

		Chapter	
laudō	laudāre, laudāvī, laudātum	1	praise
legiō	legiōnis, f	15	legion
legō	legere, lēgī, lēctum	8	read; choose
lentus	lenta, lentum	15	slow
libenter		15	willingly; gladly
liber	librī, m	8	book
līberī	līberōrum, m pl	1	children
līberō	līberāre, līberāvī, līberātum	7	set free
lībertus	lībertī, m	7	freedman; ex-slave
locus	locī, m	6	place
longus	longa, longum	8	long
loquor	loquī, locūtus sum	13	speak; talk
lūdus	lūdī, m	5	school; game; public games / festival (pl)
lūx	lūcis, f	10	light; daylight
magis		8	more
magister	magistrī, m	8	teacher
magnopere		5	greatly; very much
magnus	magna, magnum	3	big; large; great
maior	maius	8	bigger; larger; greater
mālō	mālle, māluī	13	prefer
malus	mala, malum	3	evil; bad
maneō	manēre, mānsī, mānsum	2	remain; stay
manus	manūs, f	13	hand; group of people
mare	maris, n	3	sea
marītus	marītī, m	10	husband
māter	mātris, f	1	mother
maximē		8	very greatly
maximus	maxima, maximum	8	greatest; largest; biggest
medius	media, medium	8	middle
melior	melius	8	better
meus	mea, meum	6	my
mīles	mīlitis, m	9	soldier
mīlia	mīlium	6	1000s
mīlle		6	1000
minimus	minima, minimum	8	smallest; least
minor	minus	8	smaller; less
mīrābilis	mīrābile	10	wonderful; extraordinary
mīror	mīrārī, mīrātus sum	13	wonder at; admire
miser	misera, miserum	4	miserable; wretched; sad
mittō	mittere, mīsī, missum	9	send
modus	modī, m	16	manner; way; kind
moneō	monēre, monuī, monitum	6	warn; advise
mōns	montis, m	3	mountain
morior	morī, mortuus sum	13	die
mors	mortis, f	9	death
mortuus	mortua, mortuum	5	dead
moveō	movēre, mōvī, mōtum	9	move

Latin-to-English Vocabulary List

		Chapter	
mox		5	soon
mulier	mulieris, f	10	woman; wife
multus	multa, multum	1	much; many
mūrus	mūrī, m	7	wall
nam		12	for
nārrō	nārrāre, nārrāvī, nārrātum	12	tell; relate
nauta	nautae, m	10	sailor
nāvigō	nāvigāre, nāvigāvī, nāvigātum	10	sail
nāvis	nāvis, f	10	ship
-ne		4	(introduces question)
ne	+ subjunctive	16	that . . . not; so that . . . not; that; lest
necesse		10	necessary
necō	necāre, necāvī, necātum	9	kill
nēmō	nūllīus	12	no one; nobody
neque, nec		11	and not; nor; neither
nesciō	nescīre, nescīvī	14	not know
nihil		10	nothing
nisi		15	if . . . not; unless; except
nōbilis	nōbile	8	of noble birth; renowned
nōlī / nōlīte	+ infinitive	6	don't . . .
nōlō	nōlle, nōluī	4	not want; refuse
nōmen	nōminis, n	4	name
nōn		2	not
nōnne . . . ?		4	surely . . . ?
nōnnūllī	nōnnūllae, nōnnūlla	13	some; several
nōnus	nōna, nōnum	6	ninth
nōs	nostrum	8	we; us
noster	nostra, nostrum	6	our
nōtus	nōta, nōtum	8	famous; well-known
novem		6	9
novus	nova, novum	6	new
nox	noctis, f	12	night
nūllus	nūlla, nūllum	12	not any; no
num		16	whether
num . . . ?		4	surely . . . not?
numquam		6	never
nunc		5	now
nūntiō	nūntiāre, nūntiāvī, nūntiātum	11	announce; report
nūntius	nūntiī, m	7	messenger
ō	+ vocative	6	O
occīdō	occīdere, occīdī, occīsum	9	kill
occupō	occupāre, occupāvī, occupātum	9	take possession of; occupy
octāvus	octāva, octāvum	6	eighth
octō		6	8
offerō	offerre, obtulī, oblatum	13	offer
ōlim		3	once; some time ago
omnis	omne	7	all; every

Latin-to-English Vocabulary List

		Chapter	
oppidum	oppidī, n	9	town
opprimō	opprimere, oppressī, oppressum	15	crush; overwhelm
oppugnō	oppugnāre, oppugnāvī, oppugnātum	9	attack
optimus	optima, optimum	8	best
ōrō	ōrāre, ōrāvī, ōrātum	16	beg
ostendō	ostendere, ostendī, ostentum	6	show
paene		14	almost; nearly
parēns	parentis, m / f	10	parent
parō	parāre, parāvī, parātum	5	prepare; provide
pars	partis, f	10	part
parvus	parva, parvum	6	small
pater	patris, m	1	father
patior	patī, passus sum	13	suffer; endure
patria	patriae, f	9	country; homeland
paucī	paucae, pauca	7	few; a few
pāx	pācis, f	11	peace
pecūnia	pecūniae, f	4	money
peior	peius	8	worse
pellō	pellere, pēpulī, pulsum	15	drive
per	+ accusative	2	through; along
pereō	perīre, periī, peritum	8	die; perish
perīculum	perīculī, n	2	danger
persuādeō	persuādēre, persuāsī, persuāsum (+ dative)	4	persuade
perterritus	perterrita, perterritum	4	terrified
pēs	pedis, m	14	foot
pessimus	pessima, pessimum	8	worst
petō	petere, petīvī, petītum	3	make for; seek; beg/ask for
plūrēs	plūra	8	more
plūrimus	plūrima, plūrimum	8	most; very many
plūs	+ genitive	8	more
poena	poenae, f	14	punishment
poenās dō		14	pay the penalty; be punished
poēta	poētae, m	11	poet
pōnō	pōnere, posuī, positum	4	put; place; set up
porta	portae, f	11	gate
portō	portāre, portāvī, portātum	12	carry; bear; take
possum	posse, potuī	3	can; be able
post	+ accusative	10	after; behind
posteā		11	afterwards
postquam		7	after; when
postrīdiē		15	on the next day
praemium	praemiī, n	15	prize; reward; profit
prīmus	prīma, prīmum	6	first
prīnceps	prīncipis, m	15	chief; emperor
prō	+ ablative	11	in front of; for; on behalf of
prōcēdō	prōcēdere, prōcessī	14	advance; proceed
proelium	proeliī, n	9	battle

Latin-to-English Vocabulary List

		Chapter	
proficīscor	proficīscī, profectus sum	13	set out
prōgredior	prōgredī, prōgressus sum	13	advance
prōmittō	prōmittere, prōmīsī, prōmissum	14	promise
prope	+ accusative	2	near
propter	+ accusative	11	on account of; because of
proximus	proxima, proximum	16	nearest; next to
puella	puellae, f	6	girl
puer	puerī, m	6	boy
pugnō	pugnāre, pugnāvī, pugnātum	3	fight
pulcher	pulchra, pulchrum	1	beautiful; handsome
pūniō	pūnīre, pūnīvī, pūnītum	1	punish
putō	putāre, putāvī, putātum	11	think
quaerō	quaerere, quaesīvī, quaesītum	10	search for; look for; ask
quālis?	quāle	16	what sort of?
quam		8	than; how
quam	+ superlative	8	as . . . as possible
quamquam		7	although
quandō?		4	when?
quantus?	quanta? quantum?	16	how big? how much?
quārtus	quārta, quārtum	6	fourth
quattuor		6	4
-que		10	and
quī	quae, quod	7	who; which
quīdam	quaedam, quoddam	13	one; a certain; some
quīnque		6	5
quīntus	quīnta, quīntum	6	fifth
quis?	quis? quid?	7	who? what? which?
quō?		11	to where?
quod		4	because
quōmodō?		16	how?
quoque		7	also; too
quot?		16	how many?
rapiō	rapere, rapuī, raptum	9	seize; grab
reddō	reddere, reddidī, redditum	16	give back; restore
redeō	redīre, rediī, reditum	8	go back; come back; return
redūcō	redūcere, redūxī, reductum	11	lead back; bring back
referō	referre, rettulī, relātum	13	bring/carry back; report; tell
rēgīna	rēgīnae, f	1	queen
rēgnum	rēgnī, n	12	kingdom
regō	regere, rēxī, rēctum	1	rule
regredior	regredī, regressus sum	13	go back; return
relinquō	relinquere, relīquī, relictum	11	leave; leave behind
rēs	reī, f	13	thing; matter; event
resistō	resistere, restitī (+ dative)	15	resist
respondeō	respondēre, respondī, respōnsum	6	reply
rēx	rēgis, m	1	king
rīdeō	rīdēre, rīsī, rīsum	5	laugh; smile; laugh at

		Chapter	
rogō	rogāre, rogāvī, rogātum	6	ask; ask for
Rōma	Rōmae, f	7	Rome
Rōmae		7	locative: *at Rome*
Rōmānus	Rōmāna, Rōmānum	1	Roman
sacer	sacra, sacrum	5	sacred
saepe		1	often
saevus	saeva, saevum	1	savage; cruel
sagitta	sagittae, f	2	arrow
salūtō	salūtāre, salūtāvī, salūtātum	7	greet
sanguis	sanguinis, m	14	blood
satis		10	enough
scelestus	scelesta, scelestum	15	wicked
scelus	sceleris, n	15	crime
sciō	scīre, scīvī, scītum	14	know
scrībō	scrībere, scrīpsī, scrīptum	8	write
scūtum	scūtī, n	9	shield
sē	suī	8	himself; herself; itself; themselves
secundus	secunda, secundum	6	second
sed		1	but
sedeō	sedēre, sēdī, sessum	12	sit
semper		4	always
senātor	senātōris, m	7	senator
senex	senis, m	8	old man
sentiō	sentīre, sēnsī, sēnsum	14	feel; notice
septem		6	7
septimus	septima, septimum	6	seventh
sequor	sequi, secūtus sum	13	follow
servō	servāre, servāvī, servātum	11	save; protect; keep
servus	servī, m	5	slave (male)
sex		6	6
sextus	sexta, sextum	6	sixth
sī		15	if
sīc		6	thus; in this way
silva	silvae, f	2	wood
simul		15	at the same time
simulac, simulatque		15	as soon as
sine	+ ablative	13	without
socius	sociī, m	11	ally
soleō	solere, solitus sum	14	be accustomed
sōlus	sōla, sōlum	13	alone; lonely; only; on one's own
soror	sorōris, f	12	sister
spectō	spectāre, spectāvī, spectātum	5	look at; watch
spērō	spērāre, spērāvī, spērātum	14	hope; expect
spēs	speī, f	13	hope
statim		10	at once; immediately
stō	stāre, stetī, statum	11	stand
stultus	stulta, stultum	8	stupid; foolish

Latin-to-English Vocabulary List

		Chapter	
sub	+ accusative / ablative	13	under; beneath
subitō		3	suddenly
sum	esse, fuī	1	be
summus	summa, summum	16	highest; greatest; top (of)
superō	superāre, superāvī, superātum	9	overcome; overpower
surgō	surgere, surrēxī	16	get up; stand up; rise
suus	sua, suum	6	his / her / its / their (own)
taberna	tabernae, f	5	shop; inn
taceō	tacēre, tacuī, tacitum	11	be silent; be quiet
tālis	tāle	16	such; of such a kind
tam		16	so
tamen		4	however
tandem		3	at last; finally
tantus	tanta, tantum	16	so great; such a great
tempestās	tempestātis, f	16	storm
templum	templī, n	4	temple
tempus	temporis, n	11	time
teneō	tenēre, tenuī, tentum	10	hold
terra	terrae, f	3	ground; land; country
terreō	terrēre, terruī, territum	1	frighten; terrify
tertius	tertia, tertium	6	third
timeō	timēre, timuī, timitum	2	fear; be afraid
tollō	tollere, sustulī, sublātum	13	raise; lift up; hold up
tot		16	so many
tōtus	tōta, tōtum	13	whole
trādō	trādere, trādidī, trāditum	9	hand over; hand down
trahō	trahere, trāxī, tractum	12	drag
trāns	+ accusative	2	across
trānseō	trānsīre, trānsiī, trānsitum	8	go over; cross
trēs	tria	6	3
trīstis	trīste	4	sad
tū	tuī	8	you (sg)
tum		1	then
turba	turbae, f	10	crowd
tūtus	tūta, tūtum	10	safe
tuus	tua, tuum	6	your (sg); yours
ubi		7	when; where
ubi?		4	where?
umquam		15	ever
unda	undae, f	11	wave
unde?		11	from where?
ūnus	ūna, ūnum	6	1
urbs	urbis, f	5	city
ut	+ indicative	15	as; when
ut	+ subjunctive	16	that; so that; in order that
uxor	uxōris, f	1	wife
validus	valida, validum	11	strong

		Chapter	
vehementer		15	violently; loudly
vēndō	vēndere, vēndidī, vēnditum	12	sell
veniō	venīre, vēnī, ventum	5	come
ventus	ventī, m	12	wind
verbum	verbī, n	6	word
vertō	vertere, vertī, versum	16	turn
vester	vestra, vestrum	6	your (pl); yours
via	viae, f	7	street; road; way
victōria	victōriae, f	15	victory
videō	vidēre, vīdī, vīsum	6	see
videor	vidērī, vīsus sum	13	seem; appear
vīlla	vīllae, f	5	house; country villa
vincō	vincere, vīcī, victum	2	conquer; win; be victorious; defeat
vīnum	vīnī, n	5	wine
vir	virī, m	8	man; husband
virtūs	virtūtis, f	14	courage; virtue
vīta	vītae, f	16	life
vīvō	vīvere, vīxī	14	live; be alive
vocō	vocāre, vocāvī, vocātum	5	call
volō	velle, voluī	4	want; wish; be willing
vōs	vestrum	8	you (pl)
vōx	vōcis, f	14	voice; shout
vulnerō	vulnerāre, vulnerāvī, vulnerātum	9	wound; injure
vulnus	vulneris, n	14	wound